D1188925

The Estate Agents and

Property Misdescriptions Acts

Third edition

by

John Murdoch LLB ACIArb

Senior Lecturer in Law
Reading University

1993

Estates
Gazette

A member of Reed Business Publishing

The Estates Gazette Limited
151 Wardour Street, London W1V 4BN

First published 1979
Second edition 1982
Third edition 1993

ISBN 0 7282 0187 9

Typesetting by Amy Boyle Word Processing, Rochester, Kent
Printed in Finland at Werner Söderström Osakeyhitö

CONTENTS

Foreword vii
Preface ix
Table of Cases xi
Table of Statutes xiii
Table of Statutory Instruments xxiii

CHAPTER 1 The legislative background 1

A The Estate Agents Act 1979 2
Ancient history 2
Government initiatives 4
The Davies Bill 6
The Government Bill 6
Framework of the 1979 Act 8

B The second crusade 9
The changing scene 9
The 1991 reforms 10
The future 12

CHAPTER 2 Scope of the legislation 14

A Estate agency work 14
The basic definition 15
Business 16
Instructions 17
Employees 18

B Matters excluded 19
Work done by estate agents 19
Work done by other persons 21

C Interests in land 24

D Areas of uncertainty 26
Sales by auction or tender 26
Overseas property 27
Subagency 28
Leases at full rental value 29

E Property misdescriptions 30
Estate agency business 31
Solicitors 31
Property development 32

CHAPTER 3 The regulation of estate agents 33

A Initial information to clients 34
Details of charges 34
Special commission clauses 35
Services offered to purchasers 38
Time and manner of compliance 40
Sanctions for non-compliance 42

B Continuing obligations to clients 44
Variation of terms 44
Services requested by purchasers 45
Offers received 45
Disclosure of personal interest in purchase 47

C Duties to third parties 48
Disclosure of personal interest 48
Discrimination over services 54
Misrepresentation of offers 55

D Clients' money 56
Definition of clients' money 56
Clients' money as trust property 58
Restrictions on taking deposits 61
Dealing with clients' money 64

E Restrictions on the right to practise 70
Prohibition orders 71
Bankruptcy 71
Minimum standards of competence 71

CHAPTER 4 Enforcement of the 1979 Act 74

A Negative licensing 74
Types of order 75
Trigger events 76
Proceedings under the Act 82
Register of orders 87

B Criminal offences 87

CHAPTER 5 Property misdescriptions 89

A Liability under the existing law 89
Criminal liability 90
Civil liability 91

B Misdescriptions under the 1991 Act 92
Statement 92
False or misleading 93
Prescribed matter 94
Disclaimers 95

C Incidence of liability 97

D Defences 97

E Enforcement 100

APPENDIX A Estate Agents Act 1979 101

APPENDIX B Secondary legislation under the 1979 Act
The Estate Agents (Appeals) Regulations 1981 157
The Estate Agents (Entry and Inspection) Regulations 1981 . 171
The Estate Agents (Accounts) Regulations 1981 173
The Estate Agents (Provision of Information) Regulations
1991 181
The Estate Agents (Undesirable Practices) (No 2) Order
1991 187
The Estate Agents (Specified Offences) (No 2) Order 1991 . . 193

APPENDIX C Property Misdescriptions Act 1991 199

APPENDIX D Secondary legislation under the 1991 Act
The Property Misdescriptions (Prescribed Matters) Order
  1992 210

Index 215

Forward

by

ROGER CARSON FRICS, FSVA
Vice-President Incorporated Society of Valuers and Auctioneers

I was delighted to be asked to write a forward for this excellent book, for the principal reason that as an estate agency practitioner I found its predecessor to be an invaluable reference source; this third edition not only updates readers, but also – equally important in my view – does so in an eminently readable fashion.

I have had the good fortune to share a lecture platform several times with John Murdoch – first when the ISVA mounted a series of seminars on the new orders and regulations under the 1979 Act, during the summer of 1991 and second in the spring of 1993 when the Society ran a similar set of seminars on the Property Misdescriptions Act. During both series I found John's obviously deep knowledge of the legislation to be helpfully supplemented by a no-nonsense ability to communicate his expertise clearly and concisely. As one would expect, those same qualities make the information in this book much easier to absorb than might be anticipated from a text book on a subject of this weight and importance.

From the chronicling of the history of the legislation, right through to the detail on the obligations imposed by the Acts' provisions, the text is logical and thorough; it is also further enlivened in places by some lovely shafts of dry humour!

Despite the obvious temptation, John Murdoch has not – wisely in my view – attempted to teach his estate agency grandmothers "how to suck their eggs" – there are no lists of "do's" or "don'ts" in respect of practical compliance – but an abundance of material from which the thinking agent can distil his or her own salvation.

All in all this is an essential handbook for the busy estate agent; the skilled integration of the 1991 Orders and Regulations and the

Property Misdescriptions Act bring it immediate contemporary force and make it required reading for those of us in the profession who intend to remain within the law.

Preface

The 11 years which have elapsed since the second edition of this book was published have seen fundamental changes in the world of estate agency. Quite apart from the riches-to-rags tale of the property markets in the late 1980s, the apparently insatiable appetite of lending institutions for chains of offices through which to market their financial services has placed estate agency firmly in the corporate sector. In so doing, it has placed considerable strains on traditional relationships and loyalties, as erstwhile senior partners have found themselves redefined as mere cogs in enormous financial machines.

As with any other brave new world, these changes in estate agency have brought with them new abuses, both real and imagined, and these have in turn led inexorably to Government intervention. First, a wide range of new requirements has been laid down under the Estate Agents Act 1979 which, having kept a fairly low profile for its first few years of operation, looks set to be a major thorn in the flesh of agents in the future. Second, and fulfilling a legislative threat made almost 20 years ago, the Property Misdescriptions Act has introduced into the marketing of land and buildings a regime of criminal liability for false statements akin to that which operates under the Trade Descriptions Act.

These major developments have provided the impetus for a new edition of this book, the preparation of which leaves me indebted to many people. My thanks are due first to Roger Carson, FRICS, FSVA, Vice-President of the Incorporated Society of Valuers and Auctioneers, not only for contributing a forward to this edition, but also for educating me in the harsh realities of estate agency life, in the course of some very enjoyable seminars on the new legislation. My thanks also to the publishers, who have produced this edition with the speed, efficiency and accuracy which I have by now come to expect from them and who, in Audrey Boyle and Colin Greasby, have a particularly "user friendly front end". Lastly, as always, heartfelt gratitude to Sandi, not only for moral support in times of deadline-related stress, but for a good deal of sound legal advice into the bargain.

International Women's Day 1993   John Murdoch

TABLE OF CASES

Aitchison v Reith & Anderson (Dingwall & Tain) Ltd 1974 SLT 282; 1974
    JC 12 98
Annesley v Muggridge (1816) 1 Madd 593 58
Atlantic Estates Ltd v Ezekiel [1991] 2 EGLR 202; 33 EG 118, CA 93

Barrington v Lee [1972] 1 QB 326; [1971] 3 WLR 962; [1971] 3 All ER 1231,
    CA 58
Brentnall & Cleland Ltd v LCC [1945] 1 KB 115; [1944] 2 All ER 552; (1944) 61
    TLR 97; 43 LGR 20, DC 142
Brown v Inland Revenue Commissioners [1965] AC 244; [1964] 3 WLR 511;
    [1964] 3 All ER 119, HL 68
Burt v Claude Cousins & Co Ltd [1971] 2 QB 426; [1971] 2 WLR 930; [1971]
    2 All ER 611; [1971] EGD 565; (1971) 218 EG 413, CA 58

Christie Owen & Davies v Rapacioli [1974] QB 781; [1974] 2 WLR 723;
    [1974] 2 All ER 311, CA 38
Clayton's Case (1816) 1 Mer 529 59
Computastaff Ltd v Ingledew Brown Bennison & Garrett (1983) 268 EG 906 . . . 91
Cremdean Properties Ltd v Nash (1977) 244 EG 547, CA 96

Davis v George Trollope & Sons [1943] 1 All ER 501, CA 38

Edgell v Day (1865) LR 1 CP 80 61
Ellis v Goulton [1893] 1 QB 350 61

Fairvale Ltd v Sabharwal [1992] 2 EGLR 27, [1992] 32 EG 51, CA 37
Fiesta Girl of London Ltd v Network Agencies [1992] 2 EGLR 28;
    [1992] 32 EG 55 43
Flint v Woodin (1852) 9 Hare 618 48
Furtado v Lumley (1890) 6 TLR 168 61

Goding v Frazer [1967] 1 WLR 286; [1966] 3 All ER 234; (1966) 199 EG 127 . . 58
Gordon v Selico Ltd [1986] 1 EGLR 71; (1986) 278 EG 53, CA 91
Gosling v Anderson (1972) 223 EG 1743 91

Hampton & Sons Ltd v George [1939] 3 All ER 627 37
Harington v Hoggart (1830) 1 B&Ad 577; [1824-34] All ER 471 68
Hinchcliffe v Sheldon [1955] 3 All ER 406; [1955] 1 WLR 1207 . . . . 140, 209
Hoddell v Smith [1976] EGD 217; (1975) 240 EG 295, CA 16
Hughes, Re, Rea v Black [1943] Ch 296; [1943] 2 All ER 269; (1943) 112
    LJCh 234; 59 TLR 375 . . . . 142, 204

Luxor (Eastbourne) Ltd v Cooper [1941] AC 108; [1941] 1 All ER 33, HL 41

McGuire v *Sittingbourne Co-operative Society Ltd* (1976) 140 JP 306 99
May v *Vincent* [1991] 1 EGLR 27; [1991] 04 EG 144 96
Mullens v *Miller* (1882) 22 ChD 194 91

Norman v *Bennett* [1974] 1 WLR 1229; [1974] 3 All ER 351 96

Ojelay v *Neosale Ltd* [1987] 2 EGLR 167; (1987) 283 EG 1391 . . . . 61, 68

Pilkington v *Flack* (1948) 152 EG 366 48
Port Louis Corporation v *Attorney-General of Mauritius* [1965] AC IIII; [1965]
    3 WLR 67, PC 144
Potters v *Loppert* [1973] Ch 399; [1973] 2 WLR 469; [1973] 1 All ER 658;
    (1972) 25 P&CR 82; [1972] EGD 960; 224 EG 1717 68

R v *Carr-Briant* [1943] KB 607 97
R v *Commission for Racial Equality, ex parte Cottrell & Rothon* [1980]
    1 WLR 1580; [1980] 3 All ER 265; (1980) 255 EG 783, DC 80
R v *Milk Marketing Board, ex parte Austin* The Times March 21 1983 75
R v *Senior* [1899] 1 QB 283; 63 LJQB 175; 63 JP 8; 15 TLR 102 140
Registrar of Restrictive Trading Agreements v *WH Smith & Son Ltd* [1969]
    3 All ER 1065; [1969] 1 WLR 1460, CA 142
Resolute Maritime Inc v *Nippon Kaiji Kyokai* [1983] 1 WLR 857; [1983] 2 All
    ER 1; [1983] 1 Lloyds Rep 431 91
Rolfe (FP) & Co v *George* (1969) 210 EG 455, CA 16
Rowe v *May* (1854) 18 Beav 613 58
Ryan v *Pilkington* [1959] 1 WLR 403; [1959] 1 All ER 689, CA 58

Sadler v *Whittaker* (1953) 162 EG 404, CA 37
Secretary of State for Education and Science v *Tameside Metropolitan
    Borough Council* [1977] AC 1014; [1976] 3 WLR 641; [1976] 3 All ER 665;
    (1976) 75 LGR 190, CA and HL 108
Smith (Henry) & Son v *Muskett* (1978) 246 EG 655 . . . . 54, 55
Solicitors' Estate Agency (Glasgow) Ltd v *MacIver* 1990 SCLR 595; 1993
    SLT 23 . . . . 35, 43
Sorrell v *Finch* [1977] AC 728, HL 58, 60
Sutton London Borough v *Perry Sanger & Co Ltd* (1971) 135 JP 239 99

Taylor's Central Garages (Exeter) Ltd v *Roper* [1951] WN 383; (1951)
    115 JP 445 . . . . 142, 204
Tesco Supermarkets Ltd v *Nattrass* [1972] AC 153; [1971] 2 WLR 1166;
    [1971] 2 All ER 127, HL 98, 142, 204
Trinder (John E) & Partners v *Haggis* [1951] WN 416, CA 44
Toulmin v *Millar* (1887) 12 AC 746; 3 TLR 836, HL 44

Walsh v *Lonsdale* (1882) 21 ChD 9 25
Way & Waller Ltd v *Ryde* [1944] 1 All ER 9; (1944) 60 TLR 185, CA 44
Webb v *Smith* (1885) 30 ChD 192; 1 TLR 225, CA 60
Whiteman v *Weston* The Times March 15 1900 91
With v *O'Flanagan* [1936] Ch 575; [1936] 1 All ER 727, CA 94

TABLE OF STATUTES

Administration of Justice Act 1970
    section 40 194
Administration of Justice Act 1985
    section 35 . . . . 78, 194
Accommodation Agencies Act 1953 15
Airports Act 1986 . . . . 116, 117

Bankers' Books Evidence Act 1879 170
Banking Act 1979 180
Banking Act 1987 180
Bankruptcy (Scotland) Act 1985
    section 75 137
    Sched 7 137
Building Act 1984 212
Building (Scotland) Act 1959
    section 9 213
Building Societies Act 1962 173
Building Societies Act 1986
    Part III 194
    Part IV 194
Buildings Societies Act (Northern Ireland) 1967 173

Companies Act 1989
    section 25 124
    section 73 197
    section 76 197
    Part II 124
Company Directors Disqualification Act 1986
    section 11 194
    section 12 194
    section 13 194
    Sched 8 194
Competition Act 1980 . . . . 116, 117
    section 19 117
Consumer Credit Act 1974 . . . . . 5, 8, 20, 74, 77, 85, 104, 116, 120, 139,
                                           140, 141
    section 7 195
    section 39 195
    section 46 195

section 145 . . . . 20, 105
section 154 195
section 162 120
section 165 195
section 167 195
section 174 117
Part III 20
Consumer Protection Act 1987 . . . . 91, 95, 116, 117, 205
section 20 . . . . 90, 195
section 23 . . . . 90, 211
section 32 196
section 38 209
Consumer Safety Act 1978
section 4 116
Conveyancing and Feudal Reform (Scotland) Act 1970
section 9 106
Courts and Legal Services Act 1990 . . . . 116, 117
Criminal Justice Act 1982
section 37 . . . . 125, 141, 209
section 46 . . . . 125, 141
Criminal Justice Act 1991
section 17 . . . . 125, 141, 149, 202, 209
Criminal Procedure (Scotland) Act 1975 . . . . 148, 209

Data Protection Act 1984
section 5 196
section 6 196
section 10 196
section 15 . . . . 78, 196

Electricity Act 1989 . . . . 116, 117
Estate Agents Act 1979
section 1 . . . . 17, 29, 49, 201
section 1(1) . . 15, 16, 18, 19, 22, 23, 26, 31, 63, 75, 89, 100, 103, 182,
188, 201
section 1(1)(a) 201
section 1(2)(a) 21
section 1(2)(b) 20
section 1(2)(c) 21
section 1(2)(d) 19
section 1(2)(e) 19
section 1(3)(a) 23, 134
section 1(3)(b) 22
section 1(3)(c) 24

section 1(4) 22
section 1(4)(*b*) 16
section 1(5)(*a*) 21
section 1(5)(*b*) 22
section 1(5)(*c*) 18, 23
section 1(5)(*e*) 31
section 1(5)(*f*) 31
section 1(5)(*g*) 31
section 2 . . . . 25, 26, 27, 49, 103, 105, 182, 188, 201, 202
section 2(1) 103
section 2(1)(*a*) 25
section 2(1)(*b*) 25,29, 30
section 2(2) 25
section 2(3)(*a*) 25
section 3 . . . . . . 76, 79, 80, 82, 83, 84, 85, 86, 87, 103, 109, 138, 193
section 3(1) 77, 108
section 3(1)(*a*) 76, 77, 108, 193
section 3(1)(*b*) 76, 79
section 3(1)(*c*) 19, 76, 80, 108, 145
section 3(1)(*d*) 19, 76, 81, 108, 187
section 3(2) 75, 82, 108
section 3(3) 53, 81
section 3(3)(*a*) 18, 23
section 3(3)(*c*) 50, 135
section 3(5) 75
section 3(6) 186, 192
section 3(8) 84
section 4 . . . . 76, 82, 83, 84, 85, 86, 87, 103, 138
section 4(3) 76
section 5 103
section 5(2) 76, 111
section 5(4) 84
section 5(5) 84
section 6 . . . . 85, 86, 103, 138
section 6(4) 160
section 6(5) 160
section 7 . . . . 84, 86, 103, 159
section 7(2) 162, 163, 166, 169
section 7(3) 113, 158
section 8 . . . . 87, 103
section 8(3) 87
section 8(6) 87
section 9 . . . . 82, 83, 103
section 9(1) 116

section 9(3) 82
section 9(4) 82
section 9(5) 79, 80
section 9(6) 80
section 10 . . . . 82, 103, 116, 120
section 10(6) 77, 78
section 11 . . . . 83, 87, 88, 103, 120, 170
section 11(1) 120
section 11(3) 120
section 11(4) 88, 120
section 11(6) 120
section 12 . . . . 28, 56, 57, 103
section 12(1) 57, 103
section 12(2) 57, 103
section 12(3) 57, 103
section 12(4) 103
section 13 . . . . 56, 61, 70, 103
section 13(1) 58, 60
section 13(2) 59
section 13(3) 59
section 13(4) 59, 75
section 13(5) 60
section 14 . . . . 56, 64, 65, 69, 103, 173
section 14(1) 18, 64, 174
section 14(2) 64, 103
section 14(6) 67
section 14(7) 67
section 14(8) 65
section 15 . . . . 56, 68, 70, 76, 77, 80, 103
section 15(3) 70
section 15(5) 70
section 16 . . . . 56, 62, 85, 103
section 16(1) 61
section 16(2)(*b*) 127
section 16(2)(*c*) 62
section 16(2)(*d*) 62
section 16(3) 61, 127
section 16(4) 62
section 17 . . . . 56, 62, 85, 103, 138
section 18 . . . . 34, 40, 42, 43, 44, 66, 76, 77, 80, 103, 176
section 18(1) 41
section 18(2) 34, 35, 40, 183
section 18(2)(*a*) 35, 43
section 18(2)(*b*) 35

section 18(2)(*d*) 43
section 18(3) 44, 183
section 18(4) 131, 181
section 18(4)(*b*) 40
section 18(5) 42
section 18(6) 43
section 19 . . . . 63, 76, 77, 80, 103
section 20 . . . . 63, 76, 77, 80, 103
section 21 . . . . . . 23, 40, 47, 48, 50, 52, 53, 76, 77, 80, 103, 134, 135,
145, 147
section 21(1) 49, 50, 51, 63, 190
section 21(2) 49, 51, 52, 63
section 21(3) 49, 63
section 21(4) 63, 135
section 21(5) 49
section 21(6) 53, 63
section 22 . . . . 11, 72, 78, 87, 103
section 22(1) 71
section 22(2) 72, 73
section 22(2)(*a*) 73
section 22(2)(*b*) 73
section 22(2)(*c*) 73
section 22(3) 77
section 23 . . . . 78, 90, 103, 146
section 23(1) 71
section 23(3) 71
section 23(4) 77
section 26(1) 74, 103, 127
section 26(2) 79
section 26(3) 74
section 27 . . . . 88, 120
section 28 . . . . 108, 109, 116, 117, 125, 129
section 29 . . . . 112, 129
section 30 . . . . 108, 124, 131
section 30(1) 173, 181, 187, 193
section 30(3) 158, 173
section 31 . . . . 50, 52, 81, 103, 134, 146, 147
section 31(5) 103, 147
section 32 . . . . 50, 52, 103, 134, 145, 147
section 32(1) 181, 187
section 32(4) 135
section 32(6) 135
section 33(1) 71, 73, 103
section 34 103

section 36 .... 103, 129
section 36(2) 103
section 36(3) 103
Sched 1 .... 77, 79, 80, 103, 109, 159
Sched 2 103
   para 9 159
   Part 1 .... 83, 86, 111
   Part 2 .... 86, 87
Sched 3
   para 2 55

Fair Trading Act 1973 .... 116, 139, 141
   section 29 120
   section 130 205
   section 131 .... 79, 80, 115
   section 133 117
Financial Services Act 1986
   section 4 196
   section 57 196
   section 59 197
   section 105 197
   section 111 197
   section 130 197
   section 133 197
   section 199 197
   section 200 197
   Sched 6 197

Gas Act 1986 .... 116, 117

Health & Safety at Work etc Act 1974
   section 27 116
House Purchase and Housing Act 1959
   section 1 180
Housing Act 1988 26
   section 34 26

Insolvency Act 1985
   section 130(3) 59
   section 235 137
   Sched 8 137
Insolvency Act 1986
   section 437 137
   sched 11 137

Insurance Brokers (Registration) Act 1977
   section 2 21
   section 4 .... 21, 104
   section 22 21
Interpretation Act 1978 76
   section 5 .... 103, 199, 200
   section 7 .... 143, 144

Law of Property Act 1925
   section 85 25
   section 86 25
Land Registration (Scotland) Act 1979
   section 28 202
Local Government Act 1972
   section 1 .... 103, 199
   section 20 .... 103, 200
   section 201 140
   Part IV 103, 199, 200
Local Government Finance Act 1988 212
Local Government Finance Act 1992
   section 3 212
   section 72 212
Local Government Planning and Land Act 1980
   section 1 140
   Sched 4 140
   Sched 34 140
Local Government (Scotland) Act 1973
   section 149 140

Magistrates' Courts Act 1980 149
   section 32 .... 148, 200
Malicious Communications Act 1988
   section 1 197
Misrepresentation Act 1967 91

Planning (Consequential Provisions) Act 1990
   section 4 105
   Sched 2 105
Planning (Hazardous Substances) Act 1990 104
Planning (Listed Buildings and Conservation Areas)
   Act 1990 104
Property Misdescriptions Act 1991 .. 2, 12, 14, 24, 30, 31, 32, 55, 79, 89
   section 1 97
   section 1(1) 30, 92, 97, 198, 210

section 1(1)(a) 96
section 1(1)(b) 96
section 1(2) 97, 198
section 1(4) 92
section 1(5)(a) 93
section 1(5)(b) 93
section 1(5)(c) 92
section 1(5)(d) 94
section 1(5)(e) 31
section 1(5)(f) 32
section 1(5)(g) 31
section 1(6) 28
section 2(1) 97
section 2(2) 98
section 2(3) 99
section 2(4) 99
section 3 100
section 4(1) 97
Sched 100
Protection from Eviction Act 1977
section 1 79

Race Relations Act 1976 .... 79, 81
section 29 151
section 30 151
section 31 151
section 32 .... 18, 81
section 53 110
section 57 151
section 62 151
section 63(2) 151
section 63(4) 151
section 78(1) 151
section 78(4) 151
Rehabilitation of Offenders Act 1974 .... 77, 87, 110, 150
Rent Act 1977 26
section 120 26
Restrictive Trade Practices Act 1976 116
section 41 117

Sale of Land by Auction Act 1867 56
section 6 .... 56, 19
Scotland Act 1978 149
Sex Discrimination Act 1975 .... 79, 150

section 38 .... 151, 152
section 39 .... 151, 152
section 40 .... 151, 152
section 41 .... 18, 81
section 62 110
section 66 150
section 71 151
section 72(2) 151
section 72(4) 151
section 82(1) 151, 152
section 82(4) 151, 152
Part III 151
Solicitors Act 1974 105
  section 22(1) 16
Statute Law (Repeals) Act 1981
  section 1 149
  Sched 1 149
Statutory Instruments Act 1946
  section 5 144

Telecommunications Act 1984 .... 116, 117
Theft Act 1968
  section 15 90
Town and Country Planning Act 1990 104
  section 224(3) 79
Town and Country Planning (Scotland) Act 1972 105
Trade Descriptions Act 1968 ... 8, 11, 12, 89, 96, 98, 99, 100, 116, 141
  section 1 .... 90, 96, 198
  section 13 198
  section 14 198
  section 24 97
  section 28 .... 117, 120
  section 29 198
Tribunals and Inquiries Act 1971 138
  section 24 83
Tribunals and Inquiries Act 1992 138
  section 1 .... 111, 112, 129, 138
  section 14 .... 111, 112, 129, 138
  Sched 1 .... 111, 112, 129, 138
Trustee Act 1925
  section 41 122
Trustee Act (Northern Ireland) 1958 122
Trustee Savings Bank Act 1969
  section 3 180

Trustee Savings Bank Act 1981 180

Unfair Contract Terms Act 1977 91

Water Act 1989 . . . . 116, 117
Water Consolidation (Consequential Provisions) Act 1991 117
Water Industry Act 1991 116
  Section 206 116
Weights and Measures Act 1963 141

TABLE OF STATUTORY INSTRUMENTS

Building Regulations 1991 (SI 1991 No 2768) 212
Building Regulations (Northern Ireland) Order 1979 (SI 1979 No 1709)
(N.I. 16) 213
Building Societies (Commercial Assets and Services) Order 1988
(SI 1988 No 1141) 194

Companies Act 1989 (Eligibility for Appointment as Company
Auditor) (Consequential Amendments) Regulations 1991
(SI 1991 No 1997) 125
Companies (Northern Ireland) Order 1986 (SI 1986, No 1032)
(N.I. 6) 124, 195
Consumer Protection (Northern Ireland) Order 1987 (SI 1987
No 2049) (N.I. 20) 196, 211
Control of Misleading Advertisements Regulations 1988(SI 1988
No 915) 116, 117
Criminal Justice Act 1991 (Commencement No 3) Order 1992 (SI 1992
No 333) 125, 141, 149, 202, 209

Estate Agents (Accounts) Regulations 1981 (SI 1981 No 1520)
. . . . 56, 64, 65, 85, 124, 126, 173
reg 3 64
reg 4 64
reg 5 64
reg 6 . . . . 65, 67, 68
reg 6(1) 66
reg 6(3) 66
reg 7 . . . . 68, 69
reg 7(1) 69
reg 8 67
Estate Agents Act 1979 (Commencement No 1) Order 1981 (SI 1981
No 1517) 1, 103, 150
Estate Agents (Appeals) Regulations 1981 (SI 1981 No 1518) . . . 85,113
144, 158
reg 15 85
reg 17 85
reg 26 85
Estate Agents (Entry and Inspection) Regulations 1981 (SI 1981
No 1519) 120, 171
Estate Agents (Fees) Regulations 1982 (SI 1982 No 637) 86, 87

Estate Agents (Provision of Information) Regulations 1991 (SI 1991
     No 859) 34, 38, 42, 43, 44, 45, 131, 181
  reg 2 39
  reg 3(1) 41
  reg 4 40
  reg 5 36
  reg 6 36
Estate Agents (Specified Offences) Order 1991 1991 No 860) . . 78, 193
Estate Agents (Specified Offences) (No 2) Order 1991 (SI 1991
     No 1091) 78, 108, 193
Estate Agents (Undesirable Practices) Order 1991 (SI 1991 No 861)
     . . . . 12, 89, 95, 188
Estate Agents (Specified Offences) (No 2) (Amendment) Order 1992
     . . . . 79, 108, 198
Estate Agents (Undesirable Practices) (No 2) Order 1991 (SI 1991
     No 1032) 23, 27, 39, 45, 46, 47, 48, 52, 56, 81, 108
  Sched 1 51
  Sched 1 para 2 47
  Sched 2 para 1 54
  Sched 3 para 1 55
  Sched 3 para 2 . . . . 45, 55

Malicious Communications (Northern Ireland) Order 1988 (SI 1988
     No 1849)(N.I. 18) 198

Planning (Northern Ireland) Order 1991 105
Property Misdescriptions (Specified Matters) Order 1992 (SI 1992
     No 2834) 89, 94, 200, 202, 210

Rates (Northern Ireland) Order 1977 (SI 1977 No 2157) (N.I. 28) . . . 212

Sex Discrimination (Northern Ireland) Order 1976 . . . . 79, 110, 152
Solicitors (Northern Ireland) Order 1976 105

Town and Country Planning (Control of Advertisements) Regulations
     1989 (SI 1989 No) 79

CHAPTER 1

The legislative background

April 4 1979 is a very important date in the history of the estate agency profession in the United Kingdom, for it was on that day that the Estate Agents Act 1979 received the Royal Assent and thus brought to an end a series of legislative attempts stretching back for more than 90 years. From a different perspective, it also brought to an end several weeks of agonised suspense for, with the Labour Government in the last year of its term and surrounded, as usual, by rumours of an imminent General Election, the question of time was always very much to the fore. The final stages, indeed, proved to be a real cliff-hanger; with the Government already defeated on a vote of confidence in the House of Commons, and therefore merely playing out time until the dissolution of Parliament, who could say whether the very substantial amendments introduced in the House of Lords would be accepted by the Commons? The picture did not become clear until April 2, when the Bill left the House of Lords with an assurance from the Government that it would receive an uninterrupted passage in another place. And so it proved; the *en bloc* acceptance of the Lords' amendments (a process which took a mere seven minutes) was almost the last act of the dying Government for, less than two hours later, Parliament was finally adjourned.

That the Act ultimately reached the Statute Book is due in no small measure to the determination of the major professional bodies, whose unceasing efforts to promote the Bill[1] earned the commendation of both Houses of Parliament. However, enactment is one thing, implementation another, and it was not until three years later (on May 3 1982) that the Act was brought into force by statutory instrument[2]. Even then, as will be seen in due course, a

---

1 And to amend it: in extending the Bill to cover all land, as the professional societies wished, the House of Lords contradicted the expressed intentions of both the major political parties!

2 Estate Agents Act 1979 (Commencement No 1) Order 1981 (SI 1981 No 1517).

number of important provisions (in particular those involving insurance cover for clients' money and the prescribing of minimum standards of competence) were left for future consideration.

The first few years of the Act's operation passed without controversy or even much publicity. Then, in the late 1980s important changes in the structure of estate agency coincided with a booming property market in both commercial and residential sectors and, as regards the latter, produced a barrage of criticism (much of it misguided) of estate agents. Its interest aroused, the Office of Fair Trading (independently at first, later with the backing of the Department of Trade and Industry) published proposals for such innovations as a voluntary code of practice for estate agents, together with more predictable reforms such as the designation of various "undesirable practices" under the Estate Agents Act. The code of practice remains for the moment a Government dream; the rest of the package, however, is now reality. This is the result partly of statutory instruments issued in 1991 and partly of the Property Misdescriptions Act 1991 which, passing through Parliament as a Private Members' Bill, extended to estate agency a rigorous regime previously applicable only to sales of goods.

In the course of this book we shall consider the scope of the Estate Agents Act, its 1991 appendages and the Property Misdescriptions Act. For the remainder of this chapter, however, we shall look briefly at the general background to all this legislation, in an attempt to achieve a better understanding of just what it was intended to achieve.

A Estate Agents Act 1979

Ancient history

The story of estate agents' registration[1] is generally taken to have started in 1888, when a Bill was presented to Parliament for the registration of architects, engineers and surveyors. This measure, which sought to prevent an unregistered person from using the title of architect, engineer or surveyor, rather than from practising as such, foundered on second reading in the face of almost unanimous opposition from MPs, including the president of what

---

1 This story, up to the incorporation of the Estate Agents' Council in 1967, is related in a series of articles by FAR Bennion: (1968) 206 EG 427, 543, 661, 779, 887.

was then the Surveyors' Institution. The president's argument was one which has frequently been used by the professional societies in relation to subsequent legislative attempts; it was that, unless registration was limited to those practitioners who were professionally qualified, its effect would be to confer, in the eyes of the public, an official stamp of approval upon what were inferior beings.

It was not until 1914 that an attempt was made to secure registration for estate agents as such (together, in this instance, with auctioneers). This Bill, like all its successors[1], was aimed at registration of the estate agency function, rather than simply appellation; further, like every measure prior to the Davies Bill in 1977, it envisaged a system of *positive* registration administered by a board which would be representative of the profession. However, despite attracting the support of the Auctioneers' and Estate Agents' Institute (though not that of the Surveyors' Institution), this was merely one of many attempts which made virtually no progress at all.

There is little to be gained from an exhaustive recital of all the setbacks and frustrations which were encountered during the period from 1914 to 1962 by those dedicated to the cause of registration. The catalogue of disasters does, however, contain two connecting threads which have applied more or less consistently throughout this period (and, indeed, beyond it). In the first place, as each fresh scheme for control of the profession has been proposed by the major institutions, so new "breakaway" organisations have been formed to oppose it in the interests of unattached or unqualified agents. These groups have in due course become part of the "establishment" and helped to promote future attempts at legislation, only to find other opposing organisations springing up in their place. In this respect, the Corporation of Estate Agents, which so resolutely opposed both the Davies and Government Bills, was merely following the path already trodden by the Incorporated Society of Auctioneers and Landed Property Agents (1923) and the National Association of Estate Agents (1962).

The second feature which characterised the half-century in question was the continuing inability of the major professional bodies to agree among themselves upon the most suitable form of

---

1 If one includes the 1888 Bill, and the Estate Agents Act itself, there have been no fewer than 14 attempts to legislate in this area.

control to adopt. This undoubtedly hampered the cause of registration; as recently as 1972, in an adjournment debate, the Government was able to justify its failure to legislate in this area by pointing to the fact that, while the Incorporated Society of Valuers and Auctioneers wanted registration in the full sense, the Royal Institution of Chartered Surveyors and the National Association of Estate Agents advocated a simple bonding scheme to protect the public against the loss of deposits.

The Bill which came closest to success was that introduced by Arthur Jones MP, in 1965. Based on an earlier Bill[1], this attracted unusually widespread support from the profession, being backed by a committee which represented no fewer than 10 societies. The proposal was for a full-blown registration scheme, administered by an Estate Agents' Council, which would have power to impose rules of conduct upon practitioners. The Bill reached a Standing Committee before running out of time, but its momentum carried over to provide the impetus for the setting up of the voluntary Estate Agents' Council. This body, which was regarded by the profession as a step towards statutory control, rather than as a substitute for it, was set up in October 1967; by 1969, however, disillusioned by a Monopolies Commission Report which seemed to deny the possibility of raising professional entry standards, the ISVA withdrew, and the Council was formally wound up after two years in operation.

Government initiatives

Throughout the period described above, successive Governments were constant in their refusal to introduce legislation on the subject of estate agents, or to give any official support (other than assistance at the drafting stage) to Private Members' Bills dealing with this matter. It may be that no particular Government department felt itself sufficiently responsible for what was, after all, not a very pressing social problem; if so, then the decision of the Labour Government in 1974 to set up a Department of Prices and Consumer Protection may be seen in retrospect to have been a

---

1 Introduced by Sir Harry Legge-Bourke in 1962.

very significant event in estate agency history[1].

First indications that the new department might lead to a breakthrough in this field came with its publication, in November 1975, of a Green Paper entitled *The Regulation of Estate Agency: a Consultative Document*. This found no evidence of frequent malpractice among estate agents, but referred to "a continuing groundswell of complaint" about certain matters, notably some well-publicised cases involving the loss of deposits. The major suggestion contained in this document was that there should be established a scheme for the licensing of any persons seeking to carry on the business of estate agency, and that this should be administered, not by the profession itself, but by the Director-General of Fair Trading, on whose licensing functions under the Consumer Credit Act 1974 the new proposals were based. The opportunity was also taken to suggest some possible standards of conduct (though not, interestingly, of competence), observance of which might be made a precondition for the grant of a licence; these included many of the matters which are now embodied in the Estate Agents Act.

The consultations which were stimulated by the Green Paper convinced the Government that, while the time was ripe for statutory control of estate agents, the desired degree of consumer protection could be achieved without what the minister termed "a bureaucracy of control involving compulsory registration or licensing". Hints of a new approach to the problem appeared as early as September 1976, but it was not until a year later that details of the department's proposals were revealed. The main feature of these proposals, which distinguished them from every previous attempt to secure the statutory control of estate agents, lay in the "negative licensing" form of supervision to be exercised by the Director-General of Fair Trading[2]. Perhaps because this sought "to strike a balance between effective control and economy in administrative resources" it proved attractive to both the Government and the Opposition; sufficiently attractive, as we now know, to have passed into law.

---

1 The previous Conservative Government had paved the way for this by the appointment in 1972 of Sir Geoffrey Howe QC as the first Minister for Trade and Consumer Affairs at the Department of Trade and Industry.
2 Also noteworthy was the proposal to lay down minimum standards of competence.

The Davies Bill

Natural excitement among estate agents at the prospect of Government-sponsored legislation was kept within bounds by the concluding sentence of the article in which the proposals were revealed: "The Government has not yet decided on when these proposals should be brought forward in the form of legislation". There was, however, not long to wait; a mere three months later there appeared, as if springing fully armed from the head of Bryan Davies MP, a Private Member's Bill of no fewer than 32 sections and two schedules, spread over 36 pages, which covered all the matters referred to and more besides. This ambitious measure was supported by MPs from all the major political parties; indeed, as was made clear by an Opposition spokesman, Conservative objections to the measure (many of which were based on views submitted by the professional bodies) were concerned with matters of detail rather than with the general principles on which it was founded. In particular, the Opposition felt that the jurisdiction of the Director-General could be somewhat oppressive, since an estate agent might be subject thereby to "double jeopardy"; as a result, it was suggested that the powers given to enforcement authorities should be restricted, and the provisions for agents to appeal improved. Despite strong pressure from the professional institutions, however, the Opposition did *not* seek to extend the scope of the Bill beyond the field of residential property, since it agreed with the sponsor that this was a consumer protection measure, rather than one designed to impose statutory regulation upon a profession.

The Davies Bill passed through a Standing Committee with very few amendments and hopes were high that, despite the shortage of time, it might become law by the end of the Parliamentary session. However, on report to the House of Commons it was "talked out" for political reasons, most of which had nothing to do with estate agency. Once again, therefore, the profession was disappointed; such consolation as might be found lay only in the knowledge that the Bill had travelled further than any previous one upon the long road to enactment.

The Government Bill

On November 3 1978 there was introduced into the House of Commons a Government Bill which bore a remarkable resemblance (down to the misspelling of the word "niece") to the Davies Bill as amended by the Standing Committee. Whether this meant that the

Government had taken a strong fancy to a genuine Private Member's Bill, or whether (as seems more likely) the earlier measure was in truth a Government Bill in disguise, is not now of great significance; either way, there is no doubt that the passage of the new Bill was substantially eased by its earlier run-through.

In the eyes of the professional societies, the Government Bill exhibited most of the defects of the Davies Bill which preceded it. The powers of the Director-General of Fair Trading were naturally viewed with considerable suspicion, but (perhaps surprisingly) the main criticism was that the Bill was too restricted; it should, it was felt, have been so drafted as to include *all* persons carrying out estate agency work, *all* forms of property, and *all* sums of money in an agent's hands.

Once again, a Standing Committee of the House of Commons made little impact upon an Estate Agents Bill. Of all the proposed amendments, only those introduced by the Government were accepted, and this process was repeated at the report stage. By January 30 1979, a date which gave it a good chance of reaching the Statute Book, the Bill was passed to the House of Lords, thus becoming the first of its kind to reach this stage in the legislative process.

Having come so far along the road, the professional bodies might have been expected to rest content with what they had achieved. However, despite a very real risk (with the Government tottering) that any delay might prove fatal to the Bill, they continued to press for various amendments to be made and, in due course, were twice successful. First, the Bill was extended to cover all land, rather than merely residential property; second, the enforcement officers' power of entry, which would have enabled them to make "spot checks" on estate agents, was replaced by a more limited power, exercisable only upon reasonable suspicion that an offence has been committed. Whether these amendments would, in normal circumstances, have proved acceptable to the Government is an open question; a sudden quirk of Parliamentary fate, however, ensured that the prevailing circumstances were very far from normal. The Government was defeated on a vote of confidence in the House of Commons and, after negotiations with the Opposition, agreed to speed through a number of matters which were regarded by the parties as non-controversial. Among these was the Estate Agents Bill, which duly became one of 25 such Bills to receive the Royal Assent on April 4 1979.

This last twist in the tale produces the surprising result that a piece of legislation, which both Government and Opposition believed should apply only to residential property, in fact applies to land of any kind. The professional societies must have seen this strange outcome as an unexpected bonus; in the light of their patience and determination over 90 years, who would say that they did not deserve it?

Framework of the 1979 Act

The Estate Agents Act by its very title conjures up visions of a measure designed to regulate all members of the profession in every part of their daily work. Nothing could be further from the truth; as already mentioned, the Government in 1979 saw the problem as essentially one of consumer protection, and this view was reflected to a high degree in the limited ambitions of the Act[1]. As we shall see, many activities which are carried out by estate agents on an everyday basis (such as valuations or mortgage broking) were none the less excluded from the definition of "estate agency work" and therefore from the Act's coverage. The detailed reasons for the exclusion of these items might vary, but the thread linking them was that in each case the gain to consumers was felt insufficient to justify the public expenditure which would have been involved in extending the Act to cover them.

All that the 1979 Act seeks to achieve is the provision of a measure of protection for members of the public against the harm which may be caused by a dishonest or incompetent estate agent. Central to this idea is the imposition of a proper accounting system for deposit money, and it is noteworthy that this is the only area in which an estate agent is made subject to possible criminal penalties for failure to run the business properly[2]. Apart from this, enforcement of the Act lies, not with the criminal courts, but in the hands of the Director-General of Fair Trading, through the novel concept of "negative licensing".

---

1 Many of the enforcement provisions, for example, were taken almost verbatim from other statutes such as the Trade Descriptions Act 1968 and the Consumer Credit Act 1974.

2 Most of the other criminal offences created by the Act are those, standard in "consumer protection" statutes, connected with obstruction of authorised enforcement officers and so on.

This innovation (which satisfied both the determination of the Labour Government to avoid creating a professional "closed shop" and its reluctance to spend public money on a bureaucratic licensing machine) allows anyone to practise as an estate agent unless and until they demonstrate, in the opinion of the Director (and subject to rights of appeal), their "unfitness to practise". Even in this context, the majority of offences which were specified as "triggers" for the enforcement powers of the Director-General of Fair Trading bore no necessary relation to estate agency; in fact the only specific "estate agency" duties in the Act were the requirements that agents should disclose any personal interest in property, hand over interest earned on deposit money and inform clients of likely charges.

B The second crusade

In the first six years of its operation, the Estate Agents Act kept a fairly low profile. Although 89 Prohibition and Warning Orders were made by the end of October 1988 (out of a total of 146 proceedings commenced), by far the majority of these arose out of criminal convictions for offences involving dishonesty, such as theft of clients' money. Indeed, in the only case which cast any light on estate agency practice as such[1], and which was well-publicised as a result, the Warning Orders issued by the Director-General of Fair Trading were quashed following an appeal to the Secretary of State.

The changing scene

This comparatively low level of enforcement activity might be taken to suggest that estate agency itself was in a quiet phase during the 1980s. Any such conclusion would, of course, be a thoroughly misleading one, for the period was one of frenzied activity and fundamental change within the profession. Not only were both the residential and commercial property markets in an unprecedentedly buoyant state, the headlong rush by financial institutions (and other companies) to acquire chains of estate agency practices was creating an entirely new operating environment, as agents accustomed to operating in partnerships on behalf of clients now

---

1 Proceedings against the firm of *Burling Morrison* and one of its partners for failure to give a client sufficient notice of charges.

found themselves to be mere cogs in an enormous corporate machine.

Given the unfamiliar pressures and divisions of loyalty which these changes brought in their wake, it is hardly surprising that various aspects of estate agency practice came in for some sharp criticism from consumer bodies. Nor were the professional bodies unaware of the problems created by these new developments, and the need to improve estate agency's somewhat tarnished public image. Action was perhaps inevitable; the only doubt was as to the direction from which it would come.

The 1991 reforms

The first clear signs of official interest in the current state of the profession appeared in December 1988, when the Director-General of Fair Trading published a review of the Estate Agents Act 1979. That review stated that the OFT had "no evidence to suggest that the majority of estate agents fail to treat consumers fairly and efficiently". Furthermore, the OFT was not convinced that the advantages to be gained by implementing the 1979 Act provisions on minimum standards of competence or bonding for client's money (both of which were consistently advocated by the professional bodies) were sufficient to outweigh the cost and inconvenience which this would involve. None the less, the review identified a number of areas in which the Act might usefully be amended or extended, in relation to both the substance of estate agents' duties and the procedures for their enforcement. And, as will be seen, many of those substantive proposals have, following a long and arduous process of consultation, finally emerged as legislation.

Meanwhile, apparently quite independently of the OFT's initiatives, the Department of Trade and Industry began to show an interest in estate agency. In the latter part of 1988 John Butcher MP, who was then Minister for Consumer Affairs at the DTI, reacted to unfavourable press coverage of estate agency services[1] by inviting various organisations concerned with the transfer of property to take part in a series of consultations. The fruits of that consultation process were seen in June 1989 when the DTI (whose Industry and

---

1 Including a highly critical survey in *Which?*, the magazine of the Consumers' Association.

Consumer Affairs section was by now under the control of Eric Forth MP) published its *Review of Estate Agency*.

That document recognised that much of the public concern related to "a perception of shortcomings in the property transfer system itself rather than estate agents". Furthermore, it was made clear that the DTI's priority was "to identify a means of improving practices and enhancing the protection of clients and prospective purchasers without imposing a stifling layer of regulation". To this end, the review expressed a firm preference for an industry-led code of practice (to which estate agents would adhere on a purely voluntary basis, and which would be backed up by either an arbitration procedure or an Ombudsman scheme), and an equally firm indication that the Government would *not* heed the calls of the professional bodies for the introduction of minimum standards of competence under section 22. However, the DTI did express agreement with the Director-General of Fair Trading's suggestion that certain aspects of estate agency should be curbed by being designated "undesirable practices". Most important among these were the use of certain agency terms such as "sole selling rights"; non-disclosure of various interests not already covered by the 1979 Act; bidding-up of prices by misleading purchasers; abuses relating to tie-in sales; and misleading advertising[1].

Responsibility for putting some more detailed flesh on the bare bones of the DTI's review was given to the Director-General of Fair Trading. Action followed swiftly: a consultation document was produced in September 1989, and this led in March 1990 to a final report. This last document acknowledged with considerable regret the impracticability of obtaining industry-wide agreement on a voluntary code of practice[2]. It also followed what had by now clearly become the "official" line on misdescriptions, namely that the Trade Descriptions Act should be extended to property. And, following on from the earlier discussions of "undesirable practices", the report contained drafts of what were later to be the 1991 Orders and Regulations.

---

1 The DTI also favoured extending the Trade Descriptions Act 1968 to property.

2 The report stressed the difficulty of reaching consensus in what is a highly fragmented area of activity. However, it is fair to point out that the reason why the main professional bodies rejected the proposal was that they wanted a code with statutory sanctions for non-compliance.

After the publication of the OFT report, things moved at what, in legislative terms, must be regarded as a cracking pace. The first official draft of orders and regulations to be issued under the 1979 Act appeared in June 1990 and, after an informal consultation process had tightened up the wording somewhat, these were laid before Parliament in March and came into force on July 29 1991.

There was, however, one notable omission. The Government's intention to amend the Trade Descriptions Act 1968 to cover property, and in the meantime to treat an estate agent's misdescription of property as an "undesirable practice", had been pre-empted by the introduction into Parliament on December 5 1990 of the Estate Agents (Property Misdescriptions) Bill. This Private Members' Bill, which was drafted by the Consumers' Association, was sponsored by none other than John Butcher MP, whose term as Minister of Consumer Affairs at the DTI had seen the start of this entire process. Ill health unfortunately prevented Mr Butcher from seeing his Bill through but, under the guidance of Antony Coombs MP and with Government support, it duly passed into law as the Property Misdescriptions Act 1991[1]. Once it was clear that this measure would indeed reach the statute book, to continue with misdescription as an "undesirable practice" would have been a severe case of overkill, and so all reference to it was duly removed from the Undesirable Practices Order. And, with that amendment, the 1991 legislative package was complete.

The future

What the future holds, in terms of legislative control of estate agency, is not easy to predict. Time for primary legislation (such as would be needed to amend the Estate Agents Act itself) is not easy to find, and Governments tend to react to whatever attracts public attention at the time. However, it seems likely that both the Office of Fair Trading and the Department of Trade and Industry will continue to press the profession to set up a voluntary code of practice, backed by some method of dealing with complaints such as an arbitration procedure or ombudsman scheme; it seems equally likely that the major professional bodies will continue to resist this, on the

---

1 The change of name came about when the Standing Committee widened the scope of the Bill to include statements made in the course of property development as well as estate agency.

ground that what is really required is statutory regulation to deal with the unethical fringe.

Apart from this issue, there are a number of suggestions for legislative intervention which have been made by the OFT but which have not as yet been implemented. Some of these have simply disappeared at various stages of the consultation process; others the OFT has promised (or threatened) to keep under review. A glance into the crystal ball, therefore, may well reveal some or all of the following developments:

i   The Estate Agents Act extended explicitly to cover property overseas[1].

ii   The Director-General of Fair Trading given power to ban an agent from practising "other than as an employee".

iii The DGFT given power to issue a Warning Order in *all* cases (including those where the "trigger" is a criminal offence).

iv   The DGFT given the same right as an estate agent to appeal to the court against a decision of the Secretary of State.

v   Estate agents acting for a vendor required to tell applicants when they wish to purchase the client's property for themselves.

vi   Non-disclosure of an estate agent's personal interest to give rise to a civil claim for damages.

vii Estate agents required to cease acting as agent altogether when they wish to purchase a client's property for themselves.

viii Estate agents required to disclose that they are selling a property anywhere in the same "chain".

ix   Estate agents absolutely prohibited from offering tie-in services.

---

1 For the possibility that the Act already applies to such property, see p 27.

CHAPTER 2

Scope of the legislation

As seen in the previous chapter, the Estate Agents Act 1979, even with its 1991 extensions, falls well short of providing a comprehensive system of statutory control for the estate agency profession as a whole. What the Act covers may be described as "estate agency work in relation to freehold and leasehold interests in land, subject to a number of exclusions", a definition which must now be examined in some detail. It will be seen that many of the services which are provided as a matter of course by estate agents are nevertheless outside the scope of the 1979 Act, either because they do not satisfy the rather limited definition of "estate agency work" or because they have been specifically excluded. As to precisely *why* these matters have been excluded, the detailed reasons vary, but the common thread is that in each case the element of "consumer protection" involved was felt insufficient to justify the public expenditure required to extend the coverage of the legislation.

Although the matter will be considered in more detail later[1], it may be noted at this point that the scope of the Property Misdescriptions Act 1991 is wider than that of the 1979 Act in two important respects. First, while its definition of an "estate agency business" is based on the earlier definition of "estate agency work", it extends to *solicitors* who carry on such work. Second, the 1991 Act also governs the activities of property developers who market their buildings directly, rather than through the medium of estate agents.

A Estate agency work

An estate agent is easy enough to recognise and fairly easy to describe; a satisfactory *definition*, however, is much harder to achieve, as the instigators of previous attempts at legislative control

---

1 See p 30.

discovered. Rather than try yet again to attain this difficult objective, the Estate Agents Act adopts an alternative approach, namely that of defining the estate agency *function*. As a result, this definition requires extremely careful study, since any person who carries out the functions described will be caught by the Act, whether or not he or she would otherwise be regarded as an "estate agent".

Section 1(1) provides:

This Act applies, subject to subsections (2) to (4) below to things done by any person in the course of a business (including a business in which he is employed) pursuant to instructions received from another person (in this section referred to as "the client") who wishes to dispose of or acquire an interest in land –

(a) for the purpose of, or with a view to, effecting the introduction to the client of a third person who wishes to acquire or, as the case may be, dispose of such an interest; and

(b) after such an introduction has been effected in the course of that business, for the purpose of securing the disposal or, as the case may be, the acquisition of that interest;

and in this Act the expression "estate agency work" refers to things done as mentioned above to which this Act applies.

The basic definition

It will be clearly seen from the above that the basic definition of "estate agency work" is an extremely wide one. "Things done" is not, perhaps, the most elegant of expressions, but it serves to indicate that the Act is capable of applying to any form of activity, provided that its object is *either* to effect an introduction between potential contracting parties *or* to bring such an introduction, once made, to a successful conclusion. Furthermore, the specific reference to both acquisitions and disposals of interests in land makes it clear that the Act covers estate agents, not only where they act for vendors or landlords who are seeking to dispose of property, but also where they represent purchasers or tenants who are seeking to acquire it[1]. However, it may be noted that certain of the statutory duties are worded in such a way that they can only apply to agents acting for vendors or landlords.

As to the first of the statutory alternatives (the effecting of introductions), few problems of definition seem likely to arise, especially given that persons who do nothing more than publish

---

1 Where an estate agent acts for a person seeking the tenancy of a dwellinghouse, care is needed to avoid any contravention of the Accommodation Agencies Act 1953.

advertisements are specifically excluded from the operation of the Act by section 1(4). Para (b), however, leaves a curious loophole in relation to post-introduction work, by providing that such work is only covered when it takes place in the course of the same business as the introduction which it follows. If it were not for this restriction, it might perhaps be argued that building societies agreeing to lend money on mortgage, or Land Registry clerks dealing with searches, were doing things for the purpose of bringing transactions to fruition and were therefore within the scope of section 1(1). Common sense suggests that such persons should not come within the Act; however, in seeking to prevent them from doing so, the wording also serves to exclude the work of an estate agent who is instructed to *negotiate* a sale or lease on behalf of one of the parties, at a time when the *introduction* has already been made by another agent or by the parties themselves. Such work is not uncommon; indeed, the meaning of "negotiation" in this context has twice received the attention of the Court of Appeal[1]. Nevertheless, and despite the fact that such an agent, if called in to advise a vendor, might well receive a deposit from the purchaser (control of which is one of the primary objectives of the Act), it is quite clear that this situation is not covered by the statutory definition of "estate agency work".

Business

Many of the introductions which lead to a sale of property are made by a mutual acquaintance of the parties on a purely social basis. It would not of course be desirable to subject these to the provisions of the Act and, one might have thought, a simple way to avoid this would be to confine the operation of the statute to cases where the person concerned is to be paid for this trouble[2]. This, however, has not been done; the Act applies to all work, whether paid or not, provided only that it is done both "in the course of a business" and "pursuant to instructions received".

The first point to be noted in relation to this chosen form of words is that the "business" in question need not be an estate agency

---

1 *Rolfe (FP) & Co v George* (1969) 210 EG 455; *Hoddell v Smith* (1975) 240 EG 295.
2 Compare the restriction of the legal profession's so-called "conveyancing monopoly" to work done "for or in expectation of any fee, gain or reward": Solicitors Act 1974, section 22(1).

business; indeed, it need have little or no ostensible connection with the property world at all. For example, it has been said that bank managers not infrequently mention to one client who is seeking to sell a house the name of another client who may be interested in buying it, and there can be no doubt that any such introduction would fall within the course of the bank manager's business. The same would of course be true of members of other professions, such as accountants, who might well happen to introduce two of their clients and thereby indirectly bring about a sale of property.

As to the meaning of "business" itself, the Act provides no definition. If previous decisions of the courts upon other legislation may be relied upon as a guide, it seems that a "business" connotes both a degree of continuity (ie more than one isolated transaction) and the general idea of gain or reward. However, it is not essential that a person intends to make a gain out of each and every transaction, nor need the "business" show an overall profit; thus, for example, any activities of a local authority, the housing corporation or a housing association which satisfy the rest of the definition of "estate agency work" will come within the Act.

Instructions

It is not every introduction made by a person in the course of business that will constitute "estate agency work" for the purposes of section 1, but only those which are effected "pursuant to instructions received". "Instructions", like "business", are not defined by the Act, but it seems clear that they may quite validly be given by word of mouth, whether or not they are subsequently confirmed in writing. None the less, there must always be some element of instruction, however informal; if this is lacking, then the person concerned is not engaged in "estate agency work". As a result, the Act does not apply to sales of land effected by such people as the personal representative of a deceased landowner, a trustee in bankruptcy or the liquidator of a company; all these "officials" act by virtue of their position, rather than pursuant to instructions received.

It has been suggested that the concept of "instructions" will serve to exclude from the Act those other professional persons, such as bank managers and accountants, mentioned above, who may in the course of business introduce one of their clients wishing to sell a house to another client wishing to buy one. No doubt this is true of some cases, where the intermediary acts on his or her own initiative, but equally there must be many occasions where a bank manager is specifically asked by a prospective vendor to keep an ear to the ground, and here the requirement of "instructions" would seem to be satisfied.

Employees

Much of an estate agent's work is carried out by employees, who may (depending on their type and status) be remunerated on a salary basis or by the payment of commission on business done. Section 1(1) makes it quite clear that such an employee is engaged in "estate agency work" and is therefore subject to all the provisions of the Act and its supporting regulations. Indeed, it is not necessary for a person to be acting pursuant to instructions which *that person* has received from a client; the instructions may have been received by the employer or by a fellow-employee.

The effect of this is to bring every member of an estate agent's staff[1] within the Act. As a result, each employee must comply with all the various statutory duties[2]; any failure to do so may lead to investigation of the individual employee by the Director-General of Fair Trading, with all the consequences that this may involve. In practical terms, such coverage is essential in order to provide for the case of a firm with branch offices, some of which may be under the sole control of a person who is an employee rather than a principal in the business.

Not only is the employee of an estate agency firm subject to the provisions of the Act; responsibility for what that employee does in the course of business may also be placed upon the firm itself. This may involve criminal liability[3] or, under other legislation[4], a finding that the firm is guilty of discrimination. Further, in connection with the events which empower the Director-General of Fair Trading to make an order prohibiting an estate agent from practising, section 3(3)(a) imposes vicarious liability upon the employer in respect of those duties under the 1979 Act which do not lead to criminal

---

1 At least, all those who are employed under "contracts of employment": see section 1(5)(c).

2 Except the duty to open a "client account"; section 14(1) permits an employee to pay clients' money into a client account maintained by the employer.

3 There may be vicarious liability in respect of crimes which do not require the prosecution to prove guilty intent.

4 Sex Discrimination Act 1975, section 41; Race Relations Act 1976, section 32.

sanctions and also any "undesirable practices" as defined by statutory instrument[1].

B Matters excluded

Section 1(1) defines "estate agency work"; the remainder of section 1 specifies no fewer than nine situations in which work apparently satisfying this definition is nevertheless not covered by the Act. Although these exclusions are not classified by the Act itself, they may be seen as falling into two groups. In the first place, there are a number of things which may well be done by an estate agent, either in connection with the disposal of a particular property or quite independently of it, which have been thought for one reason or another not to warrant statutory control. Second, certain work carried out by persons who are not themselves "estate agents" is also excluded.

Work done by estate agents

(a) *Planning matters*
Section 1(2)(e) excludes from the operation of the Act things which are done "in connection with applications and other matters" which arise under current planning legislation. The reason for this exclusion, which appears to cover such advice even where it is given in the course of "estate agency work", is not immediately apparent. Presumably it was felt by those responsible for drafting the Act that the need for consumer protection, which was its motivating force, was much less evident in this connection than in relation to those functions more directly connected with the actual disposal of property.

(b) *Surveys and valuations*
Things done "in the course of carrying out any survey or valuation pursuant to a contract which is distinct from that under which other things falling within subsection (1) above are done" are excluded by section 1(2)(d). This again gives a sharper focus to "estate agency work" by making it clear that it is only when such work is already being done that an *incidental* survey or valuation is included within

---

1 Section 3(1) (c) and (d): see p 81.

the definition. This, it is suggested, would cover the case where a valuation forms part of the service which is offered by an estate agent to a prospective vendor. It would not, however, apply to a mortgage valuation carried out on behalf of a building society, even if the valuer's firm had been responsible for introducing the property to the borrower concerned[1]. What, then, of the case where an agent retained by a prospective purchaser, having found a suitable property, then carries out a structural survey of that property on the client's behalf? This is more doubtful, but it would probably be held to fall outside the scope of the Act, as such a survey would normally be done under a separate contract.

(c) *Credit brokerage*

"Estate agency work" does not include things done "in the course of credit brokerage, within the meaning of the Consumer Credit Act 1974"[2]. The reference is to section 145(2) of that Act, which deals with "the effecting of introductions – in the case of an individual desiring to obtain credit to finance the acquisition or provision of a dwelling occupied or to be occupied by himself or his relative, to any person carrying on a business in the course of which he provides credit secured on land". This clearly applies to the common case of an estate agent who arranges mortgages, and such a person will therefore need to be licensed under Part III of the 1974 Act as carrying on an "ancillary credit business". In view of the strict control which this involves, and the supervisory functions exercised by the Director-General of Fair Trading, to have brought credit brokerage within the Estate Agents Act as well was seen as an unnecessary duplication. It should be noted, however, that mortgage-broking in respect of *non-residential* premises is beyond the scope of the Consumer Credit Act; as a result, an estate agent carrying out this particular function remains within the Estate Agents Act, provided of course that the agent's firm is responsible for introducing the parties.

---

1 If the firm had not effected the introduction, the Act would in any case not apply, since the valuation would not then follow an introduction made in the course of *the agent's* business.
2 Section 1(2)(b).

(d) *Insurance brokerage*

Similar reasoning underlies section 1(2)(c), which excludes things done "in the course of insurance brokerage by a person who is for the time being registered under section 2, or enrolled under section 4, of the Insurance Brokers (Registration) Act 1977"[1]. It should be noted, however, that this provision is of much narrower scope than that relating to credit brokerage. The 1977 Act does not compel all those who *practise* insurance broking to register or enrol; it applies only to those who wish to use the *title* of "insurance broker"[2]. Hence, if an estate agent arranges insurance, without using a restricted title or falsely claiming to be registered, these activities will be governed, not by the Insurance Brokers (Registration) Act, but by the Estate Agents Act.

Work done by other persons

(a) *Solicitors*

Things which are done "in the course of his profession by a practising solicitor or a person employed by him" are excluded from the operation of the Act by section 1(2)(a). Since the normal conveyancing work of a solicitor, although undoubtedly of assistance in bringing about a completed transaction, does not follow an introduction made in the course of the *solicitor's* business, this would not in any case be covered by the Act. Section 1(2)(a), therefore, is concerned to exclude cases where a solicitor is in effect acting as an estate agent, for example by operating a "property shop".

This apparent privilege given to solicitors was heavily criticised by estate agents' professional bodies, especially in its application to Scotland, where solicitors have traditionally played a much more active role in the actual selling of property and have therefore been in direct competition with estate agents. The Government's response to such criticism has been to argue that existing controls on solicitors[3] are at least as rigorous as those imposed upon estate

---

1 Registration applies to individuals, enrolment to companies.

2 For the precise nature of the restrictions which are imposed upon unregistered persons, see the Insurance Brokers (Registration) Act 1977, section 22.

3 Section 1(5)(a) defines solicitors in such a way that those who are *not* subject to their own professional code are caught by the Estate Agents Act.

agents and that to subject solicitors to both régimes would, from the point of view of consumer protection, be superfluous.

Whether or not the Government view is correct depends upon one's assessment of the relative burdens imposed by two different sets of regulations. However, it is interesting to note that one of the main grounds of estate agents' complaints (that solicitors were not obliged to give their clients advance warning of charges for estate agency services) has since been remedied by a Guidance Note from the Council of the Law Society, which requires a written agreement signed by the client at the time when instructions to negotiate a sale are given and accepted.

(b) *Publishers of advertisements*

In order to avoid an unnecessary extension of statutory control to newspapers, computerised house-finding agencies and the like, whose activities in the estate agency field consist *solely* of the provision of information, it is laid down by section 1(4) that the Act does not apply to "the publication or the dissemination of information by a person who does no other acts which fall within subsection (1)". However, the exemption applies only where the organisation goes no further than merely providing information; any further measures designed to effect introductions for clients *are* governed by the Act.

(c) *Receivers of mortgage income*

Following expressions of anxiety by accountants through their professional bodies, it was suggested that the Estate Agents Act should specifically exclude the activities of liquidators, trustees in bankruptcy, executors and so on who might, in that capacity, sell property belonging to another person. The official view, however, was that, with one exception, such a person would be acting by virtue of an office rather than "pursuant to instructions" and would not therefore in any case be caught by the Act. The exceptional case (which, it was felt, might come within the definition of estate agency work but ought not to) was dealt with by section 1(3)(*b*), which excludes things done by any person "in relation to any interest in any property if the property is subject to a mortgage and he is the receiver of the income of it"[1].

---

[1]"Mortgage" is defined by section 1(5)(*b*).

(d) *Employees*

Section 1(3)(a) excludes from the operation of the Act things done by any person "pursuant to instructions received by him in the course of his employment in relation to an interest in land if his employer is the person who, on his own behalf, wishes to dispose of or acquire that interest". The purpose of this provision may have been simply to avoid the creation of a client-agent relationship between an estate agent and an individual employee[1] where that estate agent seeks to buy or sell a property through the firm, but the effect of the statutory wording appears to be wider than this in at least two respects.

In the first place, it seems that, while an estate agent who has a personal interest in property will be in breach of section 21 of the Act[2] if this is not disclosed in any negotiations, the employee who actually conducts those negotiations with a third party will owe no such duty of disclosure. This could of course lead to the removal of the Act's protection in the very circumstances in which it is most needed. Second, it is at least arguable that the exemption may also apply where the "instructions" mentioned in section 1(3)(a) come, not from the employer, but from an independent client, and where the employee then carries out those instructions by selling to his or her own employer. This can hardly have been intended, and it is to be hoped that a court would resist this conclusion by interpreting the phrase "the person who, on his own behalf, wishes to dispose of or acquire that interest" as referring back to the person described as a "client" in section 1(1).

It is not only the employees of estate agents who may be removed from the operation of the Act by section 1(3)(a), but anyone carrying out what would otherwise constitute "estate agency work" on behalf of his or her own employer[3]. This means, for example, that office workers may safely assist the employer in arranging a "private" sale of the employer's own house without finding that they have inadvertently become estate agents. More importantly, where a firm of builders or developers sells its houses

---

1 It is clear that an employee is, potentially at least, subject to all the statutory controls: see p 18.
2 And of the Estate Agents (Undesirable Practices) (No 2) Order 1991: see pp 48–53.
3 Provided that the relationship between them is a true "contract of employment": see section 1(5)(c).

direct to the public, the activities of its employees in negotiating sales, collecting deposits, etc are outside the scope of the Estate Agents Act[1].

(d) *Employers*

Far less controversial is section 1(3)(*c*), which excludes things done by any person "in relation to a present, prospective or former employee of his or of any person by whom he also is employed if the things are done by reason of the employment (whether past, present or future)". As a result of this provision, a firm which assists its employees in buying or selling their own houses will not be treated as carrying on "estate agency work", and nor will the specific employees whose job it is to provide that assistance. The exemption also covers cases where the "employee" assisted has not yet started work or has ceased to work for this employer (eg where he or she is moving into the area to take up the employment or leaving the area at the end of it).

C Interests in land

The Estate Agents Act was originally intended to apply only to estate agency work which related to residential property, or at least to property with a substantial residential element. To critics who regarded the buyer of a small business as being as much in need of "consumer protection" as the buyer of a house, the Government made two replies: first, that "small" business deals were difficult to define and there was no evidence to suggest that large ones caused any problems; and, second, that the consultations which had been carried out prior to the introduction of the Bill had dealt only with residential property. Unconvinced by these explanations, however, the critics redoubled their efforts to extend the Bill's coverage beyond the residential sector, and these efforts ultimately proved successful during the committee stage in the House of Lords. Political events then denied the Government the opportunity to restore the earlier restriction, so that the legislation in its final form applies to all forms of property, be it residential, commercial,

---

1 Though they will be subject to the Property Misdescriptions Act: see p 32.

industrial or agricultural or of course any combination of these[1].

Section 2 sets out the particular *interests* in land whose acquisition or disposal attracts the operation of the Act. The legislation is not concerned with minor interests in land, such as rights of way or mortgages[2]; the basic concept is that of *ownership*. First and foremost, therefore, the Act applies to the transfer of "a legal estate in fee simple absolute in possession", that is, to the simple case where a freehold is marketed. About this little need be said, except to note that the restriction to *legal* estates will exclude subsales of property, at least those in which a person is selling the right to acquire the property directly from the original vendor, rather than undertaking to acquire the property and sell it on[3].

If freehold transactions are relatively straightforward, the same unfortunately cannot be said of those involving the creation or transfer of leases. The first point to be made is that the absence of the word "legal" in section 2(1)(*b*) (by contrast with section 2(1)(*a*)) suggests that equitable as well as legal leases are included. In fact, even if this interpretation were not accepted, those equitable leases which are deemed to arise where the parties fail through lack of the proper formalities (ie use of a deed) to create a legal lease[4] would in any event be brought within the Estate Agents Act by section 2(2), which provides that "the expression 'lease' includes the rights and obligations arising under an agreement to grant a lease".

The major problems in respect of leases arise from the Government's belief that the Estate Agents Act should not apply to agents involved in arranging rentals or property management, since it was felt that other statutes governing such activities already offered sufficient in the way of consumer protection. Attempting to define precisely what was to be excluded from the Act was, however, no simple task, and the formulation finally adopted sought to make the crucial question whether or not the lease was one for

---

1 There is no mention of price, so that the Act will even apply to a wholly gratuitous transfer, provided that an estate agent is involved in arranging it.

2 Section 2(3)(*a*) makes it clear that this is so, even where the mortgagee's security consists of a leasehold interest in the property under the Law of Property Act 1925, sections 85 and 86.

3 In the former case what the sub-purchaser receives is an equitable right to call for a conveyance of the property.

4 Under the principle of *Walsh* v *Lonsdale* (1882) 21 ChD 9. The vast majority of equitable leases are of this kind.

which a premium could lawfully be charged on either creation or assignment[1]. As we shall see, this formulation may have the unintended effect of excluding leases of *any* property at a full market rent[2]. However, whether or not this is so, the very idea of defining the scope of the Estate Agents Act by reference to the lawfulness or otherwise of premiums today bears an irrelevant, indeed rather arbitrary, air. This is because the prohibition on requiring or receiving a premium on the grant or assignment of a protected tenancy under the Rent Act 1977 does not extend to an assured or assured shorthold tenancy under the Housing Act 1988. In consequence, the vast majority[3] of residential tenancies created after January 15 1989 will not be excluded from the operation of the Estate Agents Act by this provision. However, it remains generally unlawful[4] to require or receive a premium on the assignment of a protected tenancy (which means most residential tenancies created before that date) and thus an estate agent involved in the assignment of such a tenancy is not subject to the Estate Agents Act.

D Areas of uncertainty

The discussion in this chapter of sections 1 and 2 of the Estate Agents Act has highlighted a number of potential uncertainties in the definition of "estate agency work", and thus in the scope of the legislation. We may now examine several areas of estate agency activity where, for various reasons, the applicability of the Act is a matter of some debate.

Sales by auction or tender

As we have seen, section 1(1) defines estate agency work by reference to the "introduction" of two parties (the client and another) who wish respectively to acquire and to dispose of an interest in

---

1 This effectively excluded from the Estate Agents Act the vast majority of transactions involving property within the Rent Act 1977, though that Act does permit the taking of a premium in certain cases (mainly involving assignments).
2 See p 29.
3 In exceptional cases it may still be possible to create a protected tenancy: see for example the Housing Act 1988, section 34.
4 There are some exceptions, most of which are listed in the Rent Act 1977, section 120.

land. It might be suggested that this form of words serves to exclude both auctions and sales by tender from the operation of the Act, on the ground that what is brought about by the agent in such cases is not an *introduction* of the prospective vendor and purchaser, but rather an immediate *contract* between them. However, it seems clear that the Act was intended to cover sales of land by whatever method, and it is certainly desirable that it should do so, if only because of the difficulties which might arise where, for example, an agent is instructed to sell land "by auction or otherwise". In any event, it may be suggested that the term "introduction", in the sense of bringing parties together, is wide enough in meaning to include these procedures.

The view that auctions at least are covered by the legislation is certainly shared by those responsible for drafting the Estate Agents (Undesirable Practices) (No 2) Order 1991, which is at pains to provide a specific exemption for auctioneers from one of the duties which it imposes. None the less, it must be acknowledged that some of the specific estate agency rules do not sit too easily in the auction context. In particular, auctioneers may find severe difficulty in complying with the requirement that every offer received for a property is to be communicated to the vendor "promptly and in writing"![1]

Overseas property

There is a basic presumption, rebuttable only by very clear words, that the effect of an Act of Parliament does not extend beyond the United Kingdom. In consequence, the legislation now under discussion can only apply to "estate agency work" which is carried out in England, Wales, Scotland or Northern Ireland. However, a separate question, which the presumption does nothing to answer, is whether the Estate Agents Act can apply to UK agents who market overseas property. This is a common enough activity, and it offers as much scope for abuse as does domestic property; none the less, it is doubtful to say the least whether it falls within the Act.

The view that sales of overseas property lie outside this legislation[2] is based largely upon section 2 of the 1979 Act. This

---

1 See p 45.
2 A view which is held by both the Department of Trade and Industry and the Office of Fair Trading: see the OFT's *Estate Agency Guide*, published July 1991, p 3.

section, in describing the interests in land which are covered, adopts the language of English (and Scottish) land law, using phrases such as "legal estate in fee simple absolute in possession" and "Register of Sasines". Such terms may well be inappropriate when referring to immoveable property in other countries whose land law is fundamentally different from that of the UK, which suggests that the Act cannot apply to such property[1].

Although the view outlined above is probably the correct one, it should be pointed out that it is based upon inference, rather than upon any express provision. What is more, some support for the opposing view, that the Act does in fact extend to UK transactions involving overseas property, may be extracted from section 12. This defines "clients' money" as deposits relating to "an interest in land in the United Kingdom". Why, one might ask, is it necessary to place this qualification on the definition in section 12, if the entire Act only applies to UK property? If nothing else, the existence of such doubts leads to the practical conclusion that estate agents handling overseas sales should adhere to the same principles as they adopt in relation to their domestic work.

Subagency

The question of how far, if at all, the estate agency legislation applies to subagents is a surprisingly complex and difficult one to answer. It is clearly desirable that subagents should be subject to the statutory controls, especially those which seek to protect members of the public rather than clients, since the various abuses at which these are aimed are just as capable of arising at the subagency level. However, it is clear that the legislation has not been drafted with subagency specifically in mind, and there is consequently some difficulty in bringing it within the statutory wording.

The basic problem lies in the 1979 Act's definition of "estate agency work", which requires the agent's instructions to have been "received from another person (in this section referred to as 'the client') who wishes to dispose of or acquire an interest in land". In considering whether these words apply to subagents, the most natural interpretation is surely that a subagent's "instructions" are

---

1 The wording of section 1(6) of the Property Misdescriptions Act 1991 seems even more clearly to rest on this assumption.

received from the main agent, and that the main agent is not a person who wishes to dispose of or acquire an interest in land. If this is correct, then what the subagent does is not "estate agency work" as defined by the Act.

In order to bring subagents within the Act (and, for that matter, within the Property Misdescriptions Act), it might be argued that the main agent *is* a person who wishes to dispose of or acquire land, albeit only as an agent for someone else. This argument, if accepted, would lead to the conclusion that the subagent's "client" is the main agent, and that all the statutory controls therefore apply "one step down". The conclusion is attractive, but the argument itself does not seem very convincing.

A third possible interpretation of the legal position would be to treat the subagent as working pursuant to instructions which emanate from the real client (ie the vendor or purchaser) and which are merely transmitted to the subagent through the main agent. This avoids the need to strain the meaning of the word "client" in section 1; unfortunately, it creates a situation in which the subagent and the "client" do not have a direct contractual relationship with each other. This in turn leads to the conclusion that, while most of the statutory obligations would apply to a subagent, the duty to give the client written notice of charges could not, since that duty requires a direct contract between the "agent" and the "client"[1].

Leases at full rental value

As has already been pointed out, the original intention was that the Estate Agents Act should apply in principle to transactions involving leasehold interests, while excluding residential lettings and property management. However, the chosen method of expressing this distinction raises the uncomfortable possibility that the baby may have been thrown out with the bath water. The problem lies in section 2(1)(*b*), which applies the Act to "a lease which ... has a capital value which may be lawfully realised on the open market". Had this description been: "a lease whose capital value *if any* may be lawfully realised", it would have indicated clearly that what mattered was whether any premium value could legitimately be extracted, rather than whether there was any such value to extract. As it stands, however, the wording of this provision suggests that,

---

1 Section 18(1): see p 41.

where a lease has no capital value (because the property is let at full rental value), no transaction involving that lease can fall within the Estate Agents Act[1].

If this is indeed the true position, it seems to introduce an unnecessary and unproductive complication into what should be a simple matter of deciding whether the Act applies[2]. The crucial question, be it noted, is not whether a premium has been paid as part of a transaction, but whether the lease actually *has* a capital value. And this question is of course one which may receive different answers at different times, as fluctuations in the property market determine whether or not the current rent is a rack-rent[3].

It can hardly have been intended that an estate agent should have to carry out a complex valuation exercise in order to discover whether the Estate Agent Act applies. However, unless a somewhat extended interpretation can be given to the term "capital value"[4], that appears to be the inevitable consequence of section 2(1)(*b*).

E Property misdescriptions

This chapter has so far been concerned exclusively with the area covered by the Estate Agents Act 1979 and the various orders and regulations made under it. It remains to consider the Property Misdescriptions Act 1991 which, though similar in scope to the 1979 Act, goes further in two important respects. The crucial provision is found in section 1(1) of the 1991 Act, which makes it applicable "where a false or misleading statement ... is made in the course of an estate agency business or a property development business, otherwise than in providing conveyancing services". This wording requires closer examination.

---

1 Unless, perhaps, it can be argued that any lease has in principle a capital value, albeit one which, depending on the rent charged, may be "nil" at any given time.

2 The problem would of course have been far less serious if the Act, as was intended, had been limited in scope to residential property.

3 In a falling market, as agents will be painfully aware, leases can rapidly acquire a *negative* value.

4 See note 1.

Estate agency business

The primary target of the Property Misdescriptions Act is undoubtedly the world of estate agency, and this is achieved by section 1(5)(e). That paragraph cross-refers to section 1(1) of the Estate Agents Act 1979 and provides that, if the 1979 Act regards a statement as "estate agency work" and thus applies to it, the statement shall also be treated as made "in the course of an estate agency business" for the purposes of the 1991 Act. To this extent, therefore, everything said in the earlier parts of this chapter about the scope of the 1979 Act is also relevant to property misdescriptions.

Solicitors

As noted earlier, the Estate Agents Act provides a specific exemption for things done by a practising solicitor (or by any employee of a solicitor) "in the course of his profession". The Property Misdescriptions Act confers no such immunity, and thus includes within its definition of "estate agency business" anything which *would* have been caught by the 1991 Act were it not for the solicitor loophole. As a result, any solicitor who provides estate agency services will be subject to the 1991 Act.

However, the extent of this provision should not be overestimated. There is no intention to subject solicitors *generally* to the Property Misdescriptions Act, but only in so far as they practise estate agency. The Act achieves this by excluding statements made in the course of providing "conveyancing services", which are defined by section 1(5)(g) as "the preparation of any transfer, conveyance, writ, contract or other document in connection with the disposal or acquisition of an interest in land, and services ancillary to that".

Although in most cases it should not prove too difficult to draw a line between "estate agency work" and "conveyancing services", there may be some situations in which that line becomes somewhat blurred. For example, a solicitor's answers to preliminary inquiries would normally be regarded as part of standard conveyancing procedure and thus as falling outside the Act, even if the prospective vendor and purchaser had been introduced by that solicitor in the capacity of estate agent. However, if those same "answers to standard preliminary inquiries" were prepared in advance so as to be available to any prospective purchaser, the position would appear far less straightforward. The truth is that estate agency work and conveyancing services are adjacent or even overlapping parts of the same spectrum, and one fades into the other without any clearly defined boundary.

Property development

The most important difference between the respective coverage of the Estate Agents Act and the Property Misdescriptions Act lies in the fact that the latter governs property developers as well as estate agents. The Act applies to a statement made in the course of a "property development business" (which is defined by section 1(5)(f) as "a business ... concerned wholly or substantially with the development of land"), provided that the statement is made "with a view to disposing of an interest in land consisting of or including a building, or a part of a building, constructed or renovated in the course of that business".

The latter part of this definition serves to rule out businesses which merely *deal* in property rather than *developing* it. On the other hand, builders and developers who sell houses and flats directly (eg from a sales office on a housing estate) are certainly included. It remains to be seen what a court would make of the situation where such a sales office is set up by the builder but staffed by a local estate agent. A statement in such a case might quite reasonably be regarded as made in the course of the estate agency business, the property development business, or indeed both.

CHAPTER 3

The regulation of estate agents

From the point of view of the practising estate agent, the most important aspect of the Estate Agents Act 1979, and the orders and regulations made under it, is the imposition of detailed rules governing the way in which day-to-day estate agency business is carried on. The legislation creates a number of specific duties which are owed, not only to clients, but also to third parties with whom an estate agent deals, and breaches of these duties can lead in appropriate cases to penalties ranging from loss of commission through a criminal prosecution to an order from the Director-General of Fair Trading which bans the agent altogether from continuing to practise.

It is perhaps unfortunate that, when the Estate Agents Bill was on its way to the statute book, the specifically "estate agency" provisions received relatively little Parliamentary attention. As a result, the wording of these sections has created a number of problems when applied to the realities of estate agency operations, something which might have been avoided or at least reduced if there had been more detailed debate. At the same time it should be acknowledged that the 1991 Orders and Regulations, which were drafted following considerable consultation with the profession, have gone some way towards repairing the defects of the original statute.

In this chapter we shall consider in detail the specific statutory duties of estate agents. In doing so however we shall not follow the order in which these duties appear in the legislation, but rather the approximate order in which they may be expected to affect a practitioner. Thus, in a straightforward case, an estate agent on obtaining instructions from a client must immediately furnish that client with certain information, concerned largely with the agent's charges. When the property is put on the market, the agent must keep the client informed about certain specified matters, and must also deal in a fair manner with any person with whom negotiations take place. If negotiations reach the point at which the agent is in receipt of deposit money (including a pre-contract deposit), this must be dealt with in accordance with strict statutory rules. The chapter concludes with a reminder that, while the right to practise estate agency is in principle open to anyone, whether qualified or not, there are some special restrictions on that right.

A Initial information to clients

In an effort to bring about the maximum possible transparency in dealings between estate agents and their clients, section 18 of the Estate Agents Act requires certain information to be provided by the estate agent as soon as an agency relationship is in view[1]. That requirement has been significantly extended by the Estate Agents (Provision of Information) Regulations 1991 in respect of both the information which is included and the time and manner at which it is to be provided. It should be appreciated, however, that neither the Act nor the Regulations seek in any way to restrict the terms on which an estate agent contracts with the client; all that is required is that those terms are properly set out at the correct time.

Details of charges
The main thrust of section 18 is geared to information about all the charges, whether in the nature of remuneration or otherwise, for which the client may become liable. This information, according to section 18(2), comprises:

(a) particulars of the circumstances in which the client will become liable to pay remuneration to the agent for carrying out estate agency work;

(b) particulars of the amount of the agent's remuneration for carrying out estate agency work or, if that amount is no ascertainable at the time the information is given, particulars of the manner in which the remuneration will be calculated;

(c) particulars of any payments which do not form part of the agent's remuneration for carrying out estate agency work or a contract or pre-contract deposit but which, under the contract referred to in subsection (1) above, will or may in certain circumstances be payable by the client to the agent or any other person and particulars of the circumstances in which any such payments will become payable; and

(d) particulars of the amount of any payment falling within paragraph (c) above or, if that amount is not ascertainable at the time the information is given, an

---

1 In principle, the requirement applies as much to agents acting for prospective purchasers or tenants as to those acting for vendors or landlords. However, some of the 1991 provisions make sense only in relation to vendors' agents.

estimate of that amount together with particulars of the manner in which it will be calculated.

If all this information is duly given, a client will know at what point the agent's remuneration is to become payable (whether this is on the mere introduction of a prospective purchaser, the exchange of contracts, completion of the sale or some other specified event), and either the precise amount of that commission or the method by which it is to be assessed (eg professional scales or percentage of the purchase price). It has further been accepted by a Scottish court that, where an estate agent obtains a "secret profit" from the agency work which is concealed from the client (consisting in that case of a discount which the agent was given on newspaper advertising) the agent is also guilty of a breach of section 18(2)(a), since this profit constitutes part of the agent's "remuneration"[1].

Compliance with section 18(2) also means that the client will be informed about any potential payments which do not amount to commission, such as advertising or other out-of-pocket expenses[2]. In relation to such payments, the agent must state either the exact amount which is to be charged or, where this is not possible at the outset, the method of its assessment together with an estimate. The Office of Fair Trading's view of this provision is that it requires the agent to provide as far as practicable an itemised list of expenses for which the client will be responsible, together with an estimate of the charges which will arise under each heading. It is emphatically *not* regarded as sufficient for the agent simply to agree a global maximum figure for expenses with the client, even if the agent then keeps within that figure[3].

Special commission clauses

One of the main criticisms of estate agents, in the period leading

---

1 *Solicitors' Estate Agency (Glasgow) Ltd* v *MacIver* 1993 SLT 23: see p 43.

2 A payment for abortive work (such as a "withdrawal fee") which exceeds the expenses actually incurred will be regarded as "remuneration" and will therefore fall within paras (a) and (b).

3 Warning orders issued on this ground against the firm of *Burling Morrison* and one of its partners were overturned on appeal to the Secretary of State. However, on September 8 1988 the Office of Fair Trading issued a press notice stating that, having taken counsel's opinion, it maintained its original interpretation (which furthermore had been accepted by the RICS, ISVA and NAEA).

up to the 1991 legislation, lay in their use of certain restrictive terms of business which might prove unduly onerous to inexperienced clients. Three such terms ("sole agency", "sole selling rights" and "ready, willing and able purchaser") came in for especially heavy criticism, and the Government's response was to require any estate agent using these terms to provide the client with an explanation of their meaning. Not only that; regulations 5 and 6 of the Estate Agents (Provision of Information) Regulations 1991 prescribe the exact words in which the explanation must be couched, subject only to the proviso that, if the circumstances render a statutory explanation misleading, it is the estate agent's responsibility to amend it so as to ensure accuracy.

It might be thought that the new rules could be evaded by the simple expedient of using variations on these terms, such as "exclusive agency" or "person willing to purchase"); however, this potential loophole has been foreseen and duly closed. The 1991 regulations provide that, if an estate agent uses any terms which "have a similar purport or effect" to those listed, the appropriate statutory explanation (again amended as far as necessary to avoid any misunderstanding) must be used.

The clear intention of regulations 5 and 6 is that the relevant statutory explanation should appear in whatever document is used by the agent to satisfy the general requirements of section 18. In any event, the time within which this information is to be given to the client is the same as for all information relating to the agent's terms of business. Furthermore, it is specifically provided that the statutory explanations must be given no less prominence than any other information in the document in which they are contained.

We may now examine the three statutory explanations. What is particularly interesting about them is that they all depart to a greater or lesser extent from the meaning which earlier case law has attributed to the commission terms in question. What is more, the departure in each case appears to be for the benefit of the estate agent. Ironically, therefore, it seems that an estate agent's compliance with statutory rules designed to offer protection to clients may have the effect of entitling the agent to commission, in circumstances where a claim would not have succeeded at common law.

(a) *Sole agency*

According to the 1991 Regulations, "sole agency " means that remuneration will be payable in the following situation:

if at any time unconditional contracts for the sale of the property are exchanged with a purchaser introduced by us during the period of our sole agency or with whom we had negotiations about the property during that period; or with a purchaser introduced by another agent during that period.

A number of points may be made about this clause:

i   The agent will be entitled to commission whenever the *sale* occurs, so long as the relevant *introduction* (whether made by the agent or by another agent) takes place during the period of sole agency[1].

ii There appears to be no requirement for the agent's introduction to be the "effective cause" of the sale in question[2]. Indeed, it is specifically provided that mere "negotiation" with the ultimate purchaser will sufficient.

iii The agent will be entitled to full commission, rather than an award of damages for breach of the sole agency which would normally reflect only the lost *chance* of earning commission[3].

(b) *Sole selling rights*

The definition of "sole selling rights" contained in the 1991 Regulations requires a client to pay remuneration in either of two situations. The first of these is:

if unconditional contracts for the sale of the property are exchanged in the period during which we have sole selling rights, even if the purchaser was not found by us but by another agent or by any other person, including yourself.

The second commission-earning situation is:

if unconditional contracts for the sale of the property are exchanged after the expiry of the period during which we have sole selling rights but to a purchaser who was introduced to you during that period or with whom we had negotiations about the property during that period.

Notwithstanding its different layout, the effect of this definition

---

1 Contrast *Fairvale Ltd* v *Sabharwal* [1992] 2 EGLR 27.
2 Contrast *Sadler* v *Whittaker* (1953) 162 EG 404.
3 See, for example, *Hampton & Sons Ltd* v *George* [1939] 3 All ER 627, where the agents recovered as damages approximately three-quarters of what would have been earned as commission.

seems very similar to that of "sole agency" (apart, of course, from the fact that it catches private introductions as well as those made by a rival estate agent). In consequence, all the comments made above about the earlier definition apply with equal force to this one.

(c) *Ready, willing and able purchaser*

The 1991 Regulations define a "ready, willing and able purchaser" as a person who "is prepared and is able to exchange unconditional contracts for the purchase of your property". The significance of using such a term is then made clear by a paragraph which states:

> You will be liable to pay remuneration to us, in addition to any other costs or charges agreed, if such a purchaser is introduced by us in accordance with your instructions and this must be paid even if you subsequently withdraw and unconditional contracts for sale are not exchanged, irrespective of your reasons.

The first point which may be made about this definition is that the phrase itself appears wholly inappropriate in cases where an estate agent is seeking a *tenant* for property (though it is probably suitable where the agent is acting on behalf of an existing tenant who is seeking to assign the leasehold interest). More serious, however, is the fact that, while the statutory definition appears accurately to reflect the case law on "person ready willing and able to purchase"[1], it is strongly arguable that the use of the word "purchaser" would normally prevent an agent from earning commission unless the transaction proceeded at least as far as exchange of contracts[2]. If this is indeed so, then compliance by an estate agent with the regulations will once again prove to offer additional benefits.

Services offered to purchasers

One area where the Estate Agents (Provision of Information) Regulations 1991 break entirely new ground is in connection with the provision, by estate agents acting on behalf of vendors, of "tie-in" services to prospective purchasers. This practice, which is perhaps especially prevalent where the estate agent concerned forms part of a larger organisation (such as a financial institution) has given rise to a range of complaints, some of which have now

---

1 *Christie Owen & Davies* v *Rapacioli* [1974] 2 All ER 311.
2 *Davis* v *George Trollope & Sons* [1943] 1 All ER 501.

been addressed in the Estate Agents (Undesirable Practices) (No 2) Order 1991. As far as *clients* are concerned, the majority of complaints centred on the fear that there might be a conflict of interest and, while the general law of agency could offer at least some protection under the doctrine of "secret profit", it is clear that by no means all services offered to purchasers would be caught in this way.

The Government's response to this problem lies in regulation 2 of the 1991 Regulations, which requires estate agents to inform their clients (at the same time that they are informed of the agents' terms of business) as to certain services which are to be offered to prospective purchasers. The services in question, which do not include any which are offered free of charge, are defined as "any services to a prospective purchaser ... which are such as would ordinarily be made available to a prospective purchaser in connection with his acquisition of an interest in land or his use or enjoyment of it". The regulation goes on to list by way of example "the provision to that purchaser of banking and insurance services and financial assistance and securing the disposal for that purchaser of an interest in land if that disposal is one which has to be made in order for him to be able to make the acquisition he is proposing or is one which is a result of that acquisition".

This wide definition (which, it is important to emphasise, is in no way limited to the examples given) will clearly include such matters as assisting a prospective purchaser in obtaining a mortgage or a required life insurance policy, or introducing the purchaser to a surveyor or a removal firm. Further, however obvious it might appear to clients who realise that estate agency is a business, an agent must solemnly inform the client that, if a prospective purchaser has a house to sell, the agent will offer to market it.

The obligation of an estate agent under regulation 2 arises in three situations. First, and simplest, there is the case where the estate agent (which, it should be remembered, may be a partnership or a company, as well as an individual) itself intends to offer relevant services. Second, the services may be offered by what the regulations call a "connected person". The meaning of "connected person" for this purpose picks up certain definitions in the Estate Agents Act itself, where they are used in setting out the scope of the agent's duty to disclose any "personal interest". These terms will accordingly be discussed in detail in relation to section 21[1]; for the moment it will suffice to point out that "connected persons" include an estate agent's employer, employee, principal or agent, and also any "associate" of either the agent or of the agent's employer, employee, principal or agent. As for "associates", these include both business associates such as partners (though not, rather oddly, fellow directors of a company) and personal associates such as spouses and a wide circle of relatives. What is more, where an estate agency consists of a partnership or company, there are detailed provisions under which it may be regarded as the "associate" of an organisation of equivalent type.

The third situation in which a client must be told about "services" is where these are to be offered by an independent third party, but where the estate agent or a "connected person" will derive a financial benefit from this. This would apply, for example, where an estate agent regularly introduces prospective purchasers to a particular mortgage or insurance broker and receives a commission from that broker for the introduction.

Although the duty created by this regulation is wide-ranging, it should be emphasised that the estate agent is not obliged to give *details* of the services in question; the regulation states "information ... as to the services", which appears to require no more than a list, and certainly does not compel the agent to reveal the amount of any financial benefit which will accrue. Still less does the regulation demand that the agent should obtain the client's *permission* to offer such services, although a client who objects strongly enough can of course withdraw the agent's instructions altogether.

Time and manner of compliance

Somewhat surprisingly, section 18 as enacted did not specify any particular manner in which the required information was to be given to clients. In consequence, while any sensible agent would give the information in writing (so as to be able if called upon to prove compliance), what mattered in law was simply whether the client had been informed[2]. However, the power given by section 18(4)(*b*) to issue regulations on this matter has now been utilised, and regulation 4 of the Estate Agents (Provision of Information) Regulations 1991 duly provides that all relevant information within

---

1 See pp 49–50.
2 See *Fiesta Girl of London Ltd* v *Network Agencies* [1992] 2 EGLR 28: p 43.

section 18 shall be given by the estate agent in writing.

The manner in which information is to be given is clear enough; the time at which it must be given is less so. Section 18(1) as enacted required this to be done "before any person (in this section referred to as 'the client') enters into a contract with another (in this section referred to as 'the agent') under which the agent will engage in estate agency work on behalf of the client". While the *intention* of this provision was probably that agents should give their clients the prescribed information at or before the time that instructions were taken, there was considerable doubt as to whether the statutory wording would have the desired effect. If, as seems probable, the normal relationship between estate agent and client is a unilateral or "if" contract[1], it is arguable that this does not ripen into a binding contract until the agent fulfils whatever commission-earning event is stipulated (which is likely to be no earlier than the exchange of contracts). Indeed, it could even be argued that this unilateral contract would not attract the operation of section 18 at all, since it would be a contract under which the agent *has engaged* in estate agency work, rather than one under which he or she *will engage* in it. If this is so, then section 18 in itself would appear unworkable.

Thankfully these problems of analysis, although interesting, can now for practical purposes be ignored, since the time at which section 18 must be complied with has been spelled out more precisely in the 1991 Regulations. According to regulation 3(1), the relevant time is "when communication commences between the estate agent and the client or as soon as is reasonably practicable thereafter provided it is a time before the client is committed to any liability towards the estate agent".

It is important to appreciate that this provision does *not* mean that agents can delay in giving the necessary information to their clients so long as they give it before the client is committed to any liability for fees or expenses. The basic requirement is to give the information as soon as communication commences, which suggests for example that an agent visiting a potential client to measure up the property which is to be marketed should take along a copy of the firm's terms of business; the agent can thus ensure that this is

---

1 *Luxor (Eastbourne) Ltd* v *Cooper* [1941] AC 108; see Murdoch (1975) 91 LQR 357 and (1977) 242 EG 609. For a contrary view, see McConnell (1983) 265 EG 547.

given to the client before any "estate agency work" is carried out[1]. This is not to say that a letter "confirming instructions", if sent out promptly, would fail to satisfy the regulations; however, there is always the risk that such a letter might not be regarded as having been sent "as soon as is reasonably practicable" and, in any event, it can *never* be in time if any charges have already been incurred[2].

An unsuspected limitation on the scope of section 18 came to light when one estate agent, who had been instructed on a "sole agency" basis to find a purchaser, complained to the Office of Fair Trading that a rival agent was trying to "tout" or seduce the client. The rival agent was, it seems, plying the client with assurances of a purchaser in waiting, but without any mention of what the agent's charges would be if the client was prepared to instruct him, and the complainant argued that this conduct was in breach of section 18. Unfortunately, the Office of Fair Trading's view[3] was that the section only comes into play where a contract for estate agency work has been entered into; once that has occurred, one can look backwards to see whether the relevant information was given by the agent to the client at the correct time. However, section 18 simply does not govern things done by an estate agent seeking to gain instructions, where no instructions are forthcoming[4].

Sanctions for non-compliance

Any breach by an estate agent of section 18 (including those matters governed by the 1991 Regulations) may have two legal consequences. First, as with the other specific duties which are imposed by the Act, such a breach may operate to "trigger" the enforcement powers of the Director-General of Fair Trading. Second, it is provided by section 18(5) that, unless the information has been given at the correct time and in the correct manner, the

---

1 Although not a statutory requirement, there is much to be said in asking the client to acknowledge in writing that a copy of the relevant information has been duly given by the agent, in case of any future dispute.

2 In a buoyant market, an estate agent may well have a prospective purchaser in mind from the outset, and may be tempted to arrange the deal before sending a "confirming letter" to the client. Such temptations are now to be avoided.

3 I am grateful to the complainant firm for allowing me to see its correspondence with the Office of Fair Trading.

4 For what it is worth, the present writer shares both the OFT's view of the statutory wording and its regret at having to reach this conclusion.

contract is unenforceable, either by legal action or by the exercise of a lien over the client's money, without a court order. Where such an order is sought, the court is given a discretion by section 18(6) either to dismiss the agent's claim altogether, where this is justified by "prejudice" caused to the client by the agent's failure to comply with this obligation and the degree of culpability for the "failure", or to reduce the amount payable so as to compensate the client for any prejudice suffered (presumably in cases where the agent's failure cannot be described as "culpable").

Attempts by clients to use section 18 as a ground for refusing to pay fees have come before the courts on at least two occasions. First, in *Solicitors' Estate Agency (Glasgow) Ltd* v *MacIver*[1], a client complained that, by not disclosing the discount of 18% which they received on the charge for advertising the client's property in a local newspaper, estate agents were in breach of either section 18(2)(*a*) or section 18(2)(*d*) or both (depending on whether the money which thereby accrued to the agents was to be regarded as part of their "remuneration"). This complaint was upheld and, having taken into account both the agents' "culpability" and the client's "prejudice", the Scottish court ruled that the commission payable should be reduced by one-half.

In *Fiesta Girl of London Ltd* v *Network Agencies*[2], a client met with less success. It was clear from the evidence in that case that, although the agent had not set out the commission terms properly in writing, the client had in fact known precisely how much would be charged and in what circumstances. Since the case arose before the 1991 Regulations came into force (and therefore at a time when agents were not compelled to give notice of charges *in writing*, it was held that the agents had in fact complied with section 18 and that there was accordingly no justification for challenging their claim for payment[3].

As a postscript to this discussion, it may be pointed out that, while a breach of section 18 may deprive an estate agent of the right to

---

1 1993 SLT 23.

2 [1992] 2 EGLR 28.

3 Similar facts would today amount to a breach of section 18 (which requires the agent's terms to be set out in writing). However, whether this would justify a court in denying the agent commission would depend on whether the client, despite knowing the truth, could be said to be "prejudiced" by the breach.

claim payment, compliance with that section does not of itself guarantee that the agent will be paid. The agent's entitlement to remuneration will depend upon the general law of contract, and it is worth noting that a contract of agency will normally be created out of an "offer" from the client which is "accepted" by the agent. It follows that, where the agent sends the client a "confirming letter" which in fact alters or extends the terms of the client's original instructions, this could well be regarded as a "counter-offer"; if so, it will carry no weight unless there is evidence to suggest that the client has accepted it. Furthermore, in searching for such evidence, it should be borne in mind that, as a general principle, silence is not consent[1].

B Continuing obligations to clients

As far as estate agents' duties to their clients are concerned, the 1979 Act itself has little to offer other than the information-giving requirement of section 18. However, the 1991 Regulations and Orders are rather more demanding in this respect, laying down a number of duties which continue throughout the agency relationship. These may now be considered.

Variation of terms

As we have noted above, section 18 of the 1979 Act and the Estate Agents (Provision of Information) Regulations 1991 impose detailed obligations upon estate agents to give their clients written notice of a number of matters at the commencement of the agency relationship. Of course, it is perfectly possible for an estate agent and a client to agree at some point that the terms of their contract shall be varied. To take just three examples, a commission rate might be altered, a ceiling on advertising expenses might be increased, or an expiring sole agency might be extended or converted into a multiple agency. In all such cases, section 18(3) requires the agent to notify the client of the new terms.

As enacted, section 18 specifies neither the time nor the manner

---

1 The House of Lords denied an estate agent's commission claim on this ground in *Toulmin* v *Millar* (1887) 3 TLR 836. However, such claims were accepted by the Court of Appeal in *Way & Waller Ltd* v *Ryde* [1944] 1 All ER 9 and *John E Trinder & Partners* v *Haggis* [1951] WN 416.

for an estate agent's compliance, but these omissions have now been rectified by the 1991 Regulations. Once again, the up-dated information must be given in writing and, in this instance, it is to be given at "the time when, or as soon as is reasonably practicable after", the changes are agreed by the parties.

Services requested by purchasers

We noted above the obligation imposed upon an estate agent by the Provision of Information Regulations, to inform the client of any "services" which the agent intends to offer to prospective purchasers. It is further provided by the Estate Agents (Undesirable Practices) (No 2) Order 1991 that, where an estate agent has introduced a prospective purchaser to the client and that purchaser has made an offer[1], the agent must also inform the client "promptly and in writing" of any services which that purchaser *requests* from the agent, or from a "connected person"[2], or from anyone else in circumstances where the agent or a connected person will derive a financial benefit. This obligation applies to all such requests, except those which are refused outright, received by the agents at any time before contracts for the sale or lease of the property are exchanged.

It is important to emphasise that this obligation is completely independent of the one discussed earlier. Even if the agent has already warned the client that, for example, the firm will offer to arrange mortgages for prospective purchasers, the client must be told when a purchaser actually requests the firm to do so. Furthermore, where an agent has *not* informed the client at the outset of a particular service (because at that time the agent had no intention of offering it), the agent must none the less report any request from a prospective purchaser unless this is immediately refused.

Offers received

The Estate Agents (Undesirable Practices) (No 2) Order 1991 seeks to ensure that estate agents are completely open with their clients over offers received from prospective purchasers. To this end, Schedule 3, para 2, defines as an undesirable practice any "failure by an estate agent to forward to his client ... accurate details

---

1 "Offer" for this purpose is expressly defined to include a conditional offer.
2 See p 40.

... of any offer the estate agent has received from a prospective purchaser in respect of an interest in the land". These details are to be forwarded "in writing" and may be sent "by hand, post or fax at the address or to the number given by the client to the estate agent".

An agent's obligation under this provision is to be complied with "promptly", which is defined to mean "within as short a period as is reasonably practicable in the circumstances, from the moment when what is to be done can reasonably be done". This, it appears, is something on which the Office of Fair Trading takes a strict line. In one instance[1] an estate agent received an offer for a client's property at about 4.30 pm on the Friday preceding a Bank Holiday weekend. The agent immediately telephoned the client with news of the offer but, because there were no secretarial staff in the office until the following Tuesday morning, waited until then to send written confirmation. The OFT's view was that this constituted a breach of the Undesirable Practices Order (albeit one which did not merit any action against the firm); the agent should, it was suggested, have sent a handwritten note on the Friday afternoon.

As to precisely what information must be sent to the client, the 1991 Order is not explicit. There is no explanation of what constitutes "details", although it may be suggested that these should include at least the amount of the offer, the identity of the person making it, and perhaps the form in which it is received (whether or not it is in writing). Further, and very importantly, the order makes clear that the agent's duty applies as much to *conditional* offers as to unconditional ones, which suggests that the agent should surely identify any conditions which are attached to an offer (eg whether or not it is "subject to contract").

An important exception to this "undesirable practice" lies in the fact that it does not extend to categories of offer, or categories of "details", which the client has indicated *in writing* need not be forwarded. For example, a client might agree that the agent need not pass on offers which are less than a certain percentage of the asking price, or which the prospective purchaser is not prepared to put in writing. Whether estate agents should habitually seek to agree such exemptions with their clients is a matter of opinion, but

---

1 I am grateful to the estate agent concerned for allowing me to see the firm's correspondence with the Office of Fair Trading.

one situation in which it would surely be sensible to do so is in relation to sales by auction. If this is not done, and assuming that such sales are covered by the Estate Agents Act and therefore by the Undesirable Practices Order[1], the auctioneer will be under an obligation to give the vendor "promptly and in writing" accurate details of every single bid!

Disclosure of personal interest in purchase

Section 21 of the Estate Agents Act imposes a duty of disclosure in respect of certain interests which either the agent or a person connected with the agent has in property to be disposed of or acquired. The main thrust of that provision concerns disclosure to third parties with whom the agent "enters into negotiations"; indeed the extent if any to which it can compel disclosure *to the client* is highly debatable.

This potential loophole has now been directly addressed by Schedule 1, para 2 to the Undesirable Practices Order, which requires an estate agent to disclose to the client "promptly and in writing" that the agent "has, or is seeking to acquire, a beneficial interest in the land or in the proceeds of sale of any interest in the land". A similar obligation arises where the agent "knows that any connected person[2] has, or is seeking to acquire" such an interest.

The duty of disclosure to the client which is imposed by this paragraph appears to arise in four different situations, although it may be suggested that the second and third of these are all that the provision was really intended to catch. The situations are:

i Where an agent acting for a vendor or landlord already has a "beneficial interest" in the property. This would arise, for instance, where a tenant of property instructs an estate agent to market the leasehold interest, and the agent has an existing interest (direct or through a "connected person") in the freehold.

ii Where an agent acting for a vendor or landlord wishes to acquire a beneficial interest in the property.

iii Where an agent acting for a client who is seeking property to rent or buy introduces property in which the agent or a "connected person" has a beneficial interest.

iv Where an agent, acting on behalf of a client who is seeking

---

1 See p 26.
2 The meaning of "connected person" is discussed at p 40.

property to rent or buy, introduces a property to the client but then decides to acquire that property personally or for a connected person (ie the agent intends to compete with the client for the property).

C Duties to third parties

A combination of the 1979 Act and the Estate Agents (Undesirable Practices) (No 2) Order 1991 means that, in addition to their clients, estate agents also owe certain obligations to third parties with whom they deal in the course of business. Three matters are of particular importance in this respect.

Disclosure of personal interest

Once an estate agent accepts instructions to act for a client[1], a fiduciary relationship comes into existence between them, as a result of which an equitable duty of loyalty is imposed upon the agent[2]. This duty manifests itself in various ways, but these are all related to the principle that an agent's personal interests should not be allowed to come into conflict with the interests of the client. If a potential conflict arises, it is the agent's duty to make full disclosure to the client, so that the latter can make an informed decision on what action to take. Failure to make such disclosure may render the agent liable to pay damages, disgorge any personal profit which has been made and forfeit the agreed commission.

It should be noted that this equitable duty of loyalty arises out of the agency relationship; there is no corresponding obligation owed to a third party with whom the agent deals. As a result, it appears that an auctioneer is quite entitled to sell his or her own property, without revealing its ownership to bidders[3]. Further, although there is no authority on the point, it seems likely that the same would be true of an estate agent. However, such cases are now subject to a *statutory* duty of disclosure by virtue of section 21 of the Estate Agents Act.

The first point to be noted about section 21 is that it is not limited

---

1 But not before: see *Pilkington* v *Flack* (1948) 152 EG 366.
2 See, in general, Murdoch: *Law of Estate Agency and Auctions* (2nd ed, 1984) pp 202-205, 241-244.
3 *Flint* v *Woodin* (1852) 9 Hare 618.

in its application to the carrying out of "estate agency work" as defined by section 1 of the Act. The opening words of section 21(1): "A person who is engaged in estate agency work" might, if taken out of context, mean either someone *generally* engaged in estate agency work (ie someone whom the layman would describe as an "estate agent") or someone so engaged *in the relevant transaction*. However, section 21(3) shows conclusively that the former interpretation is the correct one by providing that subsections (1) and (2) apply "where an estate agent is negotiating on his own behalf as well as where he is negotiating in the course of estate agency work". As a result, this statutory duty of disclosure applies, not only when an estate agent acts pursuant to instructions received from a client, but also when the agent decides to enter the marketplace in a personal capacity.

Before we turn to consider the actual obligations which are imposed by section 21, some attention must be paid to what that section regards as a "personal interest". In one sense, this concept is less widely drawn by statute than in equity, for it is limited to interests in the land itself. In other respects, however, the scope of the section far surpasses any duty created by the courts.

Section 21(5) provides that

For the purposes of this section, an estate agent has a personal interest in land if—
(a)   he has a beneficial interest in the land or in the proceeds of sale of any interest in it; or
(b)   he knows or might reasonably be expected to know that any of the following persons has such a beneficial interest, namely—
    (i)   his employer or principal, or
    (ii)   any employee or agent of his, or
    (iii) any associate of his or of any person mentioned in sub-paragraphs (i) and (ii) above.

The overall width of this definition is enormous. In the first place, what we may term an estate agent's "direct" personal interests in land will include any interest whatsoever[1] in either the land itself or in the proceeds of sale of any interest in it. Second, the estate agent will have what we may term an "indirect" personal interest in land if any member of a wide class of persons associated with the agent has a "direct" personal interest and the agent is or should be

---

1 Not just the freehold or lease included in section 2 but any legal or equitable interest.

aware of that fact. This class covers not only the estate agent's partner, employer[1], employee, principal and agent, but also his and their "associates", who are defined by section 32 as including spouses and an extensive circle of relatives.

In an effort to provide an exhaustive definition of "personal interest", the Act deals in sections 31 and 32 with the common situation where an estate agency practice is carried on, not by an individual, but by a partnership, company or unincorporated association. In each case, certain natural persons are named as "business associates" of the organisation, which is then under a duty to disclose any direct personal interest of those persons, their spouses and relatives. Further, complex provisions govern the possibility that two partnerships, two companies or two unincorporated associations may be "associates" where certain natural persons are common to both organisations. In any such case, one associate would be under a duty to disclose any direct personal interest of the other. Interestingly, however, no provision is made for the possibility of one type of organisation, such as a limited company, being the "associate" of another type, such as a partnership. Thus, for example, if X, a partner in a firm of estate agents, is also a director of a development company which markets its houses through X's firm, X as director will be deemed to have a personal interest in the houses, and thus a duty of disclosure. However, the partnership as a whole has no such interest or duty. As a result, so long as X does not personally conduct negotiations with any third party but leaves everything to the other partners, there is no breach by anybody of section 21. If, however, X does contravene the section, it must be remembered that the partnership (and the other individual partners) may also be responsible for that contravention as "business associates" under section 3(3)(c), provided that they are guilty of "connivance or consent".

On turning to the actual obligations as to disclosure which are created by section 21, it may be seen that the section attempts to deal with two different situations. First, section 21(1) provides that an estate agent who has a personal interest in land shall not "enter into negotiations with any person with respect to the acquisition or disposal by that person of any interest in that land until the estate

---

1 Note, however, that the agent who is acting on behalf of his own employer may in any case be outside the scope of the Act: see p 23.

agent has disclosed to that person the nature and extent of his personal interest in it". At its simplest, this covers the case where an estate agent is marketing his or her own house; here the truth about ownership must be disclosed to any prospective purchaser before negotiations commence. This, however, is only the tip of the iceberg; the agent's duty of disclosure applies equally where the personal interest is "indirect" (as described above) and also where that interest in the land is not the one which is being sold. For example, an estate agent instructed to sell the freehold reversion on business premises would come within section 21(1) if the agent's nephew happened to be the sublessee of those premises, or if the ex-wife of one of the agent's partners held a mortgage over them (provided in each case that the agent knew or ought to know the relevant facts).

The examples so far given all relate to an estate agent who is instructed to sell property, but the wording of section 21(1) clearly also covers the converse case. It may be unusual for an agent to be negotiating with a third party over land in which they both hold a personal interest without this being obvious but, given the wide definition of personal interest in this section, it is by no means impossible. Suppose, for example, that an estate agent is approached by a client who is seeking leasehold shop premises to rent. Suppose also that an "associate" of that agent is the landlord of a suitable shop. By virtue of the provision under discussion, the agent may not begin to negotiate with the present tenant for an assignment of the lease until the nature and extent of the agent's personal interest in the property have been disclosed to that tenant.

The Estate Agents Act itself does not specify precisely either how or when agent's duty of disclosure is to be fulfilled, beyond stating that this is to be done before "negotiations" commence. However, this matter has now been effectively fleshed out by Schedule 1 to the Estate Agents (Undesirable Practices) (No 2) Order 1991, which provides that any required disclosure is to be made "promptly and in writing". As to what is meant by "promptly", the order defines this as "within as short a period as is reasonably practicable in the circumstances, from the moment when what is to be done can reasonably be done".

If section 21(1) appears nightmarishly complex, what is to be made of section 21(2)? This deals with cases where the estate agent has no initial personal interest in the land in question, but where, as a result of a proposed transaction or series of transactions, such an interest will be acquired[1]. One might regard the case of an estate agent selling a client's property to an undisclosed "associate" as the obvious abuse at which this provision is aimed but, on closer examination, section 21(2) does not appear to catch this situation. Once again, the duty of disclosure is owed to any person with whom the agent "enters into negotiations", and it seems to place an unjustified strain upon the ordinary meaning of these words to suggest that they include the agent's own client. What section 21(2) covers is the case where an estate agent seems to be buying on behalf of an independent client, whereas in reality the agent intends to act personally or for an associate. Even so, it is by no means certain that the common case of an agent bidding at auction would be included, since such conduct might well not amount to "entering into negotiations".

Interestingly, a situation which appears to fall outside both section 21 of the Act and the Undesirable Practices Order, despite having been singled out for adverse comment by the Department of Trade and Industry, is where an estate agent acting on behalf of a vendor wishes to make a personal bid for the property (or to sell it to a connected person). The agent's intention must in such a case be disclosed to the client[2]; however, it seems that there is no obligation to disclose to prospective purchasers the fact that the agent intends to compete with them for the property.

Section 21 has given rise to a great deal of concern among practising estate agents, based largely on the fear that, because its provisions are so wide-ranging and complex, it may be difficult for an agent in any particular case to determine whether or not there is a disclosable personal interest. Further, these problems are thought to be compounded where an estate agency business is carried on by a partnership or a limited company, since the duties created by section 21 may then be imposed on more than one person, and may not be coextensive in scope. The difficulties inherent in the statutory definitions of "associate" and "business associate" are discussed in the notes to sections 31 and 32[3], and the possibilities of various forms of estate agency practice are

---

1 Note that disclosure in this instance need not be made "promptly and in writing", since the Estate Agents (Undesirable Practices) (No 2) Order 1991 does not apply.
2 See p 47.
3 See pp 145–148.

further explored in the notes to section 21[1]. For the moment, however, it is suggested that an estate agent seeking to discover whether there is a disclosable personal interest should adopt the following procedure:

i Make a list of the person or persons "entering into negotiations" in respect of the property concerned. Remember that more than one person may be involved (or be deemed to be involved). For instance, negotiations handled by one partner are regarded as negotiations of the entire partnership, and negotiations of an employee are also treated as those of the employer.

ii Make a separate list of all the persons who have a *direct* personal interest in the property.

iii For every person on the first list, check whether the second list contains:

   (a) that person, or

   (b) that person's employer, employee, principal or agent; or

   (c) any "associate" of that person; or

   (d any "associate" of that person's employer, employee, principal or agent.

iv A positive answer to any of these checks means that *that person* on the first list has a disclosable personal interest under section 21. Further, it should be remembered that any breach by that person may also be attributable to an employer, principal or business associate by virtue of the "vicarious liability" provisions of section 3(3).

All in all, it cannot be said that section 21 is happily drafted. In particular, it seems likely that, because the definitions are so widely drawn, many agents will find themselves in breach of its terms in cases where there is not the slightest suspicion of sharp practice. The sole consolation which can be offered is that there are no criminal or civil sanctions for a breach of these provisions[2]; the only effect is that a breach may be used to trigger the enforcement powers of the Director-General of Fair Trading, and one may hope that the Director is unlikely to take any action in respect of trivial or inadvertent breaches.

---

1 See p 134.
2 Section 21 (6).

Discrimination over services

One matter which was identified by the Office of Fair Trading in the late 1980s as giving cause for concern related to those estate agents who, while acting for a vendor, sought directly or indirectly to profit from the provision of services (financial or other) to prospective purchasers. It was felt that such practices, which had naturally increased considerably with the move by financial institutions into the estate agency field, could have adverse effects on both purchasers and clients. Unless restrained, an unethical agent might well be tempted for example to favour a prospective purchaser who would require a mortgage from the agent's linked financial services division over one who had already arranged the necessary finance. This would obviously be detrimental to the rejected purchaser; it could also of course work to the disadvantage of the client, who might thereby be deprived of a higher offer for the property. True, the client (if able to prove what had occurred) could take action against the agent for any loss suffered and could also refuse to pay commission[1]; however, the enforcement authorities felt that the situation called for legislative intervention.

We have already noted[2] those provisions in the 1991 Orders and Regulations which require an estate agent to inform (and keep informed) the client as to services which are provided directly or indirectly to prospective purchasers. However, the legislation goes further by defining as an undesirable practice any "discrimination against a prospective purchaser by an estate agent on the grounds that that purchaser will not be, or is unlikely to be, accepting services"[3].

While "services" for the purpose of this provision bears the meaning which we have discussed earlier, "discrimination" is not further defined in the order. However, other statutory provisions in the fields of sexual and racial equality define discrimination in terms of treating a person less favourably than one treats or would treat others in similar circumstances, and there seems no reason to doubt that such ideas would also be applied in the estate agency context. It would surely be discrimination, for example, to seek to

---

1 See *Henry Smith & Son* v *Muskett* (1978) 246 EG 655.
2 See pp 38, 45.
3 Estate Agents (Undesirable Practices) (No 2) Order 1991, Schedule 2, para 1.

persuade the client to prefer one applicant to another[1], to delay in passing on an offer from an unfavoured purchaser[2], or to send out details of suitable properties only to those applicants identified as likely to require services. Such cases appear obvious; practising estate agents can no doubt think of other more subtle tactics which might be used to discourage unwelcome purchasers, and which would thereby constitute "discrimination".

Misrepresentation of offers

An estate agent acting on behalf of a vendor will naturally try to obtain the best possible price for the client and, to that end, to emphasise the attractions and desirability of the property in question. Such conduct is only to be expected, although a feeling that agents have on occasion been somewhat over-enthusiastic in this respect is what has led to the passing of the Property Misdescriptions Act 1991[3]. However, one type of misdescription which is *not* covered by that Act is any false or misleading statement as to the state of competition for a particular property. This is because claims designed to play off one prospective purchaser against another (for example by suggesting that the other has made a higher offer or is a "cash buyer") do not appear on the list of "prescribed matters" which define the scope of the 1991 Act.

This particular matter is addressed by Schedule 3, para 1 to the Estate Agents (Undesirable Practices) (No 2) Order 1991, which provides that it is an undesirable practice for an estate agent to make any misrepresentation "(a) as to the existence of, or details relating to, any offer[4] for the interest in the land; or (b) as to the existence or status of any prospective purchaser of an interest in the land". This applies to all false or misleading statements, whether made in writing or orally; however, an agent is only in breach where the offending statement is made "knowingly or recklessly".

Pretending to one prospective purchaser that a rival has made a higher offer for the property might be regarded by cynics as the

---

1 As occurred in *Henry Smith & Son* v *Muskett* (1978) 246 EG 655.
2 This would of course also be an undesirable practice under Schedule 3, para 2.
3 See Chapter 5.
4 This is defined so as to include a conditional offer. However, the *exclusion* of offers which the client has agreed need not be passed on by the agent appears to be a drafting error; it surely cannot have been the intention that agents should be free to lie about such offers.

equivalent in private treaty sales of an auctioneer's taking of bids "off the wall". While that practice is clearly illegal[1], an auctioneer may quite lawfully bid *on behalf of the vendor* provided that the right to do so has been properly reserved in the particulars or conditions of sale[2]. The 1991 Order accordingly provides that an auctioneer who bids on behalf of the vendor in accordance with the 1867 Act is not to be regarded as guilty of an "undesirable practice".

Although the provision under discussion is aimed at statements made by an estate agent to prospective purchasers, the drafting is wide enough to include statements made to the client. However, it seems that the order would not apply to an estate agent who attempts to procure instructions from a vendor by inventing tales of eager purchasers known to the agent who are already queuing to secure the property. Since the agent's conduct in such a situation would by definition precede the receipt of any instructions from the client, it would unfortunately fall outside the definition of "estate agency work" and thus beyond the reach of the legislation altogether.

D Clients' money

The Estate Agents Act has always been seen, both in and out of Parliament, as a consumer protection measure, and nowhere does this appear more strongly than in relation to those provisions which deal with "clients' money". The intention which underlies sections 12 to 17 of the Act, and the regulations which support those sections[3], is that estate agents should deal properly with clients' money and that, in the event of an agent's default, the public should be protected as far as possible against any resulting loss. In considering this matter, it will be convenient to look first at the statutory definition of "clients' money", before turning to the specific obligations which the Act imposes in respect of such money.

Definition of clients' money

Estate agents who are members of a professional body will be accustomed to members' account rules governing their treatment

---

1 See Murdoch: *Law of Estate Agency and Auctions* (2nd ed, 1984) p 495.
2 Sale of Land by Auction Act 1867, section 6.
3 The Estate Agents (Accounts) Regulations 1981.

of "clients' money" which, in this context, means all money belonging to other persons which is temporarily in the hands of the agent. For the purposes of the Estate Agents Act, however, "clients' money" bears a far more restricted meaning, as is apparent from the wording of section 12(1):

In this Act "clients' money", in relation to a person engaged in estate agency work, means any money received by him in the course of that work which is a contract or pre-contract deposit–
(a) in respect of the acquisition of an interest in land in the United Kingdom, or
(b) in respect of a connected contract,
whether that money is held or received by him as agent, bailee, stakeholder or in any other capacity.

Of the various sums of money which may be handed over in the course of estate agency work, therefore, the Act controls only the two types of deposit on sales of land and contracts connected to and conditional upon sales of land, such as sales of curtains and carpets. Section 12(2) provides that a "contract deposit" for this purpose means

any sum paid by a purchaser–
(a) which in whole or in part is, or is intended to form part of, the consideration for acquiring [an interest in land in the United Kingdom] or for a connected contract; and
(b) which is paid by him at or after the time at which he acquires the interest or enters into an enforceable contract to acquire it.

Section 12(3) applies a similar definition to "pre-contract deposit" except that in this case, of course, the sum is paid *before* the interest is acquired or the contract made.

In view of the obligations which attach to "clients' money" and the severe consequences of failure to meet them, the definitions in section 12 are of fundamental importance, and several points are worthy of emphasis. First, since the definition of "clients' money" includes both contract and pre-contract deposits, the question into which of these categories a particular sum falls is one of purely academic interest. Second, it matters not whether the money is received by the estate agent as agent, as stakeholder or in any other capacity[1]; the Act makes it clear that the same rules apply.

---

1 The word "bailee" seems inappropriate in this situation, as this usually refers to the deposit of goods rather than money.

Third, in cases where a sum of money is paid to an estate agent partly as a deposit and partly for other purposes (eg for transmission to a building society or an insurance company) then, if it cannot conveniently be split, the whole sum is "clients' money" and must therefore pass through the "client account"[1].

Clients' money as trust property

At common law, the question of who should bear the loss caused by the default of a deposit-holding estate agent (whether this arose from dishonest misappropriation of the money or simply insolvency) gave rise to some difficulties and uncertainties. In respect of a *pre-contract* deposit, the decision of the Court of Appeal in *Ryan* v *Pilkington*[2] placed that loss squarely on the vendor (by insisting that the vendor must reimburse the purchaser). However, this was overturned by the House of Lords in *Sorrell* v *Finch*[3], with the result that it is now the purchaser who suffers the loss. As for a *contract* deposit, there were (and are) no judicial decisions directly in point, perhaps because it is so rare for estate agents to hold such deposits. It is suggested, by analogy with the case of an auctioneer, that the loss would fall on the vendor, irrespective of whether the agent received the money "as agent" or "as stakeholder"[4].

The principle that a deposit-holder's default must inevitably cause loss to either the vendor or the purchaser was due in no small measure to the common law rule that the legal claim of a person entitled to a deposit against the deposit-holder was a purely personal one. Hence, if the deposit-holders' assets were insufficient to pay off general creditors, the deposit was in no way "earmarked" for the person entitled to it. Nor, if the deposit-holder had wrongfully used the money, could it be traced. In an attempt to alleviate the hardship caused by this rule, section 13(1) provides that where clients' money, as defined above, is received by any person in the course of estate agency work, that money–

(a)   is held by him on trust for the person who is entitled to call for it to be paid over to him or to be paid on his direction or to have it otherwise credited to him, or

---

1 See p 65.
2 [1959] 1 All ER 689: see also *Goding* v *Frazer* [1966] 3 All ER 234; *Burt* v *Claude Cousins & Co Ltd* [1971] 2 QB 426; *Barrington* v *Lee* [1972] 1 QB 326.
3 [1977] AC 728.
4 *Annesley* v *Muggridge* (1816) 1 Madd 593; *Rowe* v *May* (1854) 18 Beav 613.

(b) if it is received by him as stakeholder, is held by him on trust for the person who may become so entitled on the occurrence of the event against which the money is held[1].

This statutory creation of a trust in respect of clients' money has a number of important effects. First, it means that, if an estate agent becomes insolvent, any money which is in that agent's "client account" cannot be used to pay off general creditors; it is "property held by the bankrupt on trust for any other person"[2] and is therefore payable only to those persons entitled to the deposits[3]. Second, if the estate agent has wrongfully used money impressed with a trust, for example by paying it into his or her own bank account or buying goods with it, the person entitled to the money may be able to "trace" it, even into a different form and into the hands of a third party (though not of a *bona fide* purchaser for value without notice)[4]. Less importantly, the existence of a trust brings into operation various supervisory powers of the High Court, notably the power to appoint a new trustee where necessary, such as where the sole principal of an estate agency practice dies or becomes insane[5].

The designation of clients' money as a trust fund would normally lead to a number of other consequences under the general law of trusts. Those responsible for the drafting of the Estate Agents Act, however, adopted a more specific approach; according to section 13(3):

The provisions of sections 14 and 15 below as to the investment of clients' money, the keeping of accounts and records and accounting for interest shall have effect in

---

1 If the estate agency work is done in Scotland (no matter where in the United Kingdom the property is located) the money is held "as agent" rather than on trust (section 13(2)); the legal effect, however, is the same.

2 Insolvency Act 1985, section 130(3).

3 If there is not enough money in the client account to meet all claims, the rule in *Clayton's case* (1816) 1 Mer 529 applies. It is presumed that withdrawals from the account are made in the same order as payments in; hence, "first in, first out".

4 The equitable rules on "tracing" are complex, depending mainly upon the status of the ultimate recipient of the money and also upon whether the money remains sufficiently "identifiable". Readers are referred to any of the major works on equity.

5 In the particular case where an order made by the Director-General of Fair Trading prohibits an estate agent from holding clients' money, it is provided that the order itself may appoint a substitute trustee and make provision for his expenses and remuneration: section 13(4).

place of the corresponding duties which would be owed by a person holding clients' money as trustee, or in Scotland as agent, under the general law.

Further, it is provided by section 13(5) ("for the avoidance of doubt") that, where an estate agent has a lien over clients' money, this does not affect the trust; equally, the trust does not affect the lien[1].

The statutory trust created by section 13(1) is expressed to be for the benefit of the person who is entitled to demand the clients' money from the estate agent or, in certain circumstances where nobody is so entitled, to the person who may become entitled. In the vast majority of cases, this will be one of the parties to an actual or proposed sale; which one it is will depend upon the type of deposit in question and the capacity in which it is received and held by the estate agent. In practical terms, it appears that the "person entitled" to a pre-contract deposit is the prospective purchaser who has paid it, irrespective of whether the estate agent purports to receive that deposit "as agent for the vendor", or "as stakeholder", or without any designation[2]. The only exceptions to this general principle are where the vendor has expressly authorised the agent to receive a pre-contract deposit as agent, or where the agent purports (without authority) so to receive it and the vendor subsequently ratifies what the agent has done. If, while an estate agent is holding a pre-contract deposit, contracts are exchanged between vendor and purchaser, the status of that deposit depends upon the terms of the contract. It may well be that the money is expressed to become part of the *contract* deposit; if the contract is silent, however, the rules outlined above will continue to apply.

In relation to a contract deposit, an estate agent may receive the money either "as agent for the vendor" or "as stakeholder". In the former case (assuming that the agent is acting with the vendor's authority), it is the vendor who is the "person entitled" for the

---

1 Although it has never been specifically decided whether or not an estate agent has a lien on clients' money for remuneration and expenses, it seems in principle (by analogy with the case of an auctioneer: *Webb* v *Smith* (1885) 30 ChD 192) that there should be one on money which belongs to the client. In practice, this will only apply to a contract deposit which is still in the agent's hands after the sale is completed or (possibly) to a contract deposit which has been received "as agent" with the authority of the vendor.

2 *Sorrell* v *Finch* [1977] AC 728.

purposes of section 13[1]. In the latter case, neither party is immediately entitled to demand the money; which of them subsequently becomes entitled depends upon whether the sale is successfully completed (the vendor) or one of the parties wrongfully fails to complete (the innocent party). Perhaps because estate agents so seldom hold contract deposits, the English courts have never been called upon to decide the capacity in which they are presumed to do so in the absence of any evidence to the contrary. Given that an auctioneer is presumed to be a stakeholder[2], it would seem appropriate to regard an estate agent in a similar light; however, dicta from the Court of Appeal suggest that the presumption is in favour of holding the deposit "as agent"[3].

Restrictions on taking deposits

There are three areas in which the Act either curtails or removes altogether the power of an estate agent to accept deposit money. Surprisingly, however, in a field which is central to the Act's consumer protection philosophy, a number of the relevant provisions remain unimplemented.

(a) *Insurance cover*

Section 16(1) provides that:

Subject to the provisions of this section, a person may not accept clients' money in the course of estate agency work unless there are in force authorised arrangements under which, in the event of his failing to account for such money to the person entitled to it, his liability will be made good by another[4].

This "compulsory bonding" provision is not yet in force and, notwithstanding Government assurances that its implementation would follow that of the Act by no more than a year or so, it now seems that there is no intention to bring it into operation. Surprisingly, even if it is implemented, it will not require everyone

---

1 *Ellis* v *Goulton* [1893] 1 QB 350.

2 *Furtado* v *Lumley* (1890) 6 TLR 168. By contrast, the vendor's solicitor is presumed to hold a contract deposit as agent for his client: *Edgell* v *Day* (1865) LR 1 CP 80.

3 *Ojelay* v *Neosale Ltd* [1987] 2 EGLR 167.

4 The person entitled to the money will not of course be a party to these "authorised arrangements", but may none the less make a direct claim against the insurers: section 16(3).

who engages in estate agency work to be bonded, but only those agents who accept clients' money. However, in an effort to ensure that members of the public realise when they are dealing with an unbonded agent, section 16(4) makes it a criminal offence for any person who carries on estate agency work to "describe himself as an 'estate agent'", or in any way to indicate that he is prepared to act as a broker in the acquisition or disposal of interests in land", unless the relevant information[1] is displayed both at the agent's place of business and in all documents, such as advertisements, notices and the like, which may induce people to use the agent's services.

The details of what constitutes "authorised arrangements" are not set out in the Estate Agents Act itself but are left to be filled in by subsequent regulations. These may for example specify the circumstances in which the liability of the insurers may be excluded[2], and provide that any "ceiling" on that liability in an individual case shall not be less than a specified amount[3]. It is, of course, impossible to predict with certainty the content of such regulations, but it seems safe to assume that the insurance required would have to provide total cover, not only for the agent's deliberate misappropriation of clients' money, but also for the careless mixing of such money with the agent's own funds, which results in its loss on the agent's bankruptcy. It also appears that the insurance schemes presently operated by the major professional bodies would be designated as satisfying the requirements of the statute.

Where estate agency work is carried on by such institutions as banks, building societies or insurance companies, whose funds are adequately protected by other legislation, they may be exempted from the requirements of section 16, either under the regulations or on application to the Director-General of Fair Trading under section 17. Subject to such exemption, however, these provisions are regarded as very important; any breach is a criminal offence.

(b) *Pre-contract deposits*

There are two further provisions of the Estate Agents Act which relate solely to pre-contract deposits. First, where estate agency

---

1 The content of which will be specified in regulations.
2 Section 16(2)(c).
3 Section 16(2)(d).

work is done in Scotland (no matter where in the United Kingdom the land itself may be situated), such deposits are banned altogether; section 20 provides that no pre-contract deposit may be sought or received. Second, where estate agency work is carried out in England, Wales or Northern Ireland, there is no such absolute prohibition, but section 19 enables regulations to be made which will limit the size of the sums involved "and such a limit may be so prescribed either as a specific amount or as a percentage or fraction of a price or other amount determined in any particular case in accordance with the regulations". Once again, however, this provision has not yet been brought into operation, and there are no indications that it is likely to be implemented in the foreseeable future.

(c) *Personal interest*

Section 21(4) provides that:

An estate agent may not seek or receive a contract or pre-contract deposit in respect of the acquisition or proposed acquisition of–

(a) a personal interest of his in land in the United Kingdom; or

(b) any other interest in any such land in which he has a personal interest.

The odd thing about this provision is that it appears not to apply to the sale of an agent's own property. Such a case would not normally fall within the Estate Agents Act at all, because section 1 requires the agent to be acting "pursuant to instructions", and one can hardly be said to "instruct" oneself to act. Furthermore, the extension of the "personal interest" provisions to private deals by section 21(3) applies only to the duty of disclosure imposed by subsections (1) and (2). If this analysis is correct, the ban on seeking or receiving deposits is limited to cases where the estate agent has a "personal interest" in land but is nevertheless selling an interest in that land as agent for a client.

It should be noted that, even where an estate agent accepts a contract deposit in breach of this provision, there is no statutory obligation on the agent to refund it[1]. Section 21(6) provides that no breach of the section shall give rise to any form of legal action, either civil or criminal.

---

1 A pre-contract deposit is of course returnable on demand in any case.

Dealing with clients' money

(a) *Client accounts*

When an estate agent receives clients' money in circumstances where this is permitted, the Act leaves no doubt as to what should be done with it. It is provided by section 14(1) that:

Subject to such provision as may be made by accounts regulations, every person who receives clients' money in the course of estate agency work shall, without delay[1], pay the money into a client account maintained by him or by a person in whose employment he is.

Failure to comply with this obligation is a criminal offence carrying a fine of not more than £500.

The definition of a "client account", and the detailed rules which govern its operation, are to be found in section 14 of the Act and the Estate Agents (Accounts) Regulations 1981. According to section 14(2), a client account is a current or deposit account with an authorised institution, which is in the name of a person who is or has been engaged in estate agency work and which contains in its title the word "client". The "authorised institutions", which are listed in the Schedule to the regulations, are, broadly speaking, banks (including trustee savings banks), building societies and the Post Office. It is further provided by regulation 3 that, should any of these institutions themselves engage in estate agency work, they and their employees are exempt from the requirements relating to client accounts[2].

Regulations 4 and 5 govern the precise way in which a client account is to operate. The basic objective is to achieve the rigid separation of "clients' money", as defined by the Act, from all other money in the estate agent's hands; to this end, while clients' money must always be paid into a client account without delay, there are only two other occasions on which other money may lawfully be paid into the same account. These are, first, where the institution in question requires a minimum sum to open or maintain the account (in which case it can and should be withdrawn when it is no longer

---

1 Unfortunately perhaps, in view of the severe consequences of any breach of this provision, "without delay" is not further defined in the Act.

2 This is on the basis that depositors are given sufficient protection by other statutory codes which govern such institutions.

required for that purpose) and, second, to restore in whole or in part any money wrongfully paid out of the account[1]. The regulations also clarify the position of money which is paid to an estate agent for more than one reason. In such circumstances[2], the whole sum is deemed to be "clients' money" but, in so far as it is practicable to split that part which may be strictly described as a "deposit" from the rest, only the former may be paid into the client account. If it is not practicable to split it, then the entire sum must be paid into the account and the surplus removed.

The circumstances in which money may lawfully be paid out of the account (apart of the removal of anything which should never have been paid into it) are:

i   where money is paid to the person entitled to it[3];
ii in payment of the estate agent's remuneration or expenses, with the agreement of the person for whom the money is held;
iii in the lawful exercise of a lien[4]; and
iv where money is transferred to another client account[5].

It follows from these rules that, strictly speaking, a client account should neither be credited with interest earned on the money in it, nor debited with any bank charges. The agent must arrange for these payments in and out to be allocated to other accounts.

(b) Accounts and records

In an effort to ensure that there is a means of checking compliance by an estate agent with his duty to open a client account and to operate it properly, section 14 and the Accounts Regulations lay down details of the actual accounts and records which are to be kept[6]. The duty to keep these accounts is imposed by regulation 6 upon "any person who receives clients' money in the course of estate agency work", except an employee who always pays such money without delay into the employer's client account. It is, however, provided that the obligation (which involves keeping

---

1 This might seem odd but, without it, every wrongful payment out of a client account (which constitutes a criminal offence) would automatically be followed by another offence when the money was returned.
2 See p 58.
3 As to who is the "person entitled", see p 60.
4 See p 60.
5 In which case the records kept must enable its movements to be clearly traced.
6 Failure to keep such accounts is a criminal offence: section 14(8).

records for six years after the end of the accounting period to which they relate) may be handed over by one person to another when the former ceases to be engaged in estate agency work.

As to the nature of the accounts and records which are to be kept, regulation 6(1) provides generally that these must be sufficient to show that the estate agent's basic duty in respect of clients' money has been discharged, and "to show and explain readily at any time all dealings with the money". This latter requirement involves identifying the account itself, the institution where it is located, and so on. From the point of view of the practising estate agent, however, the more important (and more useful) provision is regulation 6(3), which gives a detailed list of the information which must be made available[1]. In relation to clients' money *received*, this consists of the date of receipt; the amount; the name and address of the depositor; the purpose of the payment (eg pre-contract deposit, contract deposit, payment in respect of a connected contract)[2]; the interest in land to which the payment relates (and the identity of the person wishing to dispose of that interest); and the person for whom, and the capacity in which, the money is from time to time held[3]. Further, it is provided that the majority of this information must also appear upon the counterfoils or duplicate copies of receipts issued to those who deposit clients' money, and that these counterfoils or copies must themselves be kept. Where payments *out of the account* are concerned, the information required to be shown is the date of the payment; the amount; the identity of the payee; the interest in land to which the payment relates; a reference to the corresponding payment in; and the purpose of the payment[4]. Finally, where money is transferred from one client account to another, the records must show the reason for the transfer and enable the original payment in to be traced.

---

1 The information is to be "indexed" by reference to the interest in land to which it relates: reg 6(3)(b).

2 If part of the sum is paid in only because it cannot be split, the purpose of that payment must be shown.

3 The regulation acknowledges that the estate agent may not know these matters, since both the person and the capacity may change while clients' money is in the agent's hands.

4 Where payment is made to the estate agent in respect of remuneration or expenses, the records must further identify any information required to be given to the client in respect of those charges under section 18 (see p 34).

However, this last requirement does not apply where sums are transferred between a current and a deposit account kept by the agent, in both of which clients' money is held generally.

(c) *Audit*

The basic obligation imposed by regulation 8 of the Estate Agents (Accounts) Regulations 1981 is to draw up the accounts and records described above in respect of consecutive "accounting periods"[1] and to have them audited within six months of the end of each period by a "qualified auditor"[2]. The auditor's report must then, under threat of criminal penalties, be produced on demand to a duly authorised officer of an enforcement authority.

The methods to be adopted by an auditor in this context are clearly defined by regulation 8. Having ascertained from the estate agent in question particulars of all bank accounts maintained by the agent or by employees in the course of estate agency work during the relevant period, the auditor is to examine the accounts and records kept by that person to see whether or not they comply with the requirements of regulation 6 described above. To this end the auditor may demand further information or explanations from the estate agent, but is not required to pursue enquiries beyond the accounts and records (as supplemented by these further explanations), nor to consider the keeping of the relevant accounts outside the period in question.

Having carried out this investigation, the auditor is required to produce a report to the estate agent, and this report may take one of four forms:

i   that all the requirements of regulation 6 have been complied with;

ii that the requirements of regulation 6 have been substantially complied with. This would be appropriate where, in the auditor's opinion, the only breaches are trivial ones due to clerical errors,

---

1 A period not exceeding 12 months. No dates are specified, but an employee who is obliged to keep such accounts must adopt the same accounting period as the employer.

2 Defined by section 14(6) so as to mean, in nearly all cases, either a chartered accountant or a member of the Association of Certified and Corporate Accountants. In the case of limited companies, certain persons such as officers and servants of the company are disqualified from acting as auditors by the Companies Acts, and the Estate Agents Act applies the same disqualifications: section 14(7).

all of which were rectified on discovery and none of which have caused any loss;

iii   that the requirements of regulation 6 have not been complied with. In this case the auditor must specify the relevant breaches; and

iv   that the auditor is unable to form an opinion as to whether or not the requirements of regulation 6 have been complied with. In this case the auditor must specify the relevant matters and explain why it is impossible to form an opinion about them.

(d) *Interest*

As a general rule, where money which belongs to one person earns interest while in the hands of another, the question whether or not that interest must be accounted for depends on the nature of the relationship between the parties. If their relationship is a fiduciary one (such as that between solicitor and client), then the rules of equity require that the interest be handed over[1]. If, on the other hand, there is merely a contractual or quasi-contractual obligation to hand back the sum involved, then the holder of the money is entitled to keep whatever interest it earns.

In the specific context of sales of land, it has been held that an auctioneer holding a contract deposit "as stakeholder" falls into the latter category and is therefore not liable for interest to the person (be it vendor or purchaser) who ultimately becomes entitled to the deposit[2]. Further, it was held in *Potters* v *Loppert*[3] that the same principle governs the case of an estate agent holding a pre-contract deposit, at least where the agent purports to receive this money "as stakeholder"[4]. This case has not escaped criticism but, as a result of section 15 of the Estate Agents Act and regulation 7 of the Estate Agents (Accounts) Regulations, it is now of little or no practical significance.

Regulation 7 deals with the situations in which a person engaged

---

1 *Brown* v *Inland Revenue Commissioners* [1965] AC 244.

2 *Harington* v *Hoggart* (1830) 1 B & Ad 577. It would seem logical to regard an estate agent in the same light, although dicta from the Court of Appeal suggest the opposite: *Ojelay* v *Neosale Ltd* [1987] 2 EGLR 167.

3 [1973] Ch 399.

4 The estate agent in this situation is not a true stakeholder, but the phrase negates the possibility that he or she receives the money as agent for the vendor (which would involve a fiduciary relationship).

in estate agency work must account for interest upon clients' money. By providing that such account is to be made to the "person who is for the time being entitled to the money", and specifically excluding any period during which the money is held "as stakeholder on trust for the person who may become entitled to it on the occurrence of" a specified event, regulation 7(1) makes it clear that the same sum of money may attract a duty to pay interest to more than one person, in respect of different periods of time. As we have already seen[1], the "person entitled" to clients' money (and therefore entitled to interest on it) may be the actual or prospective purchaser (pre-contract deposit, or contract deposit once the sale has gone off); the vendor (contract deposit held "as agent", or contract deposit after completion of the sale); or neither party (contract deposit held "as stakeholder").

To avoid the creation of a legal obligation which might necessitate an expensive book-keeping operation in respect of a trifling sum, it is provided by regulation 7 that the duty to pay interest arises only where the clients' money in question exceeds £500 and the relevant interest is at least £10[2]. The relevant interest for this purpose is computed in different ways, according to where the clients' money is held:

i   If the money is held in a separate deposit account (assuming of course that this is a valid client account), the estate agent must account for the interest which it actually earns.

ii If the money is held in a client account which is not a separate deposit account, the agent must account for interest as if it had been so held at the same authorised institution.

iii If (contrary to section 14 of the Act) the money is not held in a client account, the agent is penalised by having to pay interest at the highest rate available on the day when it should have been paid in[3].

iv In the case of an authorised institution itself, interest must be

---

1 p 60.

2 This means, not the total interest earned by the sum in question, but the amount to which the particular person is entitled.

3 If the estate agent has one or more client accounts with authorised institution, payment must be made at the highest rate available at those institutions. If the agent has no such account, payment must be made at the highest rate available at *any* of the authorised institutions.

paid at the appropriate rate for a separate deposit account at that institution.

Section 15 of the Estate Agents Act makes it clear that the obligations described above may be modified or excluded by an "arrangement in writing, whenever made" between an estate agent and any other person who has or may have an interest in clients' money. Exactly what is meant by this is not clear. Presumably the mere giving of notice in writing (for example on the receipt which is issued to a depositor) falls short of being an "arrangement between" the parties, but there is no positive requirement of *signature* by or on behalf of the person concerned. In the absence of such an arrangement, the statutory rules are practically exhaustive; section 15(3) provides that there is no other liability to account for interest on money held in a general client account[1].

It should be noted that, unlike the other provisions of the Accounts Regulations, those concerned with the duty to account for interest are not backed up by criminal sanctions. However, a breach may of course operate to trigger the powers of the Director-General of Fair Trading, and it is also specifically provided by section 15(5) that any person entitled to interest on clients' money may claim it from the estate agent in the civil courts.

E Restrictions on the right to practise

We have already noted that, unlike previous attempts to legislate in the field of estate agency, the 1979 Act does not compel would-be practitioners to obtain a licence before setting up in business. This change in approach was due partly to a desire on the part of both the main political parties to avoid the creation of a professional "closed shop", and partly to a belief that the Act's objectives of consumer protection did not require a costly and cumbersome licensing machinery. The consequence is that, as a general principle, there are no restrictions upon the right to practise this particular activity. However, there are three exceptional cases in

---

1 This presumably does not preclude the possibility of the money being held in a *separate* client account; in such a case, it seems that any liability to pay interest is governed by common law in so far as it does not fall within the Accounts Regulations. If so, a liability *will* arise, since section 13 creates a trust where none existed previously.

which it is a criminal offence to engage in estate agency work, and these we now consider.

Prohibition orders

As will be seen in the next chapter, the Director-General of Fair Trading is empowered in certain circumstances to make an order prohibiting a person from engaging in estate agency work, on the ground that that person is unfit to do so. Once such an order is made, it must be obeyed, on pain of criminal sanctions[1].

Bankruptcy

Section 23(1) provides that "an individual who is adjudged bankrupt after the day appointed for the coming into force of this section or, in Scotland, whose estate is sequestrated after that day shall not engage in estate agency work of any description except as an employee of another person"[2]. This prohibition, which ceases to have effect when the bankrupt is discharged, is backed by criminal sanctions[3]. Interestingly, however, a criminal conviction in such circumstances is not a ground on which the Director-General of Fair Trading may make an order banning the agent from practice; as a result, the bankrupt agent could still continue to practise as an employee of someone else.

Minimum standards of competence

Surprisingly, perhaps, in an Act which firmly eschews any positive system of licensing, section 22(1) enables regulations to be made prescribing minimum standards of competence for those engaged in estate agency work. This (as yet unimplemented) provision, though at first regarded as highly controversial, now commands the support of the major estate agency bodies[4]; however, without a

---

1 An unlimited fine following conviction on indictment; a fine of up to £5,000 (at present) on summary conviction: see notes to section 33(1).

2 A possible loophole, by which a bankrupt might form a company and work for it under a contract of employment, is closed by section 23(3).

3 An unlimited fine on conviction on indictment; on summary conviction, a fine of (present) maximum of £5,000: see notes to section 33(1).

4 Following a u-turn by the Royal Institution of Chartered Surveyors, which was originally concerned that "official recognition" might be given to those holding lesser qualifications.

change of Government (or a complete change of mind on the part of the present Government) there seems little likelihood of its being brought into operation. Nevertheless, in politics all things are possible, and a brief review of what might be in store therefore seems in order.

It should be noted at the outset that section 22 has received a good deal of criticism, on the ground that it could be used to restrict entry to the profession; as to this, all that can be said is that the Act was not drafted with any such intention. Further, the Government has repeatedly voiced its determination that there should be no move whatever which would create a closed shop or an exclusive organisation, or which would in any way restrict competition.

A feature of previous attempts to introduce statutory control of estate agency has been that groups of experienced, though unqualified, agents have immediately banded together to oppose any measure which would restrict the right to practise to persons holding certain professional qualifications. Recognition of the legitimate anxieties of such "unattached" agents has led to the provision in section 22(2) that, if regulations are ever made, they *must* "prescribe a degree of practical experience which is to be taken as evidence of competence" and, in addition, they *may* provide for alternative qualifications. The Government has further assured such agents that, if these provisions were to be brought into force, there would be a "clearance for competence" for anyone practising at that time against whom there had been no complaint of malpractice. In other words, section 22 would not be used so as to disqualify any existing practitioner.

The part to be played by the professional bodies in relation to the setting of minimum standards for estate agents is not immediately apparent, but some idea of what was intended may be gleaned by reading between the lines of section 22(2). This provides that, in addition to dealing with practical experience, regulations may also:

(a) prescribe professional or academic qualifications which shall also be taken to be evidence of competence;

(b) designate any body of persons as a body which may itself specify professional qualifications the holding of which is to be taken as evidence of competence;

(c) make provision for and in connection with the establishment of a body having power to examine and inquire into the competence of persons engaged or professing to engage in estate agency work; and

(d) delegate to a body established as mentioned in paragraph (c) above powers of the Secretary of State with respect to the matters referred to in paragraph (a) above.

Of these provisions, para (a) is the clearest; the meaning of the remainder is somewhat obscure until it is realised that the "body" which might be designated under (b) is not the same as that which might be established under (c). Para (b) envisaged that the existing professional bodies with their own examination systems would be designated under section 22(2)(b) to set the standards of competence for their own members, so that those arrangements would continue largely undisturbed. What was envisaged by para (c), on the other hand, was a body representative of all persons engaged in estate agency work, whether or not holding professional qualifications, to test the competence of those not wishing to join the designated bodies, to prescribe standards for them, and to provide an alternative to the arrangements which are institutionalised by the existing professional bodies. The composition of this body would be determined by the regulations, but it has been made clear that, at least at the outset, the knowledge and expertise of members of the existing professional bodies would be heavily relied upon.

If section 22 is ever brought into force, any person who engages in estate agency work "on his own account" will, unless he or she satisfies the required standard of competence, be guilty of a criminal offence[1]. Further, statutory regulations will provide what proportion of partners must satisfy the minimum standard in order to render the partnership itself "competent", and similar rules will apply to any "body corporate or unincorporated association" which engages in estate agency work.

---

1 Carrying, on conviction on indictment, an unlimited fine; on summary conviction, the maximum fine is at present £5,000: see section 33(1).

CHAPTER 4

Enforcement of the 1979 Act

Responsibility for the enforcement of the Estate Agents Act is given by section 26(1) to both the Director-General of Fair Trading and local weights and measures authorities[1]. The latter are concerned with local "on the ground" enforcement which, in this instance, means only the investigation and prosecution of specific criminal offences under the Act[2]; breaches by estate agents of the *non-criminal* obligations imposed by the Act and its supporting regulations and orders are the concern of the Director alone. Notwithstanding this division of responsibility, however, local weights and measures authorities may be called upon to report to the Director on the carrying out of their functions under the Act.

A Negative licensing

The overall supervision and enforcement of the Act is made the responsibility of the Director-General of Fair Trading. However, unlike the Consumer Credit Act 1974, which the Director also administers, the Estate Agents Act does not impose any *positive* system of licensing or registration. With very few exceptions[3], any person may practise as an estate agent until proved unfit to do so. The scheme, therefore, consists of a kind of "negative licensing", and the question of a particular agent's fitness or unfitness is a matter for the Director who may, if the requirements of the Act are satisfied, make various orders, including one which prohibits the agent altogether from continuing to practise.

The taking away of a person's livelihood is of course a drastic form of punishment and, not surprisingly, the Director's powers in

1 In Northern Ireland, the functions of the latter are given to the Department of Commerce.
2 But no enforcement authority may prosecute in Scotland: section 26(3). All prosecutions there are initiated by the Procurator Fiscal.
3 See pp 70–73.

this area are hedged about by numerous restrictions, both procedural and substantive[1]. Not only must the Director be satisfied that the agent is generally unfit; there must also have occurred one of a number of specified "trigger" events, such as a criminal conviction, before these powers come into play.

We shall shortly consider the various "triggers" and the procedures (including the question of appeals) which govern their exercise. First, however, we must look at the important matter of the exact range of orders which the Director is empowered to issue.

Types of order

The simplest and most drastic form of order which may be made under the Estate Agents Act 1979 is one which prohibits a person[2] from doing any estate agency work at all. If, however, the Director feels that the "unfitness" relates to only one aspect of estate agency work, the order may instead prohibit the agent "from doing estate agency work of a description specified in the order"[3]. A limited order of this kind might be thought appropriate, for example, where an agent's careless accounting procedures, while not reflecting upon his or her general level of honesty and competence, nevertheless make the agent unfit to hold clients' money. In such a case, the agent might simply be banned from accepting clients' money[4].

It is further provided[5] that any order, whether general or specific, may be limited in scope to a particular part of the United Kingdom, a useful provision where, for example, complaints of malpractice are restricted to one branch of a larger organisation. There is, however, no power to limit the *time* for which an order is to operate; any ban takes effect (subject to the possibility of revocation following the agent's application)[6] as a life sentence.

---

1 It has been held that, where a person's livelihood depends upon the decision of a tribunal, the strict test of proof "beyond reasonable doubt" is to be applied: see *R v Milk Marketing Board, ex parte Austin* The Times, March 21 1983.

2 Or an estate agency partnership or company as a whole: see p 76.

3 Section 3(2).

4 As to money which is already in the agent's possession when the order comes into force, the Director is empowered to appoint a new trustee in substitution for the banned agent: see section 13(4).

5 By section 3(5).

6 See p 86.

The severity of a prohibition order may be tempered under section 4, which empowers the Director in certain cases to issue a *warning* to the estate agent that, if he or she persists in infringing the law, the Director will make a declaration of unfitness to practise under section 3.

It is vital to appreciate that this warning power does *not* exist where the grounds for an order under section 3 consist of a criminal conviction (section 3(1)(*a*)) or either racial or sex discrimination (section 3(1)(*b*)). It *only* applies where the estate agent is guilty of a breach of one of the non-criminal obligations contained in sections 15 and 18 to 21 (section 3(1)(*c*)), or has engaged in an "undesirable practice" as defined by a statutory instrument made under section 3(1)(*d*). Further, it should be emphasised that a warning order can only be made where the Director is satisfied that the agent's *general* "unfitness" will justify an order under section 3 if the warning order is not heeded.

A warning order made under section 4 must indicate the type of section 3 order (general or limited) which will be made against the agent if there is a further infringement. If such an infringement does occur[1], the Director may automatically proceed to make an order under section 3; the agent's failure to comply with the warning is, by section 4(3), to be treated as conclusive evidence of unfitness to practice.

It should be noted that any prohibition or warning order under the Estate Agents Act is made against a "person" which, according to the Interpretation Act 1978, "includes a body of persons corporate or unincorporate". As a result, it seems clear that an order may be made against a partnership or a limited company, as well as an individual estate agent. Indeed, the possibility of dealing *en bloc* with a partnership is expressly envisaged by section 5(2), which provides that the order may also have effect against some or all of the partners individually. Somewhat oddly, however, there is no similar provision in relation to limited companies.

"Trigger" events

The grounds upon which an order may be made by the Director are

---

1 If the warning order is based on a breach of the Act itself (ie sections 15 and 18 to 21), a further breach of *any* of those sections may trigger a ban. If it is based on an "undesirable practice", however, it must be the *same* practice which recurs.

set out in section 3(1). This requires the Director to be satisfied that the agent:

(a) has been convicted of –
    (i)   an offence involving fraud or other dishonesty or violence, or
    (ii) an offence under any provision of this Act, other than section 10(6), section 22(3) or section 23(4), or
    (iii) any other offence which, at the time it was committed, was specified for the purpose of this section by an order made by the Secretary of State; or
(b) has committed discrimination in the course of estate agency work; or
(c) has failed to comply with any obligation imposed on him under any of sections 15 and 18 to 21 below; or
(d) has engaged in a practice which, in relation to estate agency work, has been declared undesirable by an order made by the Secretary of State.

These four categories of grounds may now be considered.

(a) *Criminal offences*

Section 3(1)(a) lists three groups of offences, conviction for which will justify the Director in making an order against the agent. In relation to all of these it should be noted that a conviction which is "spent" by virtue of the Rehabilitation of Offenders Act 1974 "or any corresponding enactment for the time being in force in Northern Ireland" is to be disregarded: Schedule 1.

The first group of offences, those involving fraud, dishonesty or violence, is identical to that which would justify the Director-General of Fair Trading in refusing to grant a licence under the Consumer Credit Act 1974. It might be thought fairly uncontroversial, but dislike of the idea of "double jeopardy" led a number of MPs to suggest that an estate agent with, say, a tendency to beat his wife (or her husband) in private ought not to be banned from practising as an estate agent, in addition to being subject to the normal penalties imposed by the criminal law. These criticisms, however, proved ineffective, and it is clear that conviction for an offence within this group is a "trigger", whether or not the offence took place in the course of estate agency work.

Ironically, this last point has been used by the Office of Fair Trading, not to persecute secret spouse-batterers, but rather to support the issue of a substantial number of prohibition orders[1] against persons who were not in fact estate agents at all! For

---

1 Approaching one-half of the total number of prohibition orders so far issued.

example, a solicitor convicted of stealing clients' money, or of participating in a large scale mortgage fraud, would in all probability be struck off the roll of solicitors. If the OFT in such a case had any reason to believe that that person might subsequently enter the field of estate agency, but regarded this as undesirable from the point of view of consumer protection, then a prohibition order under the Estate Agents Act might well be issued[1].

As to the 15 offences created by the Act (most of which are concerned either with the handling of clients' money or with obstruction of the enforcement authorities), all but three rank as "triggers". Of those which do not, section 10(6) (which makes it illegal to disclose information obtained by authorised officers under the Act) is simply irrelevant to the practice of estate agency. The other two (practising without possessing the necessary qualifications[2] or when bankrupt[3]) are such as to render a banning order superfluous. It should be noted, however, that a criminal conviction for disregarding a previous order of the Director *is* a ground for a subsequent order; this might be relevant where, for example, the first order is limited as to type or work or geographical area.

The third group includes any criminal offence which may be listed from time to time in orders made by the Secretary of State. At the time of writing, only two such orders have been made. The first of these, the Estate Agents (Specified Offences) (No 2) Order 1991[4], is not easy to summarise[5]; its contents, which include more than 40 offences arising under 13 statutes, range from the making of unauthorised disclosures by a computer bureau[6] to the impersonation of a licensed conveyancer[7]. The broad impression is that the offences have for the most part been collected from "consumer protection" statutes, rather than with any real consideration of what it is that estate agents actually do; one might

---

1 Alternatively, the OFT might demand a formal undertaking not to enter estate agency from the person concerned.

2 Section 22 (not yet in force).

3 Section 23.

4 So called because it was issued to replace the Estate Agents (Specified Offences) Order 1991, which had inadvertently not been made in accordance with Parliamentary procedure.

5 The order is reproduced in Appendix B: see p 193.

6 Data Protection Act 1984, section 15.

7 Administration of Justice Act 1985, section 35.

have expected, for example, to find specified such offences as the eviction or harassment of residential occupiers[1], but this is not the case.

The second order, the Estate Agents (Specified Offences) (No 2) (Amendment) Order 1992 is short and wholly unsurprising, in that it merely adds to the existing list offences arising under the Property Misdescriptions Act 1991. Interestingly, the first drafts of this order also included offences arising under the Town and Country Planning Act 1990, section 224(3)[2]; this proposal, however, met with a hostile reception from a number of estate agency bodies and was quietly dropped as being too controversial.

The Estate Agents Act contains two provisions which are designed to ensure that, so far as possible, the Director receives information of any relevant convictions. In the first place, when a local weights and measures authority proposes to institute proceedings for an offence under the Act, it is under a duty to notify the Director and to supply a summary of the facts upon which the prosecution is to be based[3]. Second, section 9(5) amends section 131 of the Fair Trading Act 1973 so as to empower courts, both civil and criminal, to notify the Director of any conviction or judgment which is regarded as relevant to the Director's functions under either Act.

(b) *Discrimination*

At first sight, section 3(1)(*b*) seems to be of enormous scope. This appearance, however, is deceptive; "discrimination" for the purposes of the Estate Agents Act bears only that meaning which is assigned to it by Schedule 1. In effect, this provides that the question whether or not an estate agent has committed discrimination is not one for the Director to answer; it is governed by the outcome of previous proceedings under either the Sex Discrimination Act 1975 or the Race Relations Act 1976[4]. As a result, an agent will only be guilty of discrimination under section 3 where a court has made a finding

---

1 Protection from Eviction Act 1977, section 1.
2 Involving any contravention of the Town and Country Planning (Control of Advertisements) Regulations 1989, governing the display of estate agents' boards.
3 Section 26(2).
4 In relation to Northern Ireland, the reference is to the Sex Discrimination (Northern Ireland) Order 1976 and there is *no* provision as to racial discrimination.

to that effect or where a non-discrimination notice served on the agent by the Equal Opportunities Commission or the Commission for Racial Equality has become final; in either event, the agent will have had an opportunity in judicial or quasi-judicial proceedings to contest the allegations[1].

To constitute a "trigger" for the purposes of section 3, the discrimination in question must have been committed "in the course of estate agency work". Whether or not it is so committed *is* a matter for the Director to decide, but there is an important limitation; an estate agent who discriminates *as employer* rather than *as estate agent* is not to be dealt with under the Estate Agents Act.

The general treatment of discrimination in the Act runs parallel to that which is given to criminal offences, and this similarity is heightened by two procedural provisions. In the first place, a finding or notice of discrimination under Schedule 1 becomes "spent" after five years. Second, section 9(6) makes it the duty of the statutory Commissions to notify the Director of any finding, notice, injunction or order which appears to them to be relevant to the Director's functions under the Act.

(c) *Statutory obligations*

Of the specific "estate agency" duties which are imposed by the 1979 Act[2], only those which relate to the keeping of client accounts are backed by criminal sanctions. It is, of course, essential that breaches of the other duties should serve as "triggers" for the enforcement powers of the Director-General of Fair Trading, and this is achieved by section 3(1)(*c*), which refers to "sections 15 and 18 to 21". The task of deciding whether an agent has failed to comply with any of these obligations is one for the Director's own judgment; it is possible, however, for a breach of sections 15, 18 or 20 to lead to a civil action[3], in which case the court concerned may notify the Director of its decision under section 131 of the Fair Trading Act 1973[4].

---

1 For a case of racial discrimination involving a London firm of estate agents, see *R v Commission for Racial Equality, ex parte Cottrell & Rothon* [1980] 3 All ER 265.

2 See Chapter 3.

3 The same is potentially true of section 19, but this has not yet been brought into effect.

4 As amended by section 9(5) of the Estate Agents Act.

(d) *Undesirable practices*

Section 3(1)(*d*) empowers the Secretary of State to designate as "undesirable" certain practices which may be found in estate agency work, so as to constitute them as additional "trigger" events. Six such practices have been so designated by the Estate Agents (Undesirable Practices) (No 2) Order 1991[1].

(e) *Vicarious liability*

An important feature of the last two groups of "trigger" events (statutory obligations and undesirable practices) is the extent to which an estate agent may be held responsible for someone else's default. Section 3(3) lays down three separate types of vicarious liability which can apply in this area. In the first place, a person is responsible for anything done by an employee "in the course of his employment", unless it can be can shown that the employer "took such steps as were reasonably practicable to prevent the employee from doing that act, or from doing in the course of his employment acts of that description". Second, a person is responsible for any act of an *agent* (as opposed to an *employee*) which is expressly or impliedly authorised, a provision which could well lead to problems in cases where an estate agent has sub-instructed.

These two kinds of vicarious responsibility are modelled on those found in the Sex Discrimination Act 1975, section 41 and the Race Relations Act 1976, section 32. By contrast, the third situation covered by section 3(3) creates a wider form of responsibility than one is accustomed to see. This lies in the provision that "Anything done by a business associate of a person shall be treated as done by that person as well, unless he can show that the act was done without his connivance or consent". Given the Act's broad definition of "business associate"[2], the requirement of "connivance or consent" seems a necessary safeguard against an unacceptably onerous obligation. However, it should be stressed once again that, like all "triggers", these events do not *compel* the Director to make an order against an estate agent; they merely enable such an order to be made if the agent is considered to be generally unfit to practise.

---

1 These are discussed in detail in Chapter 3.
2 See section 31.

Proceedings under the Act

(a) *Investigation*

The attention of the Director-General of Fair Trading may become focused on a particular agent or firm for a variety of reasons. There may for example be a complaint from a member of the public (either directly to the OFT or passed on by a trading standards department); a court or tribunal may report a case in which an estate agent has been held guilty of some offence; or a professional body may pass on the result of serious disciplinary proceedings against one of its members. In any of these cases, the Director may decide that an investigation of the agent should be carried out, with a view to the possible making of an order under sections 3 or 4. This investigation is extremely wide-ranging; section 3(2) provides that, in addition to "trigger" events, the Director may "also take account of whether, in the course of estate agency work or any other business activity, that person has engaged in any practice which involves breaches of a duty owed by virtue of any enactment, contract or rule of law and which is material to his fitness to carry on estate agency work". Thus, provided that at least one "trigger" can be found, an estate agent's unfitness (leading to the loss of livelihood) may ultimately rest upon the conduct of business activities in a very different field.

In carrying out an investigation, the Director is given far-reaching powers by section 9 of the Act. This empowers the Director, by simple notice, to "require any person to furnish to him such information as may be specified or described in the notice or to produce to him any document so specified or described"[1]. Once served, a notice under section 9 must be treated seriously; any positive refusal or deliberate failure to comply with it, or the giving of false or misleading information, is a criminal offence under section 9(4).

The confidentiality of information collected by the Director under the Estate Agents Act is protected by section 10, which makes it a criminal offence to disclose such information without the consent of the person concerned or, if the information is about a business still in existence, without the consent of the person carrying on that business. However, these provisions do not prevent the disclosure

---

1 However, this does not compel any counsel or solicitor to disclose privileged information: section 9(3).

of information for the purpose of criminal investigation or proceedings, civil proceedings under the Act or other consumer protection legislation, or the performance by the Director of any other statutory functions.

(b) *Preliminary proceedings*

It is by no means certain that the investigation of an estate agent will lead to formal proceedings by the Director-General of Fair Trading[1]. However, if the Director is minded to make a prohibition order under section 3 or a warning order under section 4, the procedures which are set out in Part I of Schedule 2 must be followed[2]. The first step is to notify the person concerned[3] of the Director's proposal. This must be done in some detail; notice of a proposed prohibition order must specify any relevant "trigger" on which the Director relies, list other matters which have been taken into account and, if the order is to be based on a previous warning under section 4, make that clear. The notice must give the person affected at least 21 days in which to make written representations to the Director or, if preferred, to notify the Director that an oral hearing is required. Where an oral hearing is requested, this is to be arranged by the Director, and the person affected is to be given at least 21 days' notice. The hearing itself is informal[4], although the estate agent may, if he or she wishes, be represented[5].

(c) *The making of orders*

If the Director decides (having duly taken into account any oral or

---

1 Out of the 652 case files which had been opened by the OFT up to the end of October 1992, 327 (one-half) resulted in notices of proposal to make a prohibition or warning order: John Mills, Director of Consumer Affairs at the OFT, in a speech to the Incorporated Society of Valuers and Auctioneers on November 13 1992.

2 The Director, in the exercise of these adjudicating functions, is governed by the Tribunals and Inquiries Act 1971: see section 24.

3 This initial notice need only be served on a partnership as a whole, even where it is intended that the order shall also take effect against the individual partners. However, all subsequent notices during the proceedings must be served by the Director on the partners as well.

4 Evidence may not be excluded solely on the ground that it would not be admissible in a court of law.

5 By any other person (not necessarily a barrister or solicitor). However, barristers and solicitors have the advantage that communications with them are privileged from disclosure under section 9 or section 11.

written representations) to make the order in the form of the original proposal, this may be done[1]. Alternatively, an order may be made in different form, provided that the grounds for this were contained in the original proposal (for example, the Director may abandon one or more of the original grounds, where others remain). If, however, the Director wishes to rely on new grounds, the person affected must be given a fresh notice of this proposal, whereupon the whole procedure begins again.

When the Director decides to make an order, the person or persons affected must be given notice specifying the type of order, the "trigger" on which it is based, and any other facts which justify it. That person must also be informed of the right to appeal against the order.

As a general rule, an order comes into operation only when there is no further possibility of an appeal against it, either because an appeal has failed or because it is too late for one to be made. If, however, the Director feels it necessary (for example, on the ground of consumer protection) it may take effect immediately upon the giving of the notice. Once the order is in force, it is a criminal offence under section 3(8) not to comply with it, and a conviction under this provision is itself a "trigger" event. An order, once made, remains in force until either the conviction or discrimination upon which it is based becomes "spent"[2] or until it is revoked by the Director on an application made to him under section 6 of the Act.

(d) *Appeals and similar proceedings*

Once an order is made under either section 3 or section 4, the person affected may try in two different ways to remove its effect. In the first place, it is provided by section 7 that an appeal against the Director's decision lies to the Secretary of State; if this appeal proves unsuccessful, there may be a further appeal on a point of law to the High Court. There is no right of appeal to the court on questions of fact, but it should be remembered that "points of law" include the assertion that a verdict was so contrary to all the

---

1 By the end of October 1992, 327 notices of proposal had resulted in 174 orders (a strike rate of about one-half): John Mills, Director of Consumer Affairs at the OFT, in a speech to the Incorporated Society of Valuers and Auctioneers on November 13 1992.
2 See section 5(4) and (5).

evidence that no reasonable tribunal could have reached it.

Details of the machinery governing appeals to the Secretary of State are contained, not in the Estate Agents Act itself, but in the Estate Agents (Appeals) Regulations 1981. Briefly, these regulations (which follow closely those applicable to appeals under the Consumer Credit Act 1974) provide that a person wishing to appeal against an order made by the Director[1] must give notice to the Secretary of State within 28 days[2]; if this notice does not itself specify the grounds of appeal (eg disputed reasons or findings of fact relied on by the Director, or points of law), then the appellant must serve another notice specifying these grounds before the 28-day period expires. Once the grounds of appeal are made known to the Director, the latter has 28 days to furnish the Secretary of State with a copy of the original order, together with any representations; the appellant in turn then has 28 days to set out any further representations to be made in the light of the Director's reply.

Assuming that the Secretary of State is not minded at this stage of the proceedings simply to allow the appeal (or, even if so minded, that the Director objects to this), the Secretary of State must make arrangements for the appeal to be heard, unless the appellant within 14 days requests that the matter be disposed of without a hearing[3]. 21 days' notice of the date, time and place of the hearing must be given to both parties[4].

Appeals will usually be heard by three "appointed persons", a legally qualified chairman together with two other members drawn from a panel made up of people with relevant professional experience. While procedure at the hearing is in the hands of the chairman, the regulations clearly envisage that the parties may be

---

1 This applies not only to orders under section 3 and section 4, but also to decisions of the Director under section 6 (revocation and variation of orders) and section 17 (exemption from the insurance requirements of section 16).

2 Compliance with this time-limit is crucial; it is the only one throughout the appeal procedure which the Secretary of Sate is not empowered to extend: regulation 26.

3 The appellant's wishes are not conclusive; the Secretary of State will decide after hearing from the Director.

4 An appellant who fails to appear runs the risk of the hearing taking place in his or her absence. However, regulations 15 and 17 provide that, in practice, the appellant will be given the opportunity to explain at least a single failure to the Secretary of State.

represented (by lawyers or others); may call witnesses (who may be questioned by the other party or the panel); and may make opening and closing statements. Further, it is specifically provided that evidence may be admitted whether or not it would be admissible in a court of law.

Once the appointed persons have completed the hearing (or, as the case may be, have considered the matter without a hearing), they are required to furnish the Secretary of State with a reasoned report in writing. On the basis of that report, the Secretary of State notifies the parties of the decision and the reasons for it, together with a reminder to the appellant that a further appeal, on a point of law only, lies to the High Court.

Quite apart from the appeals procedures, a person in respect of whom an order has been made under section 3 or section 4 is permitted by section 6 to make an application to the Director, asking for the order to be revoked or varied[1]. This provision, which is presumably intended for the benefit of the sinner who repents, may lead to a re-opening of the whole case for, unless the Director simply accedes to the request, the applicant must be notified of the intention to refuse it (or only to vary the order in a way which does not satisfy the applicant's wishes). Thereafter the position is once again governed by Schedule 2, Part 1 (as to representations, hearings, etc) and by the appeals provisions of section 7.

The Director, on being asked to revoke an order made under section 3, may refuse if it is considered that the applicant remains unfit within the terms of the order. Similarly, an order made under section 4 will be confirmed if the Director considers that the applicant is likely to commit further breaches of whatever obligation formed the basis of the order. Where, however, it is felt that the order may, without detriment to the public, be varied in favour of the applicant (eg by restricting it to a particular area or type of work) the Director may make such a variation.

---

1 The form of an application, and the conditions on which it may be made, are governed by section 6 and Schedule 2, Part 2. Repeated applications, especially frivolous ones, will no doubt be discouraged by the non-returnable fee involved, which is set at a swingeing £2,500: Estate Agents (Fees) Regulations 1982, SI 1982, No 637.

Register of orders

The essence of the Estate Agents Act is consumer protection and, consistently with this philosophy, section 8 imposes upon the Director-General of Fair Trading a duty to "establish and maintain a register on which there shall be entered particulars of every order made by him under section 3 or section 4 above and of his decision on any application for revocation or variation of such an order". The register states the terms of any order and, where an order is not yet in force, the date on which it will come into operation. If an appeal is pending, the order will nevertheless appear (this is a necessary safeguard for the public) but the pending appeal will also be mentioned. The register is open to public inspection, and any person is entitled to take copies or to ask the Director for a certified copy of any entry[1]. The latter is regarded as conclusive evidence of the contents of the register; further, any particulars which are entered on the register are presumed to be correct unless and until the contrary is proved[2].

It is the duty of the Director to see that the register is kept up to date, and that any change of circumstances is noted. In most cases the Director will automatically have received the information needed for this task, but could be unaware, for example, that an agent has died or that a relevant period under the Rehabilitation of Offenders Act 1974 has been extended. In consequence, while the Director's duty only arises when it is known that there is something which requires alteration, section 8(3) and Schedule 2, Part 2 ensure that an aggrieved person has the opportunity to bring such matters to the Director's attention.

B Criminal offences

As noted at the beginning of this chapter, the criminal offences created by the Estate Agents Act (which relate mainly to the handling of clients' money and failure to co-operate with the enforcement authorities) are "policed" by local weights and measures authorities. In order to assist these authorities in the

---

1 The fees for these services are modest: inspection costs £1 per file, and taking copies works out at approximately 75p per sheet: Estate Agents (Fees) Regulations 1982, SI 1982, No 637.
2 Section 8(6).

performance of their duties, section 11 gives them extensive powers of entry and inspection[1]. These powers (all of which are exercisable only by a duly authorised officer of an enforcement authority, only at a reasonable hour and only on production of credentials if demanded) are:

i   to enter premises (other than purely residential ones) on reasonable suspicion that an offence has been committed.

ii   to inspect books or documents, or a legible reproduction of information stored in other forms (eg in a computer) and to take copies, again on reasonable suspicion of an offence.

iii on reasonable belief[2] that they are required as evidence in a prosecution, to seize and detain books or documents. Further, if necessary for this purpose, to break open any container holding such books or documents (but only where the person authorised to open the container has been asked to do so but has not complied).

Where books or documents are seized under these powers, the person from whom they are seized must be informed and, except while they are actually being used as evidence, the person to whom they belong must be given the opportunity to take copies.

The "teeth" of these provisions are to be found in section 27, which makes it a criminal offence to obstruct an authorised officer who is exercising statutory powers or, in some circumstances, to fail to give the officer adequate assistance in the exercise of those powers. However, it does not appear that section 11 justifies an officer in making a *forcible* entry to premises; hence, if admission is refused, the officer must obtain a warrant from a justice of the peace in accordance with section 11(4)[3].

---

1 Although the powers are highly controversial, it should be remembered that they may *not* be used to investigate any breach of the Act which does not amount to a criminal offence.

2 This denotes something more than mere suspicion of an offence.

3 A warrant will be required in any case where the premises concerned are purely residential.

CHAPTER 5

Property misdescriptions

As explained in Chapter 1, the Government's intentions to bring land and buildings within the Trade Descriptions Act 1968, or to designated misdescription in this area an "undesirable practice" under the Estate Agents Act 1979, were overtaken by the Estate Agents (Property Misdescriptions) Bill of Mr John Butcher MP. Such was the support given to this Bill that the Estate Agents (Undesirable Practices) Order, which was already in draft, was amended so as to drop all reference to misdescription, and the Bill (in an extended form) duly passed into law as the Property Misdescriptions Act 1991[1].

We have already considered[2] the scope of the Property Misdescriptions Act, noting that its application is limited to statements made in the course of estate agency or property development businesses. In this chapter we examine in detail the criminal offence created by the new Act, against the background of the various forms of legal liability which already exist for estate agents engaged in marketing property.

A Liability under the existing law

The publicity generated by the Property Misdescriptions Act has perhaps rather obscured the fact that estate agents who provide inaccurate information about property which they are marketing already run the risk of a range of legal sanctions. It may of course be that the new Act, which is to be policed by trading standards departments, will be enforced more rigorously than the existing legal rules and, if this proves to be the case, then compliance will

---

1 The Act received the Royal Assent on June 27 1991; however, it becomes effective only on April 4 1993, when the Property Misdescriptions (Specified Matters) Order 1993 comes into force.
2 See pp 30–32.

place a serious additional burden upon practising agents. None the less, the present law, in terms of both criminal and civil liability, should not be overlooked.

Criminal liability

Telling lies in order to persuade people to part with their money is a serious matter, and this is no less true where the lies are told by an agent, rather than by a party to the resulting contract. There seems no reason to doubt that, provided the necessary ingredient of "dishonesty" is present, an estate agent who misdescribes property in the course of marketing it may be convicted of obtaining property by deception under section 15 of the Theft Act 1968[1]. This offence carries a maximum penalty of imprisonment for up to 10 years or a fine of unlimited amount.

The above offence involves proof of a dishonest intent, so that an honest estate agent should not be at risk. Furthermore, it is commonly stated that the main *strict liability* offences created by section 1 of the Trade Descriptions Act 1968 (applying a false trade description to goods, or supplying goods to which a false trade description has been applied) have no application to land or buildings. This is in general terms an accurate statement of the law, but it should not be overlooked that the definition of "goods" in the 1968 Act includes "things attached to land". In consequence, an estate agent who misdescribes items sold with a building could incur liability under the 1968 Act, at least where those items do not constitute fixtures[2].

One criminal offence of strict liability which does apply to buildings is that of giving to consumers a misleading indication as to the price at which any accommodation is available[3]. "Accommodation" for this purpose is defined[4] so as to include a dwelling (house or flat) which has not previously been occupied as a residence and which is being disposed of in the course of a business. This provision led in 1991 to the conviction of a firm of estate agents who, in marketing a new house, claimed that it had been reduced in price

---

1 Or, if no sale results from the agent's false statements, of an attempt.
2 Misdescription of fixtures (which are regarded in law as part of the land) is now governed by the Property Misdescriptions Act 1991.
3 Consumer Protection Act 1987, section 20.
4 By section 23.

by some £30,000 when in truth it had never been on the market at the higher price quoted[1].

Civil liability

It is only in exceptional circumstances that an estate agent is party to the contract of sale which results from the agent's efforts. Assuming that this is not the case, the agent cannot be liable *in contract* to a disappointed purchaser for any false or misleading statement made by the agent in negotiating the sale. Nor can the agent be sued under the Misrepresentation Act 1967, for that Act applies only to statements made by one contracting party to another[2]. However, an estate agent who *deliberately* misleads a purchaser could surely incur liability under the tort of deceit[3], and tortious liability has also been imposed upon a *negligent* agent[4].

In practice, any attempt to impose civil liability upon an estate agent for misstatement is likely to come about in a more indirect fashion. It is well established that any such misstatement may prevent the client from enforcing the sale[5] or render the client liable to pay damages to the purchaser[6]. If this occurs, the client can in turn seek damages from the agent, at least where the latter is in breach of a duty of care and skill[7].

An important aspect of the above forms of liability concerns the extent to which they may be affected by the use of disclaimers. In general terms, it may be stated that attempts to exclude or restrict liability will be of no avail in cases of fraud; the exclusion of liability for negligence is in principle possible, although any term or notice intended to have this effect must satisfy the statutory test of "reasonableness" under the Unfair Contract Terms Act 1977.

---

1 Although price in general is a "prescribed matter" for the purposes of the Property Misdescriptions Act 1991, statements falling within the Consumer Protection Act are specifically excluded.
2 *Resolute Maritime Inc* v *Nippon Kaiji Kyokai* [1983] 2 All ER 1.
3 *Gordon* v *Selico Ltd* [1986] 1 EGLR 71.
4 *Computastaff Ltd* v *Ingledew Brown Bennison & Garrett* (1983) 268 EG 906.
5 *Mullens* v *Miller* (1882) 22 ChD 194.
6 *Gosling* v *Anderson* (1972) 223 EG 1743.
7 *Whiteman* v *Weston* The Times, March 15 1900.

B Misdescriptions under the 1991 Act

From April 4 1993 the forms of liability described above are augmented by a new strict liability criminal offence under the Property Misdescriptions Act 1991[1]. The crucial provision is section 1(1), which provides that:

> where a false or misleading statement about a prescribed matter is made in the course of an estate agency business or a property development business, otherwise than in providing conveyancing services, the person by whom the business is carried on shall be guilty of an offence under this section.

The definitions of "estate agency business", "property development business" and "conveyancing services" have already been considered[2]; the question of who is liable under the Act is dealt with later in this chapter. Our present concern is with the phrase "false or misleading statement about a prescribed matter".

Statement

Much of the Parliamentary time spent in debating the Property Misdescriptions Act focused on misleading sales particulars. However, anyone tempted to believe that this is all that is covered should look carefully at section 1(5)(c), which explains what the Act regards as a "statement". Written statements are certainly included, but so are oral ones, which means that liability may arise from a sales negotiator's answer to a purchaser's question, an unguarded remark by a telephonist in reply to an enquiry, or even from an unjustified derogatory comment by an over-enthusiastic commercial agent negotiating on behalf of a purchaser or tenant!

In addition to words, the section provides that "a statement may be made by pictures", which would seem apt to include both an "artist's impression" of a new development or a new house and a photograph. Of course, the latter is unlikely to be "false" in the strict sense (unless it has been positively altered). However, it can certainly be "misleading", either because of what is left out or simply

---

1 Liability is exclusively a matter of criminal law: section 1(4) provides that contravention does not give rise to any civil right of action.
2 See pp 31–32.

by virtue of being out of date[1].

Nor is this all; a "statement" specifically includes "any other method of signifying meaning", which would presumably cover semaphore, morse code and body language, to name but three unusual methods of selling property. More to the point, this will catch "concrete lies", such as an inaccurate model of a new building or a "show house" which gives a false impression of the standard of finish to be expected in other houses in the same development[2].

Notwithstanding the breadth of this statutory definition, it should be emphasised that liability in all cases depends upon the making of something which can be described as a "statement". The Act does *not* impose any positive obligation of disclosure, even where an estate agent actually knows something detrimental about the property (eg that a previous survey has revealed serious defects). Whatever the ethics involved in keeping such information under wraps, it cannot be a source of liability under the Property Misdescriptions Act[3].

False or misleading

Section 1(5)(a) provides that a false statement is one which is "false to a material degree", which means that utterly trivial inaccuracies will not be a source of liability. As to what will be regarded as "material", the Act gives no further guidance, but it can safely be assumed that this will take into account all the circumstances of the case, including such factors as the type of property involved and the class of purchaser (residential or commercial).

Of course, words or pictures which are literally true may still convey a wrong impression, and these will fall within the Act if they are "misleading". According to section 1(5)(b), this will occur where "what a reasonable person may be expected to infer from [a

---

1 In *Atlantic Estates Ltd* v *Ezekiel* [1991] 2 EGLR 202 a photograph attached to the auction particulars of an investment property showed a thriving wine bar. Since this business could no longer be lawfully carried on (the tenant having lost the licence), the photograph was held to be a misrepresentation.

2 Or developers who stock a show house with undersized furniture in order to create a misleading sense of spaciousness!

3 Of course, if the purchaser asks whether the agent is aware of any defects in the property, or of any previous survey, the agent's answer must be neither false nor misleading.

statement], or from any omission from it, is false". To this extent only, then, liability can arise from what is *not* said as well as what *is*. A claim that "the property enjoys extensive views over open country" may be perfectly true; but failure to mention the industrial estate which blocks the whole horizon on one side will render the entire statement a misleading one.

One particular way in which a statement can mislead is by being out of date. Under the law of misrepresentation, a person who makes a statement and then discovers it to be untrue is under a legal obligation to inform the person to whom it was made before any contract is entered into[1]. The Property Misdescriptions Act does not go so far, but there is no doubt that an estate agent who continues to issue sales particulars after discovering that they are inaccurate (either because of initial errors or because what they describe has changed) may be guilty of an offence. It is thus essential that the content of particulars is kept under review, if only so that the issuer can rely on the statutory defence of "due diligence"[2].

Prescribed matter

The 1991 Act applies only where a statement is made about a "prescribed matter", and this is defined by section 1(5)(d) to mean "any matter relating to land which is specified in an order made by the Secretary of State". In consequence, although it was technically in force from June 27 1991, when it received Royal Assent, the Act had nothing on which to bite until a statutory instrument was produced containing a list of prescribed matters. This instrument, the Property Misdescriptions (Specified Matters) Order 1992[3], comes into force on April 4 1993, so that the Act has practical as well as legal effect from that date.

As to the content of the order[4], there is not much that can usefully be said, other than to point out that the list of 33 items (which has grown in length with each draft) provides virtually comprehensive coverage of both the physical and the legal aspects of property being sold. As to the former, the order mentions such

---

1 See *With* v *O'Flanagan* [1936] Ch 575.
2 See p 97.
3 SI 1992, No 2834.
4 Which is reproduced in full as Appendix D.

matters as measurements or sizes, form of construction, condition, environment and survey results. Examples of the latter include lease terms, rent, service charges, rates, easements and planning matters. Other matters which are specified, but which do not fall clearly into either of the above categories, include the property's age and history, its price and the length of time it has been on the market.

The statutory list of items is so wide-ranging that it is by no means easy to think of matters which are not covered (and of course agents should in any event seek for accuracy in *all* their descriptions, whether or not these fall within the Act). However, it is notable that the list contains no specific reference to "decorative condition"[1] and so, unless "physical characteristics" or "condition" includes decorative order, this appears to be one area where an over-enthusiastic agent will not face criminal sanctions. Furthermore, false or misleading statements as to the price of new dwellings are specifically excluded, in so far as these fall within the Consumer Protection Act 1987[2]; and misrepresentations as to offers received for the property are not mentioned at all, presumably because these are covered by the Estate Agents (Undesirable Practices) Order 1991[3].

Disclaimers

Although the Property Misdescriptions Act makes no explicit reference to disclaimer clauses, they are worth a separate mention, if only because such clauses, in one form or another, are routinely found in estate agents' particulars of sale. The Act's reticence on this matter means that it will be left to the courts to determine the extent, if any, to which these clauses may serve to exclude or restrict liability. As to what they are likely to decide, it may be confidently asserted that an exemption clause of the "no liability is accepted" kind will be of no effect whatsoever; it is simply not possible to deny one's liability for criminal offences in this way.

As to those "disclaimers" which do not seek in so many words to deny responsibility, but attempt rather to draw the sting from what

---

1 An earlier version included this item, but it was somewhat reluctantly dropped as being essentially a subjective question.
2 See p 90.
3 See p 55.

would otherwise be a false or misleading statement, the legal position is less clear. Estate agents' particulars have long carried paragraphs stating, for instance, that all statements contained therein are matters of opinion only, or that all measurements are mere approximations, or that accuracy cannot be guaranteed. Can it be said that, by denying any intention on the agent's part to assert positive facts, they effectively prevent anything in those particulars from constituting a "false or misleading statement"?

The answer to this question, it is tentatively suggested, is that matters which are essentially factual in their nature cannot be turned into matters of mere opinion by a statement that this is all they are. Nor will a refusal to "guarantee accuracy" mean that a court is precluded from holding a person liable for making an inaccurate statement[1]. Moreover, even if such terms might prove useful in relation to statements which truly *are* matters of opinion (such as a property's decorative state) or approximations (such as the area of an irregularly shaped garden), they can never amount to a licence to commit fraud. Thus, for example, an estate agent who has accurate measurements of a property cannot systematically exaggerate them under cover of a clause which states that they are mere approximations.

In cases arising under the Trade Descriptions Act 1968, the courts have ruled that disclaimers are totally ineffective where a person is charged under section 1(1)(a) with actually *applying* a false trade description to goods[2]; they can only ever provide a defence to the lesser charge of *supplying* goods to which a false trade description is attached[3]. Even assuming that the courts treat offences under the Property Misdescriptions Act as analogous to the second of these groups and do so not outlaw disclaimers altogether, they will none the less be required to satisfy stringent rules. In short, the question which will be asked is whether the effect of a false or misleading statement on the mind of the person to whom it is made has been neutralised by an express disclaimer or contradiction of its message. As explained in the leading case of *Norman* v *Bennett*[4]:

---

1 See *Cremdean Properties Ltd* v *Nash* (1977) 244 EG 547.
2 *May* v *Vincent* [1991] 1 EGLR 27.
3 Under section 1(1)(b).
4 [1974] 3 All ER 351.

To be effective any such disclaimer must be as bold, precise and compelling as the trade description itself and must be as effectively brought to the notice of any person to whom the goods may be supplied. In other words, the disclaimer must equal the trade description in the extent to which it is likely to get home to anyone interested in receiving the goods.

C Incidence of liability

Interestingly, it is not the *making* of a false or misleading statement which is defined as an offence under the 1991 Act. Instead, section 1(1) provides that, where an offending statement is made in the course of an estate agency or property development business, it is the person by whom that business is carried on who is guilty of an offence. This policy of targeting principals is seen further in section 4(1), which provides that, where the business in question is carried on by a company, liability also attaches to any actual or de facto director, manager, secretary or other similar officer who has contributed by "connivance, consent or neglect" to the commission of the offence.

The only other person who may be prosecuted under the Act is an employee through whose act or default an offending statement is made[1]. Where an employee is at fault in this way, section 1(2) makes clear that proceedings may be brought against the employee, whether or not the employer is also prosecuted.

D Defences

The criminal offence created by section 1 of the Property Misdescriptions Act 1991 is in principle one of strict liability, in that the prosecution is not required to prove either intent to deceive or even any negligence on the part of the defendant. However, section 2(1) provides that it shall be a defence for a person prosecuted "to show that he took all reasonable steps and exercised all due diligence to avoid committing the offence"[2].

There are strong echoes here of the defence under section 24 of

---

1 Again the wording may impose liability, not only for making a statement, but also for causing one to be made (eg by failing to check sales particulars before publication).

2 The burden is clearly on the defendant, and will require proof on the balance of probabilities: *R* v *Carr-Briant* [1943] KB 607.

the Trade Descriptions Act 1968 and, while the analogy cannot be pushed too far (for example because the earlier provision contains some additional elements), there is reason to suppose that the courts will pay attention to cases decided under the 1968 Act when called upon to interpret the new provision. Assuming that this is indeed the case, it is likely that "reasonable steps" and "due diligence" will be treated as cumulative requirements and, moreover, as demanding evidence that the defendant has done something positive to avoid the commission of an offence. To sit back and do nothing, even where this is based on the view that there is nothing to be done, can hardly be described as taking "all reasonable steps".

As a general principle, the case law[1] suggests that a defendant wishing to use this defence must prove that a system was set up to avoid contravention of the statute and that this system was subjected to periodic checks to see that it was working satisfactorily. In the estate agency context, such a "system" might involve such things as training staff on how to respond to enquiries, ensuring that sales particulars are always checked before printing, and so on. In this connection it should be noted that it is not enough for an employer merely to give instructions and assume that they will be carried out[2]. However, an employer *is* entitled to delegate responsibility for the firm's compliance system to employees at a senior (supervisory) level, provided that they are not so senior as to rank as the company's "alter ego"[3].

One aspect of the "due diligence" defence is singled out for separate treatment by the 1991 Act, presumably because it is the one which is most likely to arise in practice. This is the question of reliance by the defendant on information given by another person. Section 2(2) provides that, in order to rely on this as a defence against liability, the defendant must prove that reliance on the information was reasonable in all the circumstances. It is further explicitly stated that, in considering the "reasonableness" of reliance,

---

1 Which is collected in *O'Keefe: The Law relating to Trade Descriptions*, para 250 *et seq.*
2 *Aitchison* v *Reith & Anderson (Dingwall & Tain) Ltd* 1974 SLT 282, where auctioneers were held liable for a false description which an employee had placed on a car despite having been told that no descriptions were to be given.
3 See *Tesco Supermarkets Ltd* v *Nattrass* [1972] AC 153.

three questions are of particular importance. These are:

i what steps (if any) were taken to check the information;

ii what steps (if any) might reasonably have been taken to check it; and

iii whether there was any reason to disbelieve the information.

Time will tell how the courts will interpret these matters. Presumably an estate agent who has no grounds for suspicion will not be regarded as acting unreasonably in accepting at face-value specialist information about a property, which is provided by members of other professions such as solicitors or surveyors. On the other hand, the courts in Trade Descriptions Act cases have shown little sympathy towards defendants who accept uncritically information provided by unqualified persons, especially where those persons have a vested interest in the success of a transaction[1]. Estate agents should accordingly be wary of relying on a client's assurances as to features of the property, especially where the agent's professional instincts raise the slightest doubts about what is claimed.

Section 2(3) and (4) make additional provision for the situation in which a defendant's plea of "due diligence" amounts in effect to placing the blame on someone else. If the defence involves an allegation that the offence is due to either the "act or default" of, or "reliance on information given by" another person, the defendant must serve notice on the prosecution, at least seven days before the trial, giving as much information as possible to help identify the person concerned[2]. It has further been held, in cases arising under the Trade Descriptions Act, that it is not sufficient for a defendant merely to name all employees and claim that the offence must have been caused by one of them; the defendant must go on to show that all reasonable steps have been taken to identify the culprit[3].

---

1 Eg *Sutton London Borough* v *Perry Sanger & Co Ltd* (1971) 135 JP 239, where dog dealers were liable for describing a cross-breed dog as pure bred on the basis of an unsigned pedigree certificate and the word of the person who sold it to them.

2 Whether that person can then be prosecuted depends on whether he or she comes within the Act, as a principal or employee of an estate agency or property development business.

3 *McGuire* v *Sittingbourne Co-operative Society Ltd* (1976) 140 JP 306.

E Enforcement

The enforcement provisions of the Property Misdescriptions Act 1991, which are contained in section 3 and the Schedule to the Act, are based on those of the Trade Descriptions Act 1968. Enforcement of the Act is thus the duty of the trading standards departments of local authorities or, in Northern Ireland, of the Department of Economic Development's Trading Standards Branch[1].

The specific powers of investigation given to trading standards officers resemble those which may be used in investigating criminal offences under the Estate Agents Act 1979, although there are some important differences. Briefly, the powers (all of which are exercisable only by a duly authorised officer of an enforcement authority, only at a reasonable hour and only on production of credentials if demanded) are:

i   to enter premises (other than purely residential ones) and to inspect goods, for the purpose of ascertaining whether an offence has been committed[2];
ii on reasonable suspicion of an offence, to inspect books or documents, or a legible reproduction of information stored in other forms (eg in a computer) and to take copies;
iii on reasonable belief[3] that they are required as evidence in a prosecution, to seize and detain any books or documents.

It should be emphasised that the power of entry under this Act does not extend to premises used only as a dwelling, even where an alleged offence concerns a misdescription of that dwelling. Indeed, the power is more restrictive than that contained in the Estate Agents Act, in that, even where a warrant is issued (eg to justify an entry by force), this cannot extend to purely private premises.

Those who are subject to the Property Misdescriptions Act would be well advised to study the enforcement provisions, since that Act makes it a criminal offence to obstruct an authorised officer who is exercising statutory powers or, in some circumstances, to fail to give the officer adequate assistance in the exercise of those powers.

---

1 However, all prosecutions in Scotland are initiated by the Procurator Fiscal.
2 Note that, in contrast to the Estate Agents Act, there is no requirement of reasonable suspicion; these powers can be exercised in order to carry out spot checks.
3 This denotes something more than mere suspicion of an offence.

APPENDIX A

ESTATE AGENTS ACT 1979
(1979 c.38)

ARRANGEMENT OF SECTIONS

Application of Act

Section
1. Estate agency work.
2. Interests in land.

Orders by Director General of Fair Trading

3. Orders prohibiting unfit persons from doing estate agency work.
4. Warning orders.
5. Supplementary provisions as to orders under sections 3 and 4.
6. Revocation and variation of orders under sections 3 and 4.
7. Appeals.
8. Register of orders etc.

Information, entry and inspection

9. Information for the Director.
10. Restriction on disclosure of information.
11. Powers of entry and inspection.

Clients' money and accounts

12. Meaning of "clients' money" etc.
13. Clients' money held on trust or as agent.
14. Keeping of client accounts.
15. Interest on clients' money.
16. Insurance cover for clients' money.
17. Exemptions from section 16.

Regulation of other aspects of estate agency work

18. Information to clients of prospective liabilities.
19. Regulation of pre-contract deposits outside Scotland.
20. Prohibition of pre-contract deposits in Scotland.
21. Transactions in which an estate agent has a personal interest.
22. Standards of competence.
23. Bankrupts not to engage in estate agency work.

Supervision, enforcement, publicity etc.

24. Supervision by Council on Tribunals.
25. General duties of Director.
26. Enforcement authorities.
27. Obstruction and personation of authorised officers.

Supplementary

28. General provisions as to offences.
29. Service of notices etc.
30. Orders and regulations.
31. Meaning of "business associate" and "controller".
32. Meaning of "associate".
33. General interpretation provisions.
34. Financial provisions.
35. Scotland. [Repealed.]
36. Short title, commencement and extent.

SCHEDULES:

Schedule 1 - Provisions supplementary to section 3(1).
Schedule 2 - Procedure etc.

An Act to make provision with respect to the carrying on of and to persons who carry on, certain activities in connection with the disposal and acquisition of interests in land; and for purposes connected therewith.

[4th April 1979]

General notes

Definitions
"associate": s 32.
"business associate": s 31.
"client account": s 14(2).
"clients' money": s 12(1).
"connected contract": s 12(4).
"contract deposit": s 12(2).
"controller": s 31(5).
"Director": s 33(1).
"discrimination": Sched 1, paras 2-5.
"enforcement authority": s 26(1).
"England" means, subject to any alteration of boundaries under Part IV of the Local Government Act 1972, the area consisting of the counties established by s 1 of that Act, Greater London and the Isles of Scilly: Interpretation Act 1978, s 5.
"estate agency work": s 1(1).
"general notice": s 33(1).
"interest in land": s 2(1).
"land" includes buildings and other structures, land covered with water, and any estate, interest, easement, servitude or right in or over land: Interpretation Act 1978, s 5.
"person" includes a body of persons corporate or unincorporate: Interpretation Act 1978, s 5.
"pre-contract deposit": s 12(3).
"prescribed fee": s 33(1).
"Secretary of State" means one of Her Majesty's Principal Secretaries of State: Interpretation Act 1978, s 5.
"the statutory maximum": s 33(1).
"unincorporated association": s 33(1).
"United Kingdom" means Great Britain and Northern Ireland: Interpretation Act 1978, s 5.
"Wales" means, subject to any alteration of boundaries made under Part IV of the Local Government Act 1972, the area consisting of the counties established by s 20 of that Act: Interpretation Act 1978, s 5.

Commencement
The Act, which received the Royal Assent on April 4 1979, was left to be brought into force on a day (or days) to be appointed: see s 36(2). The Estate Agents Act 1979 (Commencement No 1) Order 1981 brought into operation on May 3 1982 sections 1 to 15, 18, 20, 21, 23 to 34 and 36, together with Schedules 1 and 2. The remaining provisions (sections 16, 17, 19 and 22) had still not been implemented at the time of writing.

Extent
Subject to a number of minor modifications, the Act applies to Northern Ireland: s 36(3). With the exception of s 19, the Act also applies to Scotland (s 20, which deals

with similar matters to s 19, applies *only* to Scotland). Again there are various minor amendments.

Parliamentary Debates

HC vol 958, col 618; Standing Committee E, November 28, 30, December 5, 1978; HC vol 961, col 1373; HL vol 398, col 1216; vol 399, cols 77, 870, 1745; HC vol 965, col 1358.

For debates on the Davies Bill, see HC vol 943, col 885; Standing Committee C, April 19, 26, 1978; HC vol 949, cols 631, 1702.

Application of Act

Estate Agency Work.

1. – (1) This Act applies, subject to subsections (2) to (4) below to things done by any person in the course of a business (including a business in which he is employed) pursuant to instructions received from another person (in this section referred to as "the client") who wishes to dispose of or acquire an interest in land –

(a) for the purpose of, or with a view to, effecting the introduction to the client of a third person who wishes to acquire or, as the case may be, dispose of such an interest; and

(b) after such an introduction has been effected in the course of that business, for the purpose of securing the disposal or, as the case may be, the acquisition of that interest;

and in this Act the expression "estate agency work" refers to things done as mentioned above to which this Act applies.

(2) This Act does not apply to things done –

(a) in the course of his profession by a practising solicitor or a person employed by him; or

(b) in the course of credit brokerage, within the meaning of the Consumer Credit Act 1974; or

(c) in the course of insurance brokerage by a person who is for the time being registered under section 2, or enrolled under section 4, of the Insurance Brokers (Registration) Act 1977; or

(d) in the course of carrying out any survey or valuation pursuant to a contract which is distinct from that under which other things falling within subsection (1) above are done; or

(e) in connection with applications and other matters arising under the Town and Country Planning Act 1990, the Planning (Listed Buildings and Conservation Areas) Act 1990, the Planning (Hazardous Substances) Act 1990 or the Town and

Country Planning (Scotland) Act 1972 or the Planning (Northern Ireland) Order 1991.

(3) This Act does not apply to things done by any person –

(a) pursuant to instructions received by him in the course of his employment in relation to an interest in land if his employer is the person who, on his own behalf, wishes to dispose of or acquire that interest; or

(b) in relation to any interest in any property if the property is subject to a mortgage and he is the receiver of the income of it; or

(c) in relation to a present prospective or former employee of his or of any person by whom he also is employed if the things are done by reason of the employment (whether past, present or future).

(4) This Act does not apply to the publication of advertisements or the dissemination of information by a person who does no other acts which fall within subsection (1) above.

(5) In this section –

(a) "practising solicitor" means, except in Scotland, a solicitor who is qualified to act as such under section 1 of the Solicitors Act 1974 or Article 4 of the Solicitors (Northern Ireland) Order 1976, and in Scotland includes a firm of practising solicitors;

(b) "mortgage" includes a debenture and any other charge on property for securing money or money's worth; and

(c) any reference to employment is a reference to employment under a contract of employment.

Notes

See pp 14–24.

For what is meant by "dispose of or acquire an interest in land" in subsection (1), see s 2.

"Credit brokerage" (subsection (2)(b)) is defined by s 145(2) of the Consumer Credit Act 1974.

Subsection (2)(e) is as amended by the Planning (Consequential Provisions) Act 1990, s 4 and Sched 2 para 42; and SI 1991 No 1220, art 133(1), Sched 5.

Interests in Land.

2. – (1) Subject to subsection (3) below, any reference in this Act to disposing of an interest in land is a reference to –

(a) transferring a legal estate in a fee simple absolute in possession; or (*b*) transferring or creating, elsewhere than in Scotland, a lease which, by reason of the level of the rent, the length of the term or both, has a capital value which may be lawfully realised on the open market; or

(*c*) transferring or creating in Scotland any estate or interest in land which is capable of being owned or held as a separate interest and to which a title may be recorded in the Register of Sasines;

and any reference to acquiring an interest in land shall be construed accordingly.

(2) In subsection (1)(*b*) above the expression "lease" includes the rights and obligations arising under an agreement to grant a lease.

(3) Notwithstanding anything in subsections (1) and (2) above, references in this Act to disposing of an interest in land do not extend to disposing of –

(*a*) the interest of a creditor whose debt is secured by way of a mortgage or charge of any kind over land or an agreement for any such mortgage or charge; or

(*b*) in Scotland, the interest of a creditor in a heritable security as defined in section 9(8) of the Conveyancing and Feudal Reform (Scotland) Act 1970.

Notes

See pp 24–26.

Orders by Director General of Fair Trading

Orders prohibiting unfit persons from doing estate agency work.

3. – (1) The power of the Director General of Fair Trading (in this Act referred to as "the Director") to make an order under this section with respect to any person shall not be exercisable unless the Director is satisfied that that person –

(*a*) has been convicted of –

(i) an offence involving fraud or other dishonesty or violence, or

(ii) an offence under any provision of this Act, other than section 10(6), section 22(3) or section 23(4), or

(iii) any other offence which, at the time it was committed, was specified for the purposes of this section by an order made by the Secretary of State; or (*b*) has committed discrimination in the course of estate agency work; or

(*c*) has failed to comply with any obligation imposed on him under any of sections 15 and 18 to 21 below; or

(*d*) has engaged in a practice which, in relation to estate agency work, has been declared undesirable by an order made by the Secretary of State;

and the provisions of Schedule 1 to the Act shall have effect for supplementing paragraphs (*a*) and (*b*) above.

(2) Subject to subsection (1) above, if the Director is satisfied that any person is unfit to carry on estate agency work generally or of a particular description he may make an order prohibiting that person –

(*a*) from doing any estate agency work at all; or

(*b*) from doing estate agency work of a description specified in the order;

and in determining whether a person is so unfit the Director may, in addition to taking account of any matters falling within subsection (1) above, also take account of whether, in the course of estate agency work or any other business activity, that person has engaged in any practice which involves breaches of a duty owed by virtue of any enactment, contract or rule of law and which is material to his fitness to carry on estate agency work.

(3) For the purposes of paragraphs (*c*) and (*d*) of subsection (1) above –

(*a*) anything done by a person in the course of his employment shall be treated as done by his employer as well as by him, whether or not it was done with the employer's knowledge or approval, unless the employer shows that he took such steps as were reasonably practicable to prevent the employee from doing that act, or from doing in the course of his employment acts of that description; and

(*b*) anything done by a person as agent for another person with the authority (whether express or implied, and whether precedent or subsequent) of that person shall be treated as done by that other person as well as by him; and

(*c*) anything done by a business associate of a person shall be treated as done by that person as well, unless he can show that the act was done without his connivance or consent.

(4) In an order under this section the Director shall specify as the grounds for the order those matters falling within paragraphs (*a*) to

(*d*) of subsection (1) above as to which he is satisfied and on which, accordingly, he relies to give him power to make the order.

(5) If the Director considers it appropriate, he may in an order under this section limit the scope of the prohibition imposed by the order to a particular part of or area within the United Kingdom.

(6) An order under paragraph (*a*)(iii) or paragraph (*d*) of subsection (1) above –

(*a*) shall be made by statutory instrument;

(*b*) shall be laid before Parliament after being made; and

(*c*) shall cease to have effect (without prejudice to anything previously done in reliance on the order) after the expiry of the period of twenty-eight days beginning with the date on which it was made unless within that period it has been approved by a resolution of each House of Parliament.

(7) In reckoning for the purposes of subsection (6)(*c*) above any period of twenty-eight days, no account shall be taken of any period during which Parliament is dissolved or prorogued or during which both Houses are adjourned for more than four days.

(8) A person who fails without reasonable excuse to comply with an order of the Director under this section shall be liable on conviction on indictment or on summary conviction to a fine which on summary conviction shall not exceed the statutory maximum.

Notes

See pp 75–81.

S 3(1) requires the Director to be "satisfied" that one of a number of "trigger" events has occurred. In relation to criminal offences or discrimination, this is simply a question of whether there has been a conviction, or a finding or notice of discrimination. In relation to paras (*c*) and (*d*), the Director's "satisfaction" must be based upon reasonable evidence.

S 3(2) also requires the Director to be "satisfied" as to the agent's general unfitness to carry on estate agency work. This subjective form of wording might be thought to confer unlimited discretion upon the Director; it is submitted, however, that there must be some reasonable ground for this opinion: see *Secretary of State for Education and Science* v *Metropolitan Borough Council of Tameside* [1976] 3 All ER 665.

For a complete list of the offences, 15 in all, which are created by the Act, see notes to s 28.

Before making an order under s 3(1)(*a*)(iii) or s 3(1)(*d*), the Secretary of State has a duty of consultation: see s 30. The powers under s 3(1)(*a*)(iii) have been used to make the Estate Agents (Specified Offences) (No 2) Order 1991 and the Estate Agents (Specified Offences) (No 2) (Amendment) Order 1992: see p 193. The powers under s 3(1)(*d*) have been used to make the Estate Agents (Undesirable Practices) (No 2) Order 1991: see p 187.

"Discrimination" has a restricted meaning in this context by virtue of Schedule 1. For provisions as to criminal offences, see s 28.

Warning orders.

4. – (1) If the Director is satisfied that –

(a) in the course of estate agency work any person has failed to comply with any such obligation as is referred to in section 3(1)(c) above (in this section referred to as a "relevant statutory obligation") or has engaged in such a practice as is referred to in section 3(1)(d) above, and

(b) if that person were again to fail to comply with a relevant statutory obligation or, as the case may be, were to continue to engage in that practice, the Director would consider him unfit as mentioned in subsection (2) of section 3 above and would proceed to make an order under that section,

the Director may by order notify that person that he is so satisfied.

(2) An order under this section shall state whether, in the opinion of the Director, a further failure to comply with a relevant statutory obligation or, as the case may be, continuation of the practice specified in the order would render the person to whom the order is addressed unfit to carry on estate agency work generally or estate agency work of a description specified in the order.

(3) If, after an order has been made under this section, the person to whom it is addressed fails to comply with a relevant statutory obligation or, as the case may be, engages in the practice specified in the order then, for the purposes of this Act, that fact shall be treated as conclusive evidence that he is unfit to carry on estate agency work as stated in the order in accordance with subsection (2) above; and the Director may proceed to make an order under section 3 above accordingly.

Notes

See p 76.
As to the requirement that the Director be "satisfied", see notes to s 3.

Supplementary provisions as to orders under sections 3 and 4.

5. – (1) The provisions of Part 1 of Schedule 2 to this Act shall have effect –

(a) with respect to the procedure to be followed before an order is made by the Director under section 3 or section 4 above; and

(b) in connection with the making and coming into operation of any such order.

(2) Where an order is made by the Director under section 3 or section 4 above against a partnership it may, if the Director thinks it appropriate, have effect also as an order against some or all of the partners individually, and in such a case the order shall so provide and shall specify the names of the partners affected by the order.

(3) Nothing in section 62 of the Sex Discrimination Act 1975, section 53 of the Race Relations Act 1976 or Article 62 of the Sex Discrimination (Northern Ireland) Order 1976 (restriction of sanctions for breaches of those Acts and that Order) shall be construed as applying to the making of an order by the Director under section 3 above.

(4) In any case where –

(a) an order of the Director under section 3 above specifies a conviction as a ground for the order, and

(b) the conviction becomes spent for the purposes of the Rehabilitation of Offenders Act 1974 or any corresponding enactment for the time being in force in Northern Ireland,

then, unless the order also specifies other grounds which remain valid, the order shall cease to have effect on the day on which the conviction becomes so spent.

(5) In any case where –

(a) an order of the Director under section 3 above specifies as grounds for the order the fact that the person concerned committed discrimination by reason of the existence of any such finding or notice as is referred to in paragraph 2 of Schedule 1 to this Act, and

(b) the period expires at the end of which, by virtue of paragraph 3 of that Schedule, the person concerned would no longer be treated for the purposes of section 3(1)(b) above as having committed discrimination by reason only of that finding or notice,

then, unless the order also specifies other grounds which remain valid, the order shall cease to have effect at the end of that period.

Notes

In following the procedure laid down by Schedule 2, Part 1, the Director is clearly carrying out an adjudicating function, and is thus subject to the supervision of the Council on Tribunals: Tribunals and Inquiries Act 1992, ss 1, 14 and Schedule 1.

It should be noted that the power to make an order against a partnership and individual partners jointly (s 5(2)) has no equivalent in the case of a company or an unincorporated association.

Revocation and variation of orders under sections 3 and 4

6. – (1) On an application made to him by the person in respect of whom the Director has made an order under section 3 or section 4 above, the Director may revoke or vary the order.

(2) An application under subsection (1) above –

(a) shall state the reasons why the applicant considers that the order should be revoked or varied;

(b) in the case of an application for a variation, shall indicate the variation which the applicant seeks; and

(c) shall be accompanied by the prescribed fee.

(3) If the Director decides to accede to an application under subsection (1) above, he shall give notice in writing of his decision to the applicant and, upon the giving of that notice, the revocation or, as the case may be, the variation specified in the application shall take effect.

(4) The Director may decide to refuse an application under subsection (1) above –

(a) where it relates to an order under section 3 above, if he considers that the applicant remains unfit to carry on any estate agency work at all or, as the case may be, estate agency work of the description which is prohibited by the order; and

(b) where it relates to an order under section 4 above, if he considers that the applicant may again fail to comply with a relevant statutory obligation or, as the case may be, again engage in the practice specified in the order.

(5) If, on an application under subsection (1) above, the Director decides that –

(a) he cannot accede to the application because he considers that the applicant remains unfit to carry on any estate agency work at all in a particular part of or area within the United Kingdom or remains unfit to carry on estate agency work of a particular description (either throughout the United Kingdom or in a particular part of or area within it) or, as the case may be, remains likely to fail to comply with a relevant statutory obligation or to engage in a particular practice, but

(*b*) the order to which the application relates could, without detriment to the public, be varied in favour of the applicant,

the Director may make such a variation accordingly.

(6) The provisions of Part II of Schedule 2 to this Act shall have effect in relation to any application to the Director under subsection (1) above and the provisions of Part I of that Schedule shall have effect –

(*a*) with respect to the procedure to be followed before the Director comes to a decision under subsection (4) or subsection (5) above; and

(*b*) in connection with the making and coming into operation of such a decision.

(7) In this section "relevant statutory obligation" has the meaning assigned to it by section 4(1)(*a*) above.

Notes

See p 86.

For the giving of notice by the Director, see s 29.

It is submitted that the Director, in dealing with applications under this section, is subject to the supervision of the Council on Tribunals: Tribunals and Inquiries Act 1992, ss 1, 14 and Schedule 1.

Appeals.

7. – (1) A person who receives notice under paragraph 9 of Schedule 2 to this Act of –

(*a*) a decision of the Director to make an order in respect of him under section 3 or section 4 above, or

(*b*) a decision of the Director under subsection (4) or subsection (5) of section 6 above on an application made by him,

may appeal against the decision to the Secretary of State.

(2) On an appeal under subsection (1) above the Secretary of State may give such directions for disposing of the appeal as he thinks just, including a direction for the payment of costs or expenses by any party to the appeal.

(3) The Secretary of State shall make provision by regulations with respect to appeals under subsection (1) above –

(a) as to the period within which and the manner in which such appeals are to be brought;

(b) as to the persons by whom such appeals are to be heard on behalf of the Secretary of State;

(c) as to the manner in which such appeals are to be conducted;

(d) for taxing or otherwise settling any costs or expenses directed to be paid under subsection (2) above and for the enforcement of any such direction; and

(e) as to any other matter connected with such appeals;

and such regulations shall be made by statutory instrument which shall be subject to annulment in pursuance of a resolution of either House of Parliament.

(4) If the appellant is dissatisfied in point of law with a decision of the Secretary of State under this section he may appeal against that decision to the High Court, the Court of Session or a judge of the High Court in Northern Ireland.

(5) No appeal to the Court of Appeal or to the Court of Appeal in Northern Ireland shall be brought from a decision under subsection (4) above except with the leave of that Court or of the court or judge from whose decision the appeal is brought.

(6) An appeal shall lie, with the leave of the Court of Session or the House of Lords, from any decision of the Court of Session under this section, and such leave may be given on such terms as to costs or otherwise as the Court of Session or the House of Lords may determine.

Notes

See p 84.

The powers conferred upon the Secretary of State by s 7(3) have been used to make the Estate Agents (Appeals) Regulations 1981, SI 1981, No 1518 (see p 157). Although there was no duty of consultation in respect of these regulations (see s 30), extensive consultation did in fact take place.

Register of orders etc.

8. – (1) The Director shall establish and maintain a register on which there shall be entered particulars of every order made by him under section 3 or section 4 above and of his decision on any application for revocation or variation of such an order.

(2) The particulars referred to in subsection (1) above shall include –

(a) the terms of the order and of any variation of it; and

(b) the date on which the order or variation came into operation or is expected to come into operation or if an appeal against the decision is pending and the order or variation has in consequence not come into operation, a statement to that effect.

(3) The Director may, of his own motion or on the application of any person aggrieved, rectify the register by the addition, variation or removal of any particulars; and the provisions of Part II of Schedule 2 to this Act shall have effect in relation to an application under this subsection.

(4) If it comes to the attention of the Director that any order of which particulars appear in the register is no longer in operation, he shall remove those particulars from the register.

(5) Any person shall be entitled on payment of the prescribed fee–

(a) to inspect the register during such office hours as may be specified by a general notice made by the Director and to take copies of any entry, or

(b) to obtain from the Director a copy, certified by him to be correct, of any entry in the register.

(6) A certificate given by the Director under subsection (5)(b) above shall be conclusive evidence of the fact that, on the date on which the certificate was given, the particulars contained in the copy to which the certificate relates were entered on the register; and particulars of any matters required to be entered on the register which are so entered shall be evidence and, in Scotland, sufficient evidence of those matters and shall be presumed, unless the contrary is proved, to be correct.

Notes

See p 87.

Information, entry and inspection

Information for the Director.

9. – (1) The Director may, for the purpose of assisting him –

(a) to determine whether to make an order under section 3 or section 4 above, and

(b) in the exercise of any of his functions under sections 5, 6 and 8 above and 13 and 17 below, by notice require any person to furnish to him such information as may be specified or described in the notice or to produce to him any documents so specified or described.

(2) A notice under this section –

(a) may specify the way in which and the time within which it is to be complied with and, in the case of a notice requiring the production of documents, the facilities to be afforded for making extracts, or taking copies of, the documents; and

(b) may be varied or revoked by a subsequent notice.

(3) Nothing in this section shall be taken to require a person who has acted as counsel or solicitor for any person to disclose any privileged communication made by or to him in that capacity.

(4) A person who –

(a) refuses or wilfully neglects to comply with a notice under this section, or

(b) in furnishing any information in compliance with such a notice, makes any statement which he knows to be false in a material particular or recklessly makes any statement which is false in a material particular, or

(c) with intent to deceive, produces in compliance with such a notice a document which is false in a material particular,

shall be liable on conviction on indictment or on summary conviction to a fine which, on summary conviction, shall not exceed the statutory maximum.

(5) In section 131 of the Fair Trading Act 1973 (which provides for the Director to be notified by courts of convictions and judgments which may be relevant to his functions under Part III of that Act) after the words "this Act" there shall be inserted the words "or under the Estate Agents Act 1979".

(6) It shall be the duty of –

(a) the Equal Opportunities Commission,

(b) the Equal Opportunities Commission for Northern Ireland, and

(c) the Commission for Racial Equality,

to furnish to the Director such information relating to any finding, notice, injunction or order falling within paragraph 2 of Schedule 1 to this Act as is in their possession and appears to them to be relevant to the functions of the Director under this Act.

Notes

See Chapter 4.

The wide-ranging powers given to the Director by s 9(1) are uncommon but not unprecedented: see the Health & Safety at Work etc Act 1974, s 27 and the Consumer Safety Act 1978, s 4. Safeguards against the misuse of information so obtained are provided by s 10.

For provisions as to criminal offences, see s 28.

Restriction on disclosure of information.

10. – (1) Subject to subsections (3) to (5) below, no information obtained under or by virtue of this Act about any individual shall be disclosed without his consent.

(2)   Subject to subsections (3) to (5) below, no information obtained under or by virtue of this Act about any business shall be disclosed except, so long as the business continues to be carried on, with the consent of the person for the time being carrying it on.

(3) Subsections (1) and (2) above do not apply to any disclosure of information made –

(a) for the purpose of facilitating the performance of any functions under this Act, the Trade Descriptions Act 1968, the Fair Trading Act 1973, the Consumer Credit Act 1974 or the Restrictive Trade Practices Act 1976 or the Competition Act 1980 or the Telecommunications Act 1984 or the Gas Act 1986 or the Airports Act 1986 or the Consumer Protection Act 1987 or the Water Act 1989 the Water Industry Act 1991 or any of the other consolidation Acts (within the meaning of section 206 of that Act of 1991) or the Electricity Act 1989 or the Control of Misleading Advertisements Regulations 1988 or the Courts and Legal Services Act 1990 of any Minister of the Crown, any Northern Ireland department, the Director the Director General of Telecommunications the Director General of Gas Supply the Civil Aviation Authority, the Director General of Water Services, the Director General of Electricity Supply or the Authorised Conveyancing Practitioners Board or a local weights and measures authority in Great Britain, or

(b) in connection with the investigation of any criminal offence or for the purposes of any criminal proceedings, or

(c) for the purposes of any civil proceedings brought under or by virtue of this Act or any of the other enactments specified in paragraph (a) above.

(4) For the purpose of enabling the Director to use, in connection with his functions under this Act, information obtained by him in the exercise of functions under certain other enactments, the following

amendments shall be made in provisions restricting disclosure of information, namely, –

    (*a*) at the end of paragraph (*a*) of subsection (2) of section 133 of the Fair Trading Act 1973 there shall be added the words "the Estate Agents Act 1979, or";

    (*b*) in paragraph (*a*) of subsection (3) of section 174 of the Consumer Credit Act 1974 after the words "Fair Trading Act 1973" there shall be added the words "or the Estate Agents Act 1979"; and

    (*c*) at the end of paragraph (*a*) of subsection (1) of section 41 of the Restrictive Trade Practices Act 1976 there shall be added the words "or the Estate Agents Act 1979".

(5) Nothing in subsections (1) and (2) above shall be construed–

    (*a*) as limiting the particulars which may be entered in the register; or

    (*b*) as applying to any information which has been made public as part of the register.

(6) Any person who discloses information in contravention of this section shall be liable on summary conviction to a fine not exceeding the statutory maximum and, on conviction on indictment, to imprisonment for a term not exceeding two years or to a fine or both.

Notes

Restrictions upon the improper disclosure of information which is obtained under statutory powers are becoming more common and more wide-ranging: see the Fair Trading Act 1973, s 133 and the Consumer Credit Act 1974, s 174, as compared with the more limited protection conferred by the Trade Descriptions Act 1968, s 28. On the other hand, the power of the Director-General of Fair Trading to use information gathered under one Act in pursuance of functions under another is also increasing: consequently subsection (3) is as amended by the Competition Act 1980, s 19(4); the Telecommunications Act 1984, s 109, Sched 4, para 72; the Gas Act 1986, s 67(1), Sched 7, para 27; the Airports Act 1986, s 83(1), Sched 4, para 6; the Consumer Protection Act 1987, s 48, Sched 4; the Control of Misleading Advertisements Regulations 1988 (SI 1988 No 915) reg 7(6)(d); the Water Act 1989, s 190, Sched 25, para 57; the Electricity Act 1989, s 112(1), Sched 16, para 24; the Courts and Legal Services Act 1990, s 125(3), Sched 18, para 22, (from a day to be appointed); and the Water Consolidation (Consequential Provisions) Act 1991, s 2, Sched 1, para 33.

For provisions as to criminal offences, see s 28.

Powers of entry and inspection.

11. – (1) A duly authorised officer of an enforcement authority, at all reasonable hours and on production, if required, of his credentials may –

(a) if he has reasonable cause to suspect that an offence has been committed under this Act, in order to ascertain whether it has been committed, enter any premises (other than premises used only as a dwelling);

(b) if he has reasonable cause to suspect that an offence has been committed under this Act, in order to ascertain whether it has been committed, require any person –

(i)   carrying on, or employed in connection with, a business to produce any books or documents relating to it, or

(ii) having control of any information relating to a business recorded otherwise than in a legible form, to provide a document containing a legible reproduction of the whole or any part of the information; and take copies of, or of any entry in, the books or documents;

(c) seize and detain any books or documents which he has reason to believe may be required as evidence in proceedings for an offence under this Act;

(d) for the purpose of exercising his powers under this subsection to seize books and documents, but only if and to the extent that it is reasonably necessary for securing that the provisions of this Act are duly observed, require any person having authority to do so to break open any container and, if that person does not comply, break it open himself.

(2) An officer seizing books or documents in exercise of his powers under this section shall not do so without informing the person from whom he seizes them.

(3) If and so long as any books or documents which have been seized under this section are not required as evidence in connection with proceedings which have been begun for an offence under this Act, the enforcement authority by whose officer they were seized shall afford to the person to whom the books or documents belong and to any person authorised by him in writing reasonable facilities to inspect them and to take copies of or make extracts from them.

(4) If a justice of the peace, on sworn information in writing, or in Scotland, a sheriff or a justice of the peace, on evidence on oath –

(a) is satisfied that there is reasonable ground to believe either –

(i)   that any books or documents which a duly authorised officer has power to inspect under this section are on any premises and their inspection is likely to disclose evidence of the commission of an offence under this Act, or

(ii)   that an offence under this Act has been, or is being or is about to be, committed on any premises; and

(b) is also satisfied either –

(i)   that admission to the premises has been or is likely to be refused and that notice of intention to apply for a warrant under this subsection has been given to the occupier, or

(ii)   that an application for admission, or the giving of such a notice, would defeat the object of the entry or that the premises are unoccupied or that the occupier is temporarily absent and it might defeat the object of the entry to wait for his return,

the justice or, as the case may be, the sheriff may by warrant under his hand, which shall continue in force for a period of one month, authorise an officer of an enforcement authority to enter the premises, by force if need be.

(5) An officer entering premises by virtue of this section may take such other persons and equipment with him as he thinks necessary, and on leaving the premises entered by virtue of a warrant under subsection (4) above shall, if the premises are unoccupied or the occupier is temporarily absent, leave them as effectively secured against trespassers as he found them.

(6) The Secretary of State may by regulations provide that, in cases specified in the regulations, an officer of a local weights and measures authority is not to be taken to be duly authorised for the purposes of this section unless he is authorised by the Director.

(7) The power to make regulations under subsection (6) above shall be exercisable by statutory instrument which shall be subject to annulment in pursuance of a resolution of either House of Parliament.

(8) Nothing in this section shall be taken to require a person who has acted as counsel or solicitor for any person to produce a document containing a privileged communication made by or to him in that capacity or authorises the seizing of any such document in his possession.

Notes

The powers contained in this section are, by and large, in common form as regards consumer protection measures enforced by local weights and measures authorities: see, for example, the Trade Descriptions Act 1968, s 28; Fair Trading Act 1973, s 29; Consumer Credit Act 1974, s 162. There is, however, a significant difference in the power of *entry* on to non-residential premises, as a result of an amendment made to the Bill in the House of Lords. The power of entry is usually made independent of any requirement of "reasonable suspicion" so as to permit "spot checks". In relation to this Act, however, it was felt that spot checks would be of little value, since they would be unlikely to reveal anything without an inspection of an estate agent's books (for which reasonable suspicion *is* required). Accordingly, the power of entry too is made dependent upon reasonable suspicion that an offence under the Act has been committed.

This section also differs from the corresponding provisions of the Consumer Credit Act in that the power which it confers relate only to *offences* under the Act; an authorised officer may not enter premises or inspect books or documents in order to ascertain whether an estate agent is in breach of any other provision of the Act. Thus, of the various specific duties considered in Chapter 3, the enforcement powers conferred by s 11 are relevant only to those which govern the handling of clients' money. They may not be used in connection with the giving of information to clients, the disclosure of personal interest, the duty to account for interest on clients' money or anything defined by the 1991 Order as an "undesirable practice".

S 11(4) empowers an officer to enter premises by force under a warrant (and specifies the conditions on which such a warrant may be issued); it seems a clear inference that forcible entry is not permitted under s 11(1). It should be noted, however, that a person who refuses admission to an officer acting under this subsection commits the offence of obstruction (see s 27); this offence in itself constitutes grounds for the issue of a warrant. It is also important to appreciate that, whereas s 11(1) gives no power of entry on to premises which are purely residential, a warrant under s 11(3) may do so.

The Estate Agents (Entry and Inspection) Regulations 1981 (SI 1981, No 1519) made under s 11(6) (see p 171), provide in effect that a trading standards officer must be specifically authorised by the Director-General of Fair Trading, or have the consent of the estate agent in question, in order to exercise those powers which refer to books or documents in respect of any book or document relating to business carried on by banks. The purpose and scope of this provision is not altogether clear; in particular, there is nothing to indicate whether it applies only to books or documents in the possession of a bank (eg the bank's records of a client account) or whether it also includes a bank statement in the agent's possession.

Information which is obtained by virtue of the powers conferred by this section may not be disclosed except in specified circumstances: see s 10.

Clients' money and accounts

Meaning of "clients' money" etc.

12. – (1) In this Act "clients' money", in relation to a person engaged in estate agency work, means any money received by him in the course of that work which is a contract or pre-contract deposit –

(a) in respect of the acquisition of an interest in land in the United Kingdom, or

(b) in respect of a connected contract,

whether that money is held or received by him as agent, bailee, stakeholder or in any other capacity.

(2) In this Act "contract deposit" means any sum paid by a purchaser –

(a) which in whole or in part is, or is intended to form part of, the consideration for acquiring such an interest as is referred to in subsection (1)(a) above or for a connected contract; and

(b) which is paid by him at or after the time at which he acquires the interest or enters into an enforceable contract to acquire it.

(3) In this Act "pre-contract deposit" means any sum paid by an person –

(a) in whole or in part as an earnest of his intention to acquire such an interest as is referred to in subsection (1)(a) above, or

(b) in whole or in part towards meeting any liability of his in respect of the consideration for the acquisition of such an interest which will arise if he acquires or enters into an enforceable contract to acquire the interest, or

(c) in respect of a connected contract,

and which is paid by him at a time before he either acquires the interest or enters into an enforceable contract to acquire it.

(4) In this Act "connected contract", in relation to the acquisition of an interest in land, means a contract which is conditional upon such an acquisition or upon entering into an enforceable contract for such an acquisition (whether or not it is also conditional on other matters).

Notes

See p 56.

Clients' money held on trust or as agent.

13. – (1) It is hereby declared that clients' money received by a person in the course of estate agency work in England, Wales or Northern Ireland –

(a) is held by him on trust for the person who is entitled to call for it to be paid over to him or to be paid on his direction or to have it otherwise credited to him, or

(b) if it is received by him as stakeholder, is held by him on trust for the person who may become so entitled on the occurrence of the event against which the money is held.

(2) It is hereby declared that clients' money received by any person in the course of estate agency work in Scotland is held by him as agent for the person who is entitled to call for it to be paid over to him or to be paid on his direction or to have it otherwise credited to him.

(3) The provisions of sections 14 and 15 below as to the investment of clients' money, the keeping of accounts and records and accounting for interest shall have effect in place of the corresponding duties which would be owed by a person holding clients' money as trustee, or in Scotland as agent, under the general law.

(4) Where an order of the Director under section 3 above has the effect of prohibiting a person from holding clients' money the order may contain provision –

(a) appointing another person as trustee, or in Scotland as agent, in place of the person to whom the order relates to hold and deal with clients' money held by that person when the order comes into effect; and

(b) requiring the expenses and such reasonable remuneration of the new trustee or agent as may be specified in the order to be paid by the person to whom the order relates or, if the order so provides, out of the clients' money;

but nothing in this subsection shall affect the power conferred by section 41 of the Trustee Act 1925 or section 40 of the Trustee Act (Northern Ireland) 1958 to appoint a new trustee to hold clients' money.

(5) For the avoidance of doubt it is hereby declared that the fact that any person has or may have a lien on clients' money held by him does not affect the operation of this section and also that nothing in this section shall prevent such a lien from being given effect.

Notes

See p 58.

Keeping of client accounts.
   14. – (1) Subject to such provision as may be made by accounts regulations, every person who receives clients' money in the course of estate agency work shall, without delay, pay the money into a client account maintained by him or by a person in whose employment he is.
   (2) In this Act a "client account" means a current or deposit account which –
   (a) is with an institution authorised for the purposes of this section, and
   (b) is in the name of a person who is or has been engaged in estate agency work; and
   (c) contains in its title the word "client".
   (3) The Secretary of State may make provision by regulations (in this section referred to as "accounts regulations") as to the opening and keeping of client accounts, the keeping of accounts and records relating to clients' money and the auditing of those accounts; and such regulations shall be made by statutory instrument which shall be subject to annulment in pursuance of a resolution of either House of Parliament.
   (4) As to the opening and keeping of client accounts, accounts regulations may in particular specify –
   (a) the institutions which are authorised for the purposes of this section;
   (b) any persons or classes of persons to whom, or any circumstances in which, the obligation imposed by subsection (1) above does not apply;
   (c) any circumstances in which money other than clients' money may be paid into a client account; and
   (d) the occasions on which, and the persons to whom, money held in a client account may be paid out.
   (5) As to the auditing of accounts relating to clients' money, accounts regulations may in particular make provision –
   (a) requiring such accounts to be drawn up in respect of specified accounting periods and to be audited by a qualified auditor within a specified time after the end of each such period;

(*b*) requiring the auditor to report whether in his opinion the requirements of this Act and of the accounts regulations have been complied with or have been substantially complied with;

(*c*) as to the matters to which such a report is to relate and the circumstances in which a report of substantial compliance may be given; and

(*d*) requiring a person who maintains a client account to produce on demand to a duly authorised officer of an enforcement authority the latest auditor's report.

(6) Subject to subsection (7) below, "qualified auditor" in subsection (5)(*a*) above means –

(*a*) eligible for appointment as a company auditor under section 25 of the Companies Act 1989; or

(*b*) in Northern Ireland, is a member of one or more bodies recognised by the Department of Economic Development for Northern Ireland for the purposes of article 397(1)(*a*) of the Companies (Northern Ireland) Order 1986 or is for the time being recognised by that Department under paragraphs (5), (6) or (7) of article 397 of that Order.

(7) A person is not a qualified auditor for the purposes of subsection (5)(*a*) above, if in the case of a client account maintained by a company, he is ineligible for appointment as auditor to the company by virtue of Part II of the Companies Act 1989.

(8) A person who –

(*a*) contravenes any provision of this Act or of accounts regulations as to the manner in which clients' money is to be dealt with or accounts and records relating to such money are to be kept, or

(*b*) fails to produce an auditor's report when required to do so by accounts regulations,

shall be liable on summary conviction to a fine not exceeding level 4 on the standard scale.

Notes

See pp 64–68.

The powers conferred by this section upon the Secretary of State have been used (after due consultation as provided for by s 30) to make the Estate Agents (Accounts) Regulations 1981 (SI 1981, No 1520) (see p 173).

Subsections (6) and (7) are as substituted by the Companies Act 1989 (Eligibility for Appointment as Company Auditor) (Consequential Amendments) Regulations 1991 (SI 1991, No 1997) reg 2, Schedule, para 33.

For provisions as to criminal offences, see s 28.

The reference in subsection (8) to fines on the standard scale was introduced by the Criminal Justice Act 1982, ss 37 and 46. From October 1 1992 level 4 is £2,500: Criminal Justice Act 1991, s 17 and Criminal Justice Act 1991 (Commencement No 3) Order 1992.

Interest on clients' money.

15. – (1) Accounts regulations may make provision for requiring a person who has received any clients' money to account, in such cases as may be prescribed by the regulations, to the person who is or becomes entitled to the money for the interest which was, or could have been, earned by putting the money in a separate deposit account at an institution authorised for the purposes of section 14 above.

(2) The cases in which a person may be required by accounts regulations to account for interest as mentioned in subsection (1) above may be defined, amongst other things, by reference to the amount of the sum held or received by him or the period for which it is likely to be retained, or both.

(3) Except as provided by accounts regulations and subject to subsection (4) below, a person who maintains a client account in which he keeps clients' money generally shall not be liable to account to any person for interest received by him on money in that account.

(4) Nothing in this section or in accounts regulations shall affect any arrangement in writing, whenever made, between a person engaged in estate agency work and any other person as to the application of, or of any interest on, money in which that other person has or may have an interest.

(5) Failure of any person to comply with any provision of accounts regulations made by virtue of this section may be taken into account by the Director in accordance with section 3(1)(c) above and may form the basis of a civil claim for interest which was or should have been earned on clients' money but shall not render that person liable to any criminal penalty.

(6) In this section "accounts regulations" has the same meaning as in section 14 above.

Notes

See p 68 and the Estate Agents (Accounts) Regulations 1981, SI 1981 No 1520 (p 173).

Insurance cover for clients' money.

16. – (1) Subject to the provisions of this section, a person may not accept clients' money in the course of estate agency work unless there are in force authorised arrangements under which, in the event of his failing to account for such money to the person entitled to it, his liability will be made good by another.

(2) The Secretary of State may by regulations made by statutory instrument, which shall be subject to annulment in pursuance of a resolution of either House of Parliament –

(a) specify any persons or classes of persons to whom subsection (1) above does not apply;

(b) specify arrangements which are authorised for the purposes of this section including arrangements to which an enforcement authority nominated for the purpose by the Secretary of State or any other person so nominated is a party;

(c) specify the terms and conditions upon which any payment is to be made under such arrangements and any circumstances in which the right to any such payment may be excluded or modified;

(d) provide that any limit on the amount of any such payment is to be not less than a specified amount;

(e) require a person providing authorised arrangements covering any person carrying on estate agency work to issue a certificate in a form specified in the regulations certifying that arrangement complying with the regulations have been made with respect to that person; and

(f) prescribe any matter required to be prescribed for the purposes of subsection (4) below.

(3) Every guarantee entered into by a person (in this subsection referred to as "the insurer") who provides authorised arrangements covering another person (in this subsection referred to as "the agent") carrying on estate agency work shall enure for the benefit of every person from whom the agent has received clients' money as if –

(a) the guarantee were contained in a contract made by the insurer with every such person; and (*b*) except in Scotland, that contract were under seal; and

(*c*) where the guarantee is given by two or more insurers, they had bound themselves jointly and severally.

(4) No person who carried on estate agency work may describe himself as an "estate agent" or so use any name or in any way hold himself out as to indicate or reasonably be understood to indicate that he is carrying on a business in the course of which he is prepared to act as a broker in the acquisition or disposal of interests in land unless, in such manner as may be prescribed–

(*a*) there is displayed at his place of business, and

(*b*) there is included in any relevant document issued or displayed in connection with his business,

any prescribed information relating to arrangements authorised for the purposes of this section.

(5) For the purposes of subsection (4) above –

(*a*) any business premises at which a person carried on estate agency work and to which the public has access is a place of business of his; and

(*b*) "relevant document" means any advertisement, notice or other written material which might reasonably induce any person to use the services of another in connection with the acquisition or disposal of an interest in land.

(6) A person who fails to comply with any provision of subsection (1) or subsection (4) above or of regulations under subsection (2) above which is binding on him shall be liable on conviction on indictment or on summary conviction to a fine which, on summary conviction, shall not exceed the statutory maximum.

Notes

See p 61. It should be noted that this section has not yet been brought into force: see the notes to s 36.

S 16(2)(*b*) was amended at a late stage to take account of views expressed by the insurance industry. These indicated that *individual* bonds (where an agent was not a member of one of the major societies, and did not wish to join a local group scheme) might have to be issued to a named person; power is therefore taken to nominate an enforcement authority (as defined in s 26(1)) or other person as the recipient of the bond.

S 16(3), which was also incorporated at report stage in the House of Lords, enables a depositor whose money is lost due to an agent's default to claim directly against the insurer, notwithstanding the absence of any contract between them. In this it follows other forms of statutory indemnity insurance. However, it does not in terms cover the case where the person who is entitled to the money at the time it is lost (and on whom that loss accordingly falls) is not the original depositor (eg where a vendor has become entitled to a contract deposit paid by a purchaser).

For the Secretary of State's duty to consult before making regulations, see s 30.

For provisions as to criminal offences, see s 28.

Exemptions from section 16.

17. – (1) If, on an application made to him in that behalf, the Director considers that a person engaged in estate agency work may, without loss of adequate protection to consumers, be exempted from all or any of the provisions of subsection (1) of section 16 above or of regulations under subsection (2) of that section, he may issue to that person a certificate of exemption under this section.

(2) An application under subsection (1) above –

(*a*) shall state the reasons why the applicant considers that he should be granted a certificate of exemption; and

(*b*) shall be accompanied by the prescribed fee.

(3) A certificate of exemption under this section –

(*a*) may impose conditions of exemption on the person to whom it is issued;

(*b*) may be issued to have effect for a period specified in the certificate or without limit of time.

(4) If and so long as –

(*a*) a certificate of exemption has effect, and

(*b*) the person to whom it is issued complies with any conditions of exemption specified in the certificate,

that person shall be exempt, to the extent so specified, from the provisions of subsection (1) of section 16 above and of any regulations made under subsection (2) of that section.

(5) If the Director decides to refuse an application under subsection (1) above he shall give the applicant notice of his decision and of the reasons for it, including any facts which in his opinion justify the decision.

(6) If a person who made an application under subsection (1) above is aggrieved by a decision of the Director –

(*a*) to refuse his application, or

(*b*) to grant him a certificate of exemption subject to conditions,

he may appeal against the decision to the Secretary of State; and subsections (2) to (6) of section 7 above shall apply to such an appeal as they apply to an appeal under that section.

(7) A person who fails to comply with any condition of exemption specified in a current certificate of exemption issued to him shall be liable on conviction on indictment or on summary conviction to a fine which, on summary conviction, shall not exceed the statutory maximum.

Notes

See p 62. It should be noted that this section has not yet been brought into force: see the notes to s 36.

In dealing with an application under this section, it is submitted that the Director is subject to the supervision of the Council on Tribunals: Tribunals and Inquiries Act 1992, ss 1, 14 and Schedule 1.

For the giving of notice by the Director, see s 29.

For provisions as to criminal offences, see s 28.

Regulation of other aspects of estate agency work

Information to clients of prospective liabilities.

18. – (1) Subject to subsection (2) below, before any person (in this section referred to as "the client") enters into a contract with another (in this section referred to as "the agent") under which the agent will engage in estate agency work on behalf of the client, the agent shall give the client –

(a) the information specified in subsection (2) below; and

(b) any additional information which may be prescribed under subsection (4) below.

(2) The following is the information to be given under subsection (1)(a) above –

(a) particulars of the circumstances in which the client will become liable to pay remuneration to the agent for carrying out estate agency work;

(b) particulars of the amount of the agent's remuneration for carrying out estate agency work or, if that amount is not ascertainable at the time the information is given, particulars of the manner in which the remuneration will be calculated;

(c) particulars of any payments which do not form part of the agent's remuneration for carrying out estate agency work or a contract or pre-contract deposit but which, under the contract referred to in subsection (1) above, will or may in certain circumstances be payable by the client to the agent or any other person and particulars of the circumstances in which any such payments will become payable; and

(*d*) particulars of the amount of any payment falling within paragraph (*c*) above or, if that amount is not ascertainable at the time the information is given, an estimate of that amount together with particulars of the manner in which it will be calculated.

(3) If, at any time after the client and the agent have entered into such a contract as is referred to in subsection (1) above, the parties are agreed that the terms of the contract should be varied so far as they relate to the carrying out of estate agency work or any payment falling within subsection (2)(*c*) above, the agent shall give the client details of any changes which, at the time the statement is given, fall to be made in the information which was given to the client under subsection (1) above before the contract was entered into.

(4) The Secretary of State may by regulations –

(*a*) prescribe for the purposes of subsection (1)(*b*) above additional information relating to any estate agency work to be performed under the contract; and

(*b*) make provision with respect to the time and the manner in which the obligation of the agent under subsection (1) or subsection (3) above is to be performed;

and the power to make regulations under this subsection shall be exercisable by statutory instrument which shall be subject to annulment in pursuance of a resolution of either House of Parliament.

(5) If any person –

(*a*) fails to comply with the obligation under subsection (1) above with respect to a contract or with any provision of regulations under subsection (4) above relating to that obligation, or

(*b*) fails to comply with the obligation under subsection (3) above with respect to any variation of a contract or with any provision of regulations under subsection (4) above relating to that obligation,

the contract or, as the case may be, the variation of it shall not be enforceable by him except pursuant to an order of the court under subsection (6) below.

(6) If, in a case where subsection (5) above applies in relation to a contract or a variation of a contract, the agent concerned makes

an application to the court for the enforcement of the contract or, as the case may be, of a contract as varied by the variation –

(a) the court shall dismiss the application if, but only if, it considers it just to do so having regard to prejudice caused to the client by the agent's failure to comply with his obligation and the degree of culpability for the failure; and

(b) where the court does not dismiss the application, it may nevertheless order that any sum payable by the client under the contract or, as the case may be, under the contract as varied shall be reduced or discharged so as to compensate the client for prejudice suffered as a result of the agent's failure to comply with his obligation.

(7) In this section –

(a) references to the enforcement of a contract or variation include the withholding of money in pursuance of a lien for money alleged to be due under the contract or as a result of the variation; and

(b) "the court" means any court having jurisdiction to hear and determine matters arising out of the contract.

Notes

See pp 34–44.

The opening words: "Subject to subsection (2) below" appear meaningless; they applied originally to a different provision, deleted from the Act during its passage through Parliament, and seem to have been left in by an oversight.

For the Secretary of State's duty to consult before making regulations, see s 30. The powers conferred upon the Secretary of State by s 18(4) have been used to make the Estate Agents (Provision of Information) Regulations 1991 (SI 1991 No 859) (see p 181).

Regulation of pre-contract deposits outside Scotland.

19. – (1) No person may in the course of estate agency work in England, Wales or Northern Ireland seek from any other person (in this section referred to as a "prospective purchaser") who wishes to acquire an interest in land in the United Kingdom, a payment which, if made, would constitute a pre-contract deposit in excess of the prescribed limit.

(2) If, in the course of estate agency work, any person receives from a prospective purchaser a pre-contract deposit which exceeds the prescribed limit, so much of that deposit as exceeds the prescribed limit shall forthwith be either repaid to the prospective

purchaser or paid to such other person as the prospective purchaser may direct.

(3) In relation to a prospective purchaser, references in subsections (1) and (2) above to a pre-contract deposit shall be treated as references to the aggregate of all the payments which constitute pre-contract deposits in relation to his proposed acquisition of a particular interest in land in the United Kingdom.

(4) In this section "the prescribed limit" means such limit as the Secretary of State may by regulations prescribe; and such a limit may be so prescribed either as a specific amount or as a percentage or fraction of a price or other amount determined in any particular case in accordance with the regulations.

(5) The power to make regulations under this section shall be exercisable by statutory instrument which shall be subject to annulment in pursuance of a resolution of either House of Parliament.

(6) Failure by any person to comply with subsection (1) or subsection (2) above may be taken into account by the Director in accordance with section 3(1)(c) above but shall not render that person liable to any criminal penalty nor constitute a ground for any civil claim, other than a claim for the recovery of such an excess as is referred to in subsection (2) above.

(7) This section does not form part of the law of Scotland.

Notes

See p 63. It should be noted that this section has not yet been brought into force: see the notes to s 36.

For the Secretary of State's duty to consult before making regulations, see s 30.

Prohibition of pre-contract deposits in Scotland.

20. – (1) No person may, in the course of estate agency work in Scotland, seek or accept from any person (in this section referred to as a "prospective purchaser") who wishes to acquire an interest in land in the United Kingdom a payment which, if made, would constitute a pre-contract deposit or, as the case may be, which constitutes such a deposit.

(2) If, in the course of estate agency work in Scotland, any person receives from a prospective purchaser a payment which constitutes a pre-contract deposit, it shall forthwith be either repaid to the

prospective purchaser or paid to such person as the prospective purchaser shall direct.

(3) Failure by any person to comply with subsection (1) or subsection (2) above may be taken into account by the Director in accordance with section 3(1)(c) above but shall not render that person liable to any criminal penalty nor constitute a ground for any civil claim, other than a claim under subsection (2) above for the recovery of the pre-contract deposit.

(4) This section forms part of the law of Scotland only.

Notes

See p 63.

Transactions in which an estate agent has a personal interest.

21. – (1) A person who is engaged in estate agency work (in this section referred to as an "estate agent") and has a personal interest in any land shall not enter into negotiations with any person with respect to the acquisition or disposal by that person of any interest in that land until the estate agent has disclosed to that person the nature and extent of his personal interest in it.

(2) In any case where the result of a proposed disposal of an interest in land or of such a proposed disposal and other transactions would be that an estate agent would have a personal interest in that land, the estate agent shall not enter into negotiations with any person with respect to the proposed disposal until he has disclosed to that person the nature and extent of that personal interest.

(3) Subsections (1) and (2) above apply where an estate agent is negotiating on his own behalf as well as where he is negotiating in the course of estate agency work.

(4) An estate agent may not seek or receive a contract or pre-contract deposit in respect of the acquisition or proposed acquisition of –

(a) a personal interest of his in land in the United Kingdom; or

(b) any other interest in any such land in which he has a personal interest.

(5) For the purposes of this section, an estate agent has a personal interest in land if –

(a) he has a beneficial interest in the land or in the proceeds of sale of any interest in it; or

   (*b*) he knows or might reasonably be expected to know that any
of the following persons has such a beneficial interest,
namely–
   (i)   his employer or principal, or
   (ii) any employee or agent of his, or
   (iii) any associate of his or of any person mentioned in sub-
paragraphs (i) and (ii) above.

(6) Failure by an estate agent to comply with any of the preceding
provisions of this section may be taken into account by the Director
in accordance with section 3(1)(*c*) above but shall not render the
estate agent liable to any criminal penalty nor constitute a ground
for any civil claim.

Notes

See pp 48–53.
Where an estate agent has, or expects to acquire, a "personal interest" in property
as defined by this section, the nature and extent of that interest must be disclosed to
anyone with whom the agent enters into negotiations regarding the property. Further,
the agent must not "seek or receive a contract or pre-contract deposit" in respect of
such property. The definition of "personal interest" for this purpose is a wide one,
especially where the actual interest in land is held, not by the estate agent, but by an
"associate" (s 32), including a "business associate" (s 31). Additional problems may
arise where estate agency is carried on, not by a sole principal, but by a partnership,
limited company or unincorporated association, for here the act of a natural person
may also constitute the act of the organisation as a whole (which is itself subject to
the duties imposed by s 21). We shall accordingly look separately at the various ways
in which an estate agency business may be conducted.
   Sole principal. An estate agent who practises as a sole principal is caught by s 21
in respect of direct personal interests in property, and also by the personal interests
of employees, agents, and his and their "associates". In addition to spouses or
relatives, this means any company of which the agent is a director or controller, any
unincorporated association of which he or she is an officer or has the management
or control, and any partnership of which he or she is a member. It does not include,
however, any *private* interests of partners or of their spouses or relatives, since the
agent is only their "business associate" in respect of acts done in the course of the
partnership business.
   Where it is an employee of the sole principal who actually deals with a property,
the employee's duty under s 21 is almost coextensive with that of the employer.
However, it does not cover the interest of a fellow-employee, nor cases where the
employee's instructions come *only* from the employer (s 1(3)(*a*)). Further, if the
employee is in breach of this duty, vicarious responsibility may also attach to the
employer by virtue of s 3(3)(*a*).
   Partnership. A partner dealing with a particular property is caught by s 21 in respect
of any direct personal interest (as described above in relation to a sole principal), and
also those of fellow-partners, their spouses and relatives. He or she is not, however,

concerned with the interests of partners' "business associates", such as other partnerships, companies or unincorporated associations. If the partner in question is in breach of s 21, this breach may be attributed as well to the other partners, and to the partnership as a whole, by virtue of s 3(3)(c), in cases of "connivance or consent".

It is further suggested that the act of a partner in negotiating or accepting a deposit may, except where the partner's authority is being exceeded, be regarded as the act of the partnership itself, which may have a wider circle of "associates" by virtue of s 32(6) (which enables two partnerships to be associates). If so, then the partnership as a whole may be in breach of s 21; whether any or all of the individual partners share responsibility for this breach depends upon their "connivance or consent" under s 3(3)(c).

Limited company. A director or controller of an estate agency company who deals with property is caught by s 21 in respect of any direct personal interest (as described above), and also those of the company itself, but not those of fellow directors or controllers (unless of course they are "associates"). Liability for any breach may be attributable to the company under s 3(3)(c).

Further, it is suggested that the company itself is caught by s 21 in such circumstances, and *its* personal interest extends to the interests of all its directors and controllers, and to those of associated companies (s 32(4)). If the company is in breach of its duty, responsibility may also fall upon any or all of its directors or controllers under s 3(3)(c).

Unincorporated association. The position of an unincorporated association is similar to that of a limited company, with the substitution for "director or controller" of "officer of the association or any other person who has the management or control of its activities".

Quite apart from the matters considered above, a particular problem raised by s 21(4) is whether an estate agent will be in breach where a contract or pre-contract deposit is sought or received by someone else on the agent's behalf. If the estate agent's servants and agents are *not* covered, the subsection would appear to be open to simple evasion. If, however, they *are* covered, this might prevent a contract for the sale of a property in which an agent has an interest from making the perfectly normal stipulation for payment of a deposit on exchange of contracts to the agent's solicitors. The answer may be that there is no contravention of s 21(4) so long as the solicitor receives the deposit "as stakeholder".

Standards of competence.

22. – (1) The Secretary of State may by regulations made by statutory instrument make provision for ensuring that persons engaged in estate agency work satisfy minimum standards of competence.

(2) If the Secretary of State exercises his power to make regulations under subsection (1) above, he shall in the regulations prescribe a degree of practical experience which is to be taken as evidence of competence and, without prejudice to the generality of subsection (1) above, the regulations may, in addition –

(a) prescribe professional or academic qualifications which shall also be taken to be evidence of competence;

(b) designate any body of persons as a body which may itself specify professional qualifications the holding of which is to be taken as evidence of competence;

(c) make provision for and in connection with the establishment of a body having power to examine and inquire into the competence of persons engaged or professing to engage in estate agency work; and

(d) delegate to a body established as mentioned in paragraph (c) above powers of the Secretary of State with respect to the matters referred to in paragraph (a) above;

and any reference in the following provisions of this section to a person who has attained the required standard of competence is a reference to a person who has that degree of practical experience which, in accordance with the regulations, is to be taken as evidence of competence or, where the regulations so provide, holds such qualifications or otherwise fulfils such conditions as, in accordance with the regulations, are to be taken to be evidence of competence.

(3) After the day appointed for the coming into force of this subsection –

(a) no individual may engage in estate agency work on his own account unless he has attained the required standard of competence;

(b) no member of a partnership may engage in estate agency work on the partnership's behalf unless such number of the partners as may be prescribed have attained the required standard of competence; and

(c) no body corporate or unincorporated association may engage in estate agency work unless such numbers and descriptions of the officers, members or employees as may be prescribed have attained the required standard of competence;

and any person who contravenes this subsection shall be liable on conviction on indictment or on summary conviction to a fine which, on summary conviction, shall not exceed the statutory maximum.

(4) In subsection (3) above "prescribed" means prescribed by the Secretary of State by order made by statutory instrument, which shall be subject to annulment in pursuance of a resolution of either House of Parliament.

(5) No regulations shall be made under this section unless a draft of them has been laid before Parliament and approved by a resolution of each House.

Notes

See p 71. It should be noted that this section has not yet been brought into force: see the notes to s 36.

For the Secretary of State's duty to consult before making regulations, see s 30.

For provisions as to criminal offences, see s 28.

Bankrupts not to engage in estate agency work.

23. – (1) An individual who is adjudged bankrupt after the day appointed for the coming into force of this section or, in Scotland, whose estate is sequestrated after that day shall not engage in estate agency work of any description except as an employee of another person.

(2) The prohibition imposed on an individual by subsection (1) above shall cease to have effect if and when –

(a) the adjudication of bankruptcy against him is annulled, or, in Scotland, the sequestration of his estate is recalled; or

(b) he obtains his discharge.

(3) The reference in subsection (1) above to employment of an individual by another person does not include employment of him by a body corporate of which he is a director or controller.

(4) If a person engages in estate agency work in contravention of subsection (1) above he shall be liable on conviction on indictment or on summary conviction to a fine which on summary conviction shall not exceed the statutory maximum.

Notes

See p 71.

Subsection (2)(a) is as amended by the Bankruptcy (Scotland) Act 1985, s 75, Sched 7, para 9.

Subsection (2)(b) is as substituted by the Insolvency Act 1985, s 235, Sched 8, para 33 and the Insolvency Act 1986, s 437, Sched 11.

For a defence to criminal prosecution, see s 28(1).

Supervision, enforcement, publicity etc.

Supervision by Council on Tribunals.

24. – (1) [Repealed.]

(2) Any member of the Council on Tribunals or of the Scottish Committee of the Council, in his capacity as such, may attend any hearing of representations conducted in accordance with Part I of Schedule 2 to this Act.

Notes

Subsection (1) amended the Tribunals and Inquiries Act 1971 so as to provide that the Director (or his delegate) in exercising adjudicating functions under the Estate Agents Act would be treated as a "tribunal". The effects of this, *inter alia*, are that reasoned decisions must be given, and that the "constitution and working" of the tribunal is to be kept under review by the Council on Tribunals. The amendments also ensured that the Director's executive functions are not caught, and that judicial consent is not required for the termination of any person's membership of the "tribunal". The reason for the repeal of this subsection is simply that the 1971 Act has now been consolidated into the Tribunals and Inquiries Act 1992, which itself makes equivalent provision in ss 1, 14 and Schedule 1.

The adjudicating functions" under the Estate Agents Act are, it is submitted, those in relation to the making of orders under s 3 and s 4, the revocation and variation of such orders (s 6) and applications for exemption from the requirement of bonding (s 17).

General duties of Director.

25. – (1) Subject to section 26(3) below, it is the duty of the Director –

(a) generally to superintend the working and enforcement of this Act, and

(b) where necessary or expedient, himself to take steps to enforce this Act.

(2) It is the duty of the Director, so far as appears to him to be practicable and having regard both to the national interest and the interest of persons engaged in estate agency work and of consumers, to keep under review and from time to time advise the Secretary of State about –

(a) social and commercial developments in the United Kingdom and elsewhere relating to the carrying on of estate agency work and related activities; and

(b) the working and enforcement of this Act.

(3) The Director shall arrange for the dissemination, in such form and manner as he considers appropriate, of such information and advice as it may appear to him expedient to give the public in the United Kingdom about the operation of this Act.

Notes

Overall responsibility for the enforcement of the Act, like that of the Consumer Credit Act 1974, is given to the Director-General of Fair Trading (an office originally created by the Fair Trading Act 1973). Financial provision is made for any increase in the Director's expenditure due to this Act: s 34(1).

Enforcement authorities.

26. – (1) Without prejudice to section 25(1) above, the following authorities (in this Act referred to as "enforcement authorities") have a duty to enforce this Act –

(a) the Director,

(b) in Great Britain, a local weights and measures authority, and

(c) in Northern Ireland, the Department of Commerce for Northern Ireland.

(2) Where a local weights and measures authority in England and Wales propose to institute proceedings for an offence under this Act it shall, as between the authority and the Director, be the duty of the authority to give the Director notice of the intended proceedings, together with a summary of the facts on which the charges are to be founded, and postpone the institution of the proceedings until either –

(a) twenty-eight days have expired since that notice was given, or

(b) the Director has notified them of receipt of the notice and summary.

(3) Nothing in this section or in section 25 above authorises an enforcement authority to institute proceedings in Scotland for an offence.

(4) Every local weights and measures authority shall, whenever the Director requires, report to him in such form and with such particulars as he requires on the exercise of their functions under this Act.

Notes

This co-ordination of effort between the Director and local weights and measures authorities is based on similar provisions in the Fair Trading Act 1973 and the

Consumer Credit Act 1974. It should be noted that, while the Director is entitled to be notified of any intended prosecution, he has no power to prevent it from proceeding. Nor would a prosecution be invalid if the local authority failed to notify the Director.

For local weights and measures authorities in England and Wales, see the Local Government Act 1972, s 201 (2); as to Scotland, see the Local Government (Scotland) Act 1973, s 149.

The significance of subsection (3) is that all prosecutions in Scotland are instituted by the Procurator Fiscal.

S 26 originally made provision (in subsections (5)–(8)) for the Secretary of State to supervise, by means of local inquiries, the exercise by local weights and measures authorities of their functions under the Act. As part of a general relaxation of control by central government over local authorities, however, these provisions were repealed by the Local Government, Planning and Land Act 1980, s 1 (4) and Schedules 4 and 34.

Obstruction and personation of authorised officers.

27. – (1) Any person who –

(a) wilfully obstructs an authorised officer, or

(b) wilfully fails to comply with any requirement properly made to him under section 11 above by an authorised officer, or

(c) without reasonable cause fails to give an authorised officer other assistance or information he may reasonably require in performing his functions under this Act, or

(d) in giving information to an authorised officer, makes any statement which he knows to be false,

shall be liable on summary conviction to a fine not exceeding level 4 on the standard scale.

(2) A person who is not an authorised officer but purports to act as such shall be liable on summary conviction to a fine not exceeding level 5 on the standard scale.

(3) In this section "authorised officer" means a duly authorised officer of an enforcement authority who is acting in pursuance of this Act.

(4) Nothing in subsection (1) above requires a person to answer any question or give any information if to do so might incriminate that person or that person's husband or wife.

Notes

"Wilfully" denotes deliberate intent: *R* v *Senior* [1899] 1 QB 283, 290, 291, *per* Lord Russell of Killowen.

"Obstructs" includes, it appears, anything which makes it more difficult for the officer to carry out his duty: *Hinchcliffe* v *Sheldon* [1955] 3 All ER 406. It does, however, require some form of positive conduct; hindrance which is purely passive falls under para (*c*).

As to when an authorised officer is "acting in pursuance of this Act", see notes to s 11.

For provisions as to criminal offences, see s 28.

The references in subsections (1) and (2) to fines on the standard scale were introduced by the Criminal Justice Act 1982, ss 37 and 46. From October 1 1992, level 4 is £2,500 and level 5 is £5,000: Criminal Justice Act 1991, s 17 and Criminal Justice Act 1991 (Commencement No 3) Order 1992.

Supplementary

General provisions as to offences.

28. – (1) In any proceedings for an offence under this Act it shall be a defence for the person charged to prove that he took all reasonable precautions and exercised all due diligence to avoid the commission of an offence by himself or any person under his control.

(2) Where an offence under this Act committed by a body corporate is proved to have been committed with the consent or connivance of, or to be attributable to any neglect on the part of, any director, manager, secretary or other similar officer of the body corporate, or any person who was purporting to act in any such capacity, he as well as the body corporate shall be guilty of that offence and shall be liable to be proceeded against and punished accordingly.

Notes

Like most of the general administrative provisions of the Act, this is based upon similar sections to be found in such consumer protection measures as the Weights and Measures Act 1963, Trade Descriptions Act 1968, Fair Trading Act 1973 and Consumer Credit Act 1974.

S 28(1), by making provision for a defence to criminal prosecution of "reasonable precautions and due diligence", seems to suggest that a defendant is always liable unless he can positively establish this defence. It is submitted, however, that this does not apply to every offence which is created by the Act; some of these require proof by the prosecution of guilty intent on the defendant's part and, where this is so, the defence under s 28(1) is superfluous.

Offences in which the onus is on the prosecution are as follows:

s 9(4)(*a*) – refusing or wilfully neglecting to comply with a notice demanding information;

s 9(4)(*b*) – knowingly or recklessly giving false information in compliance with such a notice;

s 9(4)(c) – producing, in compliance with such a notice, a false or misleading document with intent to deceive;

s 27(1)(a) – wilfully obstructing an authorised officer;

s 27(1)(b) – wilfully failing to comply with an authorised officer's proper requirement under s 11;

s 27(1)(c) – failing without reasonable cause to give assistance or information to an authorised officer;

s 27(1)(d) – knowingly making a false statement to an authorised officer;

s 27(2) – impersonating an authorised officer.

Offences which do not require the prosecution to prove guilty intent and to which, therefore, s 28(1) may provide a defence, are as follows:

s 3(8) – failing to comply with a prohibition order made by the Director-General of Fair Trading;

s 10(6) – disclosing information obtained by virtue of the Act;

s 14(8) – contravening accounts regulations;

s 16(6) – failing to comply with bonding requirements;

s 17(7) – failing to comply with any condition upon which exemption from bonding requirements has been granted;

s 22(3) – engaging in estate agency work without having achieved the necessary minimum standards of competence;

s 23(4) – engaging in estate agency work when bankrupt.

Where, in a case to which s 28(1) applies, a defendant seeks to rely on the defence of "reasonable precautions and due diligence", this is a question of fact which must be proved on the balance of probabilities. In general, it seems the defendant must prove that a system was set up to avoid contravention of the statute and that this system was subjected to periodic checks to see that it was working satisfactorily: see p 98. If a large firm with many branches has done this, and an offence is committed by, for example, a branch manager who is not sufficiently senior to rank as the *alter ego* of the company, the company will have a defence: *Tesco Supermarkets Ltd v Nattrass* [1972] AC 153.

A "person under his control" includes, not only an employee, but also an agent: *Brentnall & Cleland Ltd v LCC* [1945] 1 KB 115.

S 28(2) makes provision for the personal liability of the senior officers of a company,where the company itself is guilty of an offence. "Consent" and "connivance" might be thought to require actual knowledge, but it seems that suspicion may well be enough: see *Taylor's Central Garages (Exeter) Ltd v Roper* (1951) 115 JP 445, 449, 450, *per* Devlin J.

"Neglect", according to Simonds J in *Re Hughes, Rea v Black* [1943] Ch 296, 298, "in its legal connotation implies failure to perform a duty of which the person knows or ought to know".

As to who is a "manager" or "officer", see *Registrar of Restrictive Trading Agreements v WH Smith & Son Ltd* [1969] 3 All ER 1065; *Tesco Supermarkets Ltd v Nattrass* [1972] AC 153.

Service of notices etc.

29. – (1) Any notice which under this Act is to be given to any person by the Director shall be so given –

(a) by delivering it to him, or

(*b*) by leaving it at his proper address, or

(*c*) by sending it by post to him at that address.

(2) Any such notice may –

(*a*) in the case of a body corporate or unincorporated association, be given to the secretary or clerk of that body or association; and

(*b*) in the case of a partnership, be given to a partner or a person having the control or management of the partnership business.

(3) Any application or other document which under this Act may be made or given to the Director may be so made or given by sending it by post to the Director at such address as may be specified for the purposes of this Act by a general notice.

(4) For the purposes of subsections (1) and (2) above and section 7 of the Interpretation Act 1978 (service of documents by post) in its application to those subsections, the proper address of any person to whom a notice is to be given shall be his last-known address, except that –

(*a*) in the case of a body corporate or their secretary or clerk, it shall be the address of the registered or principal office of that body;

(*b*) in the case of an unincorporated association or their secretary or clerk, it shall be that of the principal office of that association;

(*c*) in the case of a partnership or a person having the control or management of the partnership business, it shall be that of the principal office of the partnership;

and for the purpose of this subsection the principal office of a company registered outside the United Kingdom or of an unincorporated association or partnership carrying on business outside the United Kingdom shall be their principal office within the United Kingdom.

(5) If the person to be given any notice mentioned in subsection (1) above has specified an address within the United Kingdom other than his proper address, within the meaning of subsection (4) above, as the one at which he or someone on his behalf will accept notices under this Act, that address shall also be treated for the purposes mentioned in subsection (4) above as his proper address.

Notes

In the exercise of adjudicating functions under the Act (see notes to s 24) and also under s 9 (demand for information), the Director-General of Fair Trading may find it necessary to serve a notice upon a person or firm. This section lays down the various ways in which such a notice may validly be served. As to service by post, it is provided by the Interpretation Act 1978 s 7 that "the service is deemed to be effected by properly addressing, pre-paying and posting a letter containing the document and, unless the contrary is proved, to have been effected at the time at which the letter would be delivered in the ordinary course of post".

Orders and regulations.

30. – (1) Before making any order or regulations under any provision of this Act to which this subsection applies, the Secretary of State shall consult the Director, such bodies representative of persons carrying on estate agency work, such bodies representative of consumers and such other persons as he thinks fit.

(2) Subsection (1) above applies to paragraphs (*a*)(iii) and (d) of section 3(1) above and to sections 14, 15, 16, 18, 19 and 22 above.

(3) Any power of the Secretary of State to make orders or regulations under this Act –

    (*a*) may be so exercised as to make different provision in relation to different cases or classes of cases and to exclude certain cases or classes of case; and

    (*b*) includes power to make such supplemental, incidental and transitional provisions as he thinks fit.

Notes

The Secretary of State's duty to consult before making orders or regulations does *not* apply to those made under s 7(3) (appeals), s 11(6) (authorisation of enforcement officers) or s 33(2) (prescription of fees), although consultation *did* in fact take place before the Estate Agents (Appeals) Regulations 1981 were made. In other cases, it is submitted that the duty to consult the Director is likely to be construed as mandatory, so that failure to do so would invalidate the regulations: see *Port Louis Corporation* v *Attorney-General of Mauritius* [1965] AC 1111. However, it should be noted that this is the only requirement; the consultation of any other interested parties, such as professional bodies and consumer groups, is completely within the discretion of the Secretary of State.

The procedure which is prescribed for most of the orders and regulations to be made under the Act is the "negative resolution" procedure, whereby regulations are laid before Parliament after being made and cease to have effect *only* if, within 40 days (Statutory Instruments Act 1946 s 5) either House of Parliament so resolves. In two cases, however, where the subject-matter is of a somewhat sensitive nature, an attempt has been made to secure a more effective scrutiny by Parliament. In the first place, regulations which prescribe minimum standards of competence under s 22 must be positively approved in draft by each House of Parliament before being made. Second, an order which seeks to increase the number of "trigger" events under s 3 by the designation of further criminal offences (s 3(1)(a)(iii)) or undesirable practices (s 3(1)(d)), shall cease to have effect unless positively approved by each House of Parliament within 28 days.

Meaning of "business associate" and "controller".

31. – (1) The provisions of this section shall have effect for determining the meaning of "business associate" and "controller" for the purposes of this Act.

(2) As respects acts done in the course of a business carried on by a body corporate, every director and controller of that body is a business associate of it.

(3) As respects acts done in the course of a business carried on by a partnership, each partner is a business associate of every other member of the partnership and also of the partnership itself and, in the case of a partner which is a body corporate, every person who, by virtue of subsection (2) above, is a business associate of that body is also a business associate of every other member of the partnership.

(4) As respects acts done in the course of a business carried on by an unincorporated association, every officer of the association and any other person who has the management or control of its activities is a business associate of that association.

(5) In relation to a body corporate "controller" means a person –

(a) in accordance with whose directions or instructions the directors of the body corporate or of any other body corporate which is its controller (or any of them) are accustomed to act; or

(b) who, either alone, or with any associate or associates, is entitled to exercise, or control the exercise of, one third or more of the voting power at any general meeting of the body corporate or of another body corporate which is its controller.

Notes

The meaning of "business associate" is important for the purpose of vicarious liability under s 3(3)(c). It is also of relevance in determining the meaning of "associate" under s 32, and thus the scope of the duties imposed by s 21.

The meaning of "controller", which is relevant to the definition of "business associate", is also of importance in relation to the prohibition against the practice of estate agency by bankrupts; s 23.

The provisions of s 31 are fairly clear where it is an *estate agency* business which is carried on as a company, partnership or unincorporated association. In each case, certain natural persons who are important to the organisation are named as its "business associates", which means that they must disclose any interest in the property which belongs to the organisation as a whole; it in turn must disclose *their* personal interests. Further, any breach by either an individual or the organisation may be attributable to the other where there is "connivance or consent": s 3(3)(c).

The major problems with s 31 arise in relation to businesses *other than estate agencies* in which an estate agent is involved (eg as a partner in, or a director of, a wholly unconnected enterprise). Since the status of "business associate" applies only "as respects acts done in the course of" the business, it seems that an estate agent who is also a partner in, say, a firm of caterers is not the business associate of fellow-partners for the purpose of marketing their private houses. Should the catering firm's premises be sold, however, this would presumably be in the course of *its* business and the estate agent would, as the firm's "business associate", have a disclosable interest.

Limited companies and unincorporated associations pose fewer problems, for the Act does not make directors and officers of such bodies business associates of each other, but only of the organisation as a whole. Since, with the probable exception of *ultra vires* acts, any property transaction entered into by such an organisation must of necessity be within the course of its business, it seems that an estate agent holding a prescribed office in one of these bodies will always have a "personal interest" in any of its property with which he or she deals in the capacity of estate agent.

Meaning of "associate".

32. - (1) In this Act "associate" includes a business associate and otherwise has the meaning given by the following provisions of this section.

(2) A person is an associate of another if he is the spouse or a relative of that other or of a business associate of that other.

(3) In subsection (2) above "relative" means brother, sister, uncle, aunt, nephew, niece, lineal ancestor or linear descendant, and references to a spouse include a former spouse and a reputed spouse; and for the purposes of this subsection a relationship shall be established as if an illegitimate child or stepchild of a person had been a child born to him in wedlock.

(4) A body corporate is an associate of another body corporate–

(a) if the same person is a controller of both, or a person is a controller of one and persons who are his associates, or he and persons who are his associates, are controllers of the other; or (*b*) if a group of two or more persons is a controller of each company, and the groups either consist of the same persons or could be regarded as consisting of the same persons by treating (in one or more cases) a member of either group as replaced by a person of whom he is an associate.

(5) An unincorporated association is an associate of another unincorporated association if any person –

(*a*) is an officer of both associations;

(*b*) has the management or control of the activities of both associations; or

(*c*) is an officer of one association and has the management or control of the activities of the other association.

(6) A partnership is an associate of another partnership if –

(*a*) any person is a member of both partnerships; or

(*b*) a person who is a member of one partnership is an associate of a member of the other partnership; or

(*c*) a member of one partnership has an associate who is also an associate of a member of the other partnership.

Notes

The meaning of "associate" (which includes any "business associate" as defined by s 31) is important in connection with the duties imposed upon an estate agent by s 21. Apart from defining the circle of relatives who constitute the "associates" of a natural person, s 32 makes provision for an estate agency practice which is carried on as a partnership, limited company or unincorporated association to be the "associate" of another business (whether an estate agency or not) which takes a similar form, where certain natural persons or their associates are common to both organisations. Where this is so, the estate agency *organisation* (and its employees) will have a disclosable personal interest for the purposes of s 21, and no contract or pre-contract deposit may be taken by the *organisation* on the property in question. However, the other individual members of the estate agency practice (be they partners, directors or whatever) will not thereby have a personal interest, although they may of course be vicariously responsible for a breach *by the organisation* of s 21, if they are guilty of "connivance or consent" (s 3(3)(*c*).

The scope of s 32 is considerable, not least because the human beings concerned need not themselves be common to both organisations; it is sufficient if a member of one is an "associate" of a member of the other. Indeed, in the case of two partnerships, it is enough that a member of each *share* a common associate, as where a member of partnership A was once married to the niece of a member of partnership B! However, the connections are not unlimited, especially in relation to companies; it should be noted that this provision applies, not to companies with common *directors*, but only to those with common *controllers* (as defined by s 31(5)). Further, and most importantly, the Act does not provide for one type of organisation to be the "associate" of another type; thus an estate agency practice which is carried on by a partnership can never be the "associate" of a limited company (except where that company is one of the partners), even if some or all of the partners are controllers of the company in question.

General interpretation provisions.

33. - (1) In this Act, unless the context otherwise requires –

"associate" has the meaning assigned to it by section 32 above and "business associate" has the meaning assigned to it by section 31 above;

"client account" has the meaning assigned to it by section 14(2) above;

"clients' money" has the meaning assigned to it by section 12(1) above;

"connected contract", in relation to the acquisition of an interest in land, has the meaning assigned to it by section 12(4) above;

"contract deposit" has the meaning assigned to it by section 12(2) above;

"controller", in relation to a body corporate, has the meaning assigned to it by section 31(5) above;

"Director" means the Director General of Fair Trading;

"enforcement authority" has the meaning assigned to it by section 26(1) above;

"estate agency work" has the meaning assigned to it by section 1(1) above;

"general notice" means a notice published by the Director at a time and in a manner appearing to him suitable for securing that the notice is seen within a reasonable time by persons likely to be affected by it;

"pre-contract deposit" has the meaning assigned to it by section 12(3) above;

"prescribed fee" means such fee as may be prescribed by regulations made by the Secretary of State;

"the statutory maximum" in relation to a fine on summary conviction, means –

(*a*) in England and Wales and Northern Ireland, the prescribed sum within the meaning of section 32 of the Magistrates' Courts Act 1980 (at the passing of this Act £1,000); and

(*b*) in Scotland, the prescribed sum within the meaning of section 289B of the Criminal Procedure (Scotland) Act 1975 (at the passing of this Act £1,000);

and for the purposes of the application of this definition in Northern Ireland the provisions of the Magistrates' Courts Act 1980 which relate to the sum mentioned in paragraph (a) above shall extend to Northern Ireland; and

"unincorporated association" does not include a partnership.

(2) The power to make regulations under subsection (1) above prescribing fees shall be exercisable by statutory instrument which shall be subject to annulment in pursuance of a resolution of either House of Parliament.

Notes

The "statutory maximum" is the maximum fine which may be imposed where a person is convicted summarily (ie by magistrates) of an offence which is triable either way (ie by magistrates or by a jury in the Crown Court). From October 1 1992 this is £5,000: Criminal Justice Act 1991, s 17 and Criminal Justice Act 1991 (Commencement No 3) Order 1992. These provisions also make £5,000 the "prescribed sum" for Scotland.

In prescribing fees by regulation, the Secretary of State has *no* duty of prior consultation: see s 30.

Financial provisions.

34. – (1) There shall be defrayed out of moneys provided by Parliament –

(a) any expenses incurred by the Secretary of State in consequence of the provisions of this Act; and

(b) any increase attributable to this Act in the sums payable out of moneys so provided under any other Act.

(2) Any fees paid to the Director under this Act shall be paid into the Consolidated Fund.

Scotland.

35. – [Repealed.]

Notes

Under the provisions of the ill-fated Scotland Act 1978, the Estate Agents Act was a "devolved matter" (ie within the legislative competence of the proposed Scottish Assembly). However, with the repeal of that Act consequent on the result of a referendum, s 35 of the Estate Agents Act became redundant and was formally repealed by the Statute Law (Repeals) Act 1981 s 1 and Schedule I Part IV.

Short title, commencement and extent.

36. - (1) This Act may be cited as the Estate Agents Act 1979.

(2) This Act shall come into force on such day as the Secretary of State may by order made by statutory instrument appoint and different days may be so appointed for different provisions and for different purposes.

(3) This Act extends to Northern Ireland.

Notes

At the time of writing, only the Estate Agents Act 1979 (Commencement No 1) Order 1981 had been made, bringing into force on May 3 1982 the following provisions: ss 1 to 15, 18, 20, 21, 23 to 34 and 36, together with Schedules 1 and 2. Provisions not yet in force are ss 16 and 17 (insurance cover for clients' money); s 19 (limits on pre-contract deposits); and s 22 (minimum standards of competence).

SCHEDULES

SCHEDULE 1

Section 3(1).

PROVISIONS SUPPLEMENTARY TO SECTION 3(1)

Spent convictions

1. A conviction which is to be treated as spent for the purposes of the Rehabilitation of Offenders Act 1974 or any corresponding enactment for the time being in force in Northern Ireland shall be disregarded for the purposes of section 3(1)(*a*) of this Act.

Discrimination

2. A person shall be deemed to have committed discrimination for the purposes of section 3(1)(*b*) of this Act in the following cases only, namely –

(*a*) where a finding of discrimination has been made against him in proceedings under section 66 of the Sex Discrimination Act 1975 (in this Schedule referred to as "the 1975 Act") and the finding has become final;

(*b*) where a non-discrimination notice has been served on him under the 1975 Act and the notice has become final;

(*c*) if he is for the time being subject to the restraints of an injunction or order granted against him in proceedings under section 71 (persistent discrimination) or section 72(4) (enforcement of sections 38 to 40) of the 1975 Act;

(*d*) if, on an application under section 72(2)(*a*) of the 1975 Act, there has been a finding against him that a contravention of section 38, section 39 or section 40 of that Act has occurred and that finding has become final;

(*e*) where a finding of discrimination has been made against him in proceedings under section 57 of the Race Relations Act 1976 (in this Schedule referred to as "the 1976 Act") and the finding has become final;

(*f*) where a non-discrimination notice has been served on him under the 1976 Act and the notice has become final;

(*g*) if he is for the time being subject to the restraints of an injunction or order granted against him in proceedings under section 62 (persistent discriminations) or section 63(4) (enforcement of sections 29 to 31) of the 1976 Act; or

(*h*) if, on an application under section 63(2)(*a*) of the 1976 Act, there has been a finding against him that a contravention of section 29, section 30 or section 31 of that Act has occurred and that finding has become final;

and the finding, notice, injunction or order related or relates to discrimination falling within Part III of the 1975 Act or the 1976 Act (discrimination in fields other than employment).

3. After the expiry of the period of five years beginning on the day on which any such finding or notice as is referred to in paragraph 2 above became final, no person shall be treated for the purposes of section 3(1)(*b*) of this Act as having committed discrimination by reason only of that finding or notice.

4. – (1) So far as paragraphs 2 and 3 above relate to findings and notices under the 1975 Act, subsections (1) and (4) of section 82 of that Act (general interpretation provisions) shall have effect as if those paragraphs were contained in that Act.

(2) So far as paragraphs 2 and 3 above relate to findings and notices under the 1976 Act, subsections (1) and (4) of section 78 of that Act (general interpretation provisions) shall have effect as if those paragraphs were contained in that Act.

5. In the application of paragraphs 2 to 4 above to Northern Ireland references to the 1975 Act shall be construed as references to the Sex Discrimination (Northern Ireland) Order 1976, and in particular –

- (a) the references to sections 38, 39 and 40 of the 1975 Act shall be construed as references to Articles 39, 40 and 41 of that Order;
- (b) the reference to subsections (1) and (4) of section 82 of the 1975 Act shall be construed as a reference to paragraphs (1), (2) and (5) of Article 2 of that Order; and
- (c) other references to numbered sections of the 1975 Act shall be construed as references to the Articles of that Order bearing the same number;

and there shall be omitted sub-paragraphs (e) to (h) of paragraph 2, sub-paragraph (2) of paragraph 4 and so much of paragraph 3 as relates to findings or notices under the 1976 Act.

SCHEDULE 2

Sections 5, 6 and 8(3).

PROCEDURE ETC.

PART I

ORDERS AND DECISIONS UNDER SECTIONS 3, 4 AND 6

Introductory

1. In this Schedule –

- (a) subject to sub-paragraph (2) below, references to "the person affected" are to the person in respect of whom the Director proposes to make, or has made, an order under section 3 or section 4 of this Act, or who has made an application under section 6 of this Act for the variation or revocation of such an order; and
- (b) references to the Director's "proposal" are to any proposal of his to make such an order or to make a decision under subsection (4) or subsection (5) of section 6 of this Act on such an application.

(2) In the case of a proposal of the Director to make an order under section 3 or section 4 of this Act against a partnership where, by virtue of section 5(2) of this Act, he intends that the order shall have effect as an order against some or all of the partners individually, references in the following provisions of this Schedule to the person affected shall be construed, except where the contrary is provided, as references to each of the partners affected by the order, as well as to the partnership itself.

Notice of proposal

2. – (1) The Director shall give to the person affected a notice informing him of the proposal and of the Director's reason for it; but paragraph 1(2) above shall not apply for the purposes of this sub-paragraph.

(2) In the case of a proposal to make an order, the notice under sub-paragraph (1) above shall inform the person affected of the substance of the proposed order and, in the case of a proposal to make an order under section 3 of this Act, shall –

(a) set out those matters falling within subsection (1) of that section which the Director intends should be specified as the grounds for the order, and

(b) specify any other matters of which the Director has taken account under subsection (2) of that section, and

(c) if the Director proposes to rely on section 4(3) of this Act to establish the unfitness of the person affected, state that fact.

(3) The notice given under sub-paragraph (1) above shall invite the person affected, within such period of not less than twenty-one days as may be specified in the notice, -

(a) to submit to the Director his representations in writing as to why the order should not be made or, as the case may be, should be varied or revoked in accordance with the application, and

(b) to give notice to the Director, if he thinks fit, that he wishes to make such representations orally,

and where notice is given under paragraph (b) above the Director shall arrange for the oral representations to be heard.

Hearing of representations

3. Where the Director receives notice under paragraph 2(3)(*b*) above he shall give the person affected not less than twenty-one days notice, or such shorter notice as the person affected may consent to accept, of the date, time and place at which his representations are to be heard.

4. – (1) In the course of the hearing of oral representations the Director shall, at the request of the person affected, permit any other person (in addition to the person affected) to make representations on his behalf or to give evidence or to introduce documents for him.

(2) The Director shall not refuse to admit evidence solely on the grounds that it would not be admissible in a court of law.

5. If the Director adjourns the hearing he shall give the person affected reasonable notice of the date, time and place at which the hearing is to be resumed.

Decision

6. – (1) The Director shall take into account in deciding whether to proceed with his proposal any written or oral representations made in accordance with the preceding provisions of this Schedule.

(2) If the Director considers that he should proceed with his proposal but for a reason which differs, or on grounds which differ, from those set out in the notice of the proposal under paragraph 2 above he shall give a further notice under that paragraph.

(3) In any case where –

(*a*) a notice under paragraph 2 above gives more than one reason for the proposal or (in the case of a proposal to make an order under section 3 of this Act) sets out more than one matter which the Director intends should be specified as the grounds for the order, and

(*b*) it appears to the Director that one or more of those reasons should be abandoned or, as the case may be, that one or more of those matters should not be so specified,

the Director may nevertheless decide to proceed with his proposal on the basis of any other reason given in the notice or, as the case may be, on any other grounds set out in the notice.

7. If the Director decides not to proceed with his proposal he shall give notice of that decision to the person affected and, in the case of a notice of a decision on an application under section 6 of this Act, such a notice shall be combined with a notice under subsection (3) of that section.

8. If the Director decides to proceed with his proposal he may, if he thinks fit having regard to any representations made to him –

(a) where the proposal is for the making of an order, make the order in a form which varies from that of the proposed order mentioned in the notice under paragraph 2 above, or

(b) where the proposal is to vary an order, make a variation other than that mentioned in the notice under paragraph 2 above, or

(c) where the proposal is to refuse to revoke an order, vary the order.

Notification of decision

9. – (1) Notice of the decision to make the order, and of the terms of the order or, as the case may be, notice of the decision on the application for variation or revocation of the order, shall be given to the person affected, together with the Director's reasons for his decision, including the facts which in his opinion justify the decision.

(2) The notice referred to in sub-paragraph (1) above shall also inform the person affected of his right to appeal against the decision and of the period within which an appeal may be brought and of how notice of appeal may be given.

10. – (1) Subject to sub-paragraph (2) below, the order to which the decision relates or, as the case may be, any variation of an order for which the decision provides shall not come into operation until any appeal under section 7(1) of this Act and any further appeal has been finally determined or the period within which such an appeal may be brought has expired.

(2) Where the Director states in the notice referred to in paragraph 9(1) above that he is satisfied that there are special circumstances which require it, an order shall come into operation immediately upon the giving of notice of the decision to make it.

PART II

APPLICATIONS UNDER SECTION 6(1) AND 8(3)

11.   Any reference in this Part of this Schedule to an application is a reference to an application to the Director under section 6(1) or section 8(3) of this Act, and any reference to the applicant shall be construed accordingly.

12.   An application shall be in writing and be in such form and accompanied by such particulars as the Director may specify by general notice.

13.   The Director may by notice require the applicant to publish details of his application at a time or times and in a manner specified in the notice.

14.   If an application does not comply with paragraph 12 above or if an applicant fails to comply with a notice under section 9 of this Act requiring the furnishing of information or the production of documents in connection with the application, the Director may decline to proceed with the application.

SECONDARY LEGISLATION UNDER THE 1979 ACT

STATUTORY INSTRUMENTS

1981 No. 1518

ESTATE AGENTS

The Estate Agents (Appeals) Regulations 1981

Made	*26th October 1981*
Laid before Parliament	*2nd November 1981*
Coming into Operation	*3rd May 1982*

ARRANGEMENT OF REGULATIONS

Regulation
1.   Citation, commencement and interpretation.

COMMENCEMENT OF APPEAL

2.   Notice of appeal.
3.   Notice of grounds of appeal.
4.   Director's reply.
5.   Appellant's rejoinder.
6.   Amendment of grounds before directions for hearing.
7.   Director's reply to amendment.

DISPOSAL OF APPEAL WITHOUT HEARING

8.   Director's consent to allowing of appeal.

9.   Contested appeal without hearing.

DISPOSAL OF APPEAL WITH HEARING

10.   Directions for hearing.
11.   Amendment of grounds at hearing.
12.   Notice of hearing.
13.   Admission of members of Council on Tribunals, etc.
14.   Procedure at hearing.
15.   Appellant's failure to appear at hearing.
16.   Appointed person's report.
17.   Dismissal of appeal after appellant's failure to appear.

GENERAL PROVISIONS

18.   Notice of directions disposing of appeal.
19.   Appointment of appointed person.
20.   Evidence.
21.   Disclosure of documents.
22.   Protection of confidentiality, etc. of documents.
23.   Abandonment of appeal.
24.   Effect of non-compliance with these Regulations.
25.   Costs of appeals.
26.   Extensions of time.
27.   Power of Secretary of State to give procedural directions.

Schedule 1.   Notice of appeal.
Schedule 2.   Notice of grounds of appeal.

The Secretary of State, in exercise of the powers conferred on him by sections 7(3) and 30(3) of the Estate Agents Act 1979[a] and of all other powers enabling him in that behalf, hereby makes the following Regulations:–

Citation, commencement and interpretation
   1. – (1) These Regulations may be cited as the Estate Agents (Appeals) Regulations 1981 and shall come into operation on 3rd May 1982.

---

a 1979 c.38.

(2) In these Regulations, unless the context otherwise requires –
"the Act" means the Estate Agents Act 1979;

"appeal" means appeal to the Secretary of State under section 7 of the Act, and "the appeal" shall be construed accordingly;

"appellant" means a person making, or proposing to make, an appeal against a decision, being a person who received notice under paragraph 9 of Schedule 2 to the Act;

"appointed person" means a person or persons appointed by the Secretary of State in relation to an appeal in accordance with the provisions of Regulation 19;

"decision" means a decision of the Director mentioned in section 7 of the Act;

"the Director's reply" means a notice given under Regulation 4(c) together with any document given therewith;

"notice", where required or authorised to be given under these Regulations, means a notice in writing;

"notice of appeal" means a notice given under Regulation 2(1);

"notice of grounds" means a notice given under Regulation 3(1);

"notice of amendment" means a notice given under Regulation 6(3);

"party", in relation to an appeal, means any party to the appeal, including the Director;

"period for appeal" means the period mentioned in Regulation 2(1).

COMMENCEMENT OF APPEAL

Notice of appeal

2. – (1) An appellant may appeal by giving to the Secretary of State, within the period of 28 days beginning with the date on which notice under paragraph 9 of Schedule 2 to the Act is given to him ("period for appeal"), a notice ("notice of appeal"); and a notice of appeal shall comply with the requirements of Schedule 1 to these Regulations.

(2) In the case of a notice of appeal which –

(a) is given to the Secretary of State within the period for appeal; and

(b) appears to him to comply with the requirements of Schedule 1;

the Secretary of State shall –

    (i)   inform the appellant of its receipt; and

   (ii)   send a copy of it to the Director.

Notice of grounds of appeal

3. – (1) An appellant shall at or after the time when he gives notice of appeal to the Secretary of State (but not later than the end of the period for appeal) give to the Secretary of State notice of the grounds of appeal ("notice of grounds") and a notice of grounds shall comply with the requirements of Schedule 2 to these Regulations.

   (2) In the case of a notice of grounds which –

   (*a*) is given to the Secretary of State at a time which satisfies paragraph (1) above; and

   (*b*) appears to him to comply with the requirements of Schedule 2;

the Secretary of State shall –

    (i)   inform the appellant of its receipt; and

   (ii)   send a copy of it to the Director.

Director's reply

4. The Director shall, within the period of 28 days beginning with the date on which a copy of the notice of grounds is given to him, give to the Secretary of State –

   (*a*) a copy of the notice given to the appellant under paragraph 9 of Schedule 2 to the Act together with the Director's reasons for his decision, including the facts which in his opinion justify the decision;

   (*b*) in the case of an appeal against a decision of the Director under section 6(4) or (5) of the Act on an application made by the appellant, a copy of the application and of any document containing information in support of the application; and

   (*c*) notice setting out any representations which the Director wishes to make together with a copy of any document which he wishes to produce ("the Director's reply").

Appellant's rejoinder

5. The Secretary of State shall –

   (*a*) give a copy of the Director's reply to the appellant with a notice inviting him to give to the Secretary of State, within a period of 28 days beginning with the date on which the notice is given to him, notice setting out any further representations he wishes to make and a copy of any document he wishes to produce; and

(b) give a copy of any notice or other document received under paragraph (a) above to the Director.

Amendment of grounds before directions for hearing

6. – (1) The Secretary of State shall amend the notice of grounds where –

(a) the appellant has given to the Secretary of State at a time when he is permitted to do so under paragraph (2) below a notice setting out the proposed amendment; and

(b) it appears to the Secretary of State that the amendment should be made.

(2) An appellant may give notice to the Secretary of State under paragraph (1)(a) above at any time before the Secretary of State gives notice to the parties under Regulation 9(4) below that a hearing of oral representations is not necessary or gives directions under Regulation 10(1) below for oral representations to be heard by an appointed person.

(3) When the Secretary of State makes an amendment of a notice of grounds under this Regulation he shall give notice of that fact setting out the amendment ("notice of amendment") to the appellant and to the Director.

(4) Where an appellant has given notice to the Secretary of State under paragraph (1)(a) above and it does not appear to the Secretary of State that the amendment should be made he shall give the appellant notice of that fact, giving his reasons.

Director's reply to amendment

7. – (1) The Director shall within the period of 14 days beginning with the date on which a notice of amendment is given to him give to the Secretary of State notice setting out any representations he wishes to make thereon together with a copy of any further document which he wishes to produce.

(2) The Secretary of State shall –

(a) give a copy of any notice or document given under paragraph (1) above to the appellant with a notice inviting him to give to the Secretary of State, within a period of 14 days beginning with the date on which the notice is given to him, notice setting out any further representations he wishes to make and a copy of any further document he wishes to produce; and

(b) give a copy of any notice or other document received under sub-paragraph (a) above to the Director.

DISPOSAL OF APPEAL WITHOUT HEARING

Director's consent to allowing of appeal

8. – (1) The Secretary of State after taking into account any notice and any document received under Regulations 2 to 7 above, or 21 below, may at any time give notice to the Director that he proposes under section 7(2) of the Act to give the directions which the appellant seeks unless the Director objects by notice given to the Secretary of State within a period of 14 days beginning with the date on which that notice is given.

(2) If, pursuant to a notice under paragraph (1) above, the Director–

(a) does not so object, or informs the Secretary of State that he will not so object, within that period, the Secretary of State shall give those directions; or

(b) does so object within that period, the Secretary of State shall give notice to the appellant in accordance with the provisions of Regulation 9(1) below.

Contested appeal without hearing

9. – (1) In a case where Regulation 8(2)(a) above does not have effect the Secretary of State shall give notice to the appellant that he will give directions for oral representations to be heard unless, within a period of 14 days beginning with the date on which that notice is given, the appellant gives notice to him that the appellant prefers the appeal to be heard without oral representations.

(2) Where the appellant has given notice pursuant to paragraph (1) above the Secretary of State may give notice to any party–

(a) specifying any question which appears to him to be material; and

(b) inviting that party to give to him, within a period of 14 days beginning with the date on which that notice is given, notice setting out any representations which he wishes to make;

and where a notice is given to the Secretary of State under sub-paragraph (b) above he shall –

(i) send a copy of it to the other party; and

(ii) by notice invite that party to give to him, within a period of 14 days beginning with the date on which that notice is given, notice setting out any representations he wishes to make.

(3) Where the appellant has given notice pursuant to paragraph (1) above and it appears to the Secretary of State that it is not necessary for oral representations to be heard, the Secretary of State shall give notice to the Director –

(*a*) informing him of that fact; and

(*b*) inviting him, within a period of 7 days beginning with the date on which that notice is given, to give to the Secretary of State notice setting out any representations he wishes to make about the necessity of oral representations being heard.

(4) Where the appellant has given notice pursuant to paragraph (1) above and it appears to the Secretary of State after taking account of any notice given to him under this Regulation that it is not necessary for oral representations to be heard, the Secretary of State shall give notice to the parties –

(*a*) that a hearing of oral representations is not necessary; and

(*b*) that the Secretary of State is proceeding to –

  (i)   refer the appeal to an appointed person for consideration and report without a hearing of oral representations; or

  (ii) give directions under section 7(2) of the Act for disposing of the appeal;

and the Secretary of State shall so refer the appeal or give those directions.

DISPOSAL OF APPEAL WITH HEARING

Directions for hearing

10. – (1) Where the Secretary of State so directs, oral representations shall be heard by three appointed persons on his behalf unless he directs that they shall be heard by a different number of persons.

(2) The Secretary of State shall give notice to the parties of any direction under paragraph (1) above.

(3) A direction shall not be given under paragraph (1) above that oral representations shall be heard by a different number of persons unless the Secretary of State has afforded the parties an opportunity of making representations to him thereon.

Amendment of grounds at hearing

11. – (1) An appellant may amend a notice of grounds in the course of the hearing of oral representations if the appointed person gives leave for the amendment which is proposed to be made.

(2) The appointed person shall not give such leave unless he has informed the Director that he is minded to do so and afforded to him an opportunity of making representations on the proposed amendment.

Notice of hearing

12.   In any case other than a case where the appeal is –

(a) disposed of under Regulation 8(2)(a) above or 9(4)(b)(ii) above; or

(b) referred to an appointed person under Regulation 9(4)(b)(i) above; the Secretary of State shall, after taking into account any notice, statement and other document which has been sent to the Secretary of State under the foregoing provisions of these Regulations and not less than 21 days before the date on which oral representations are to be heard, give notice to the parties of the date, time and place of the hearing.

Admission of members of Council on Tribunals, etc

13.   A member of the Council on Tribunals or of the Scottish Committee of the Council shall be permitted to attend the hearing or oral representations in his capacity as such a member.

Procedure at hearing

14. – (1) The appointed person shall give such directions at the hearing of oral representations as appear to him to be appropriate for the proper conduct thereof.

(2) Without prejudice to the generality of paragraph (1) above, the appointed person shall –

(a) permit any person authorised by any party to do so ("representative") to conduct that party's case on his behalf;

(b) afford to the parties or their representatives an opportunity to make an opening and a closing statement;

(c) if he adjourns the hearing, inform the parties a reasonable time before its resumption of the date, time and place of that resumption;

(d) permit each party or his representative to call witnesses;

(e) address any questions which appear to him to be appropriate to each party and to any witness; and

(f) permit any questions which appear to him to be appropriate to be addressed by each party or his representative to any party who is present and to any witness.

Appellant's failure to appear at hearing

15.   Where the appellant or his representative does not appear at the date, time and place of the hearing the appointed person may –

(a) adjourn the hearing; or

(b) if there appears to him to be good reason to do so –

   (i)   proceed to hear the Director, or his representative, if he appears; or

   (ii) proceed forthwith to prepare his report in accordance with Regulation 16 below.

Appointed person's report

16. – (1) Where the appeal is referred to the appointed person under Regulation 9(4)(b)(i) above or the appointed person has completed the hearing of oral representations under Regulations 10 to 15 above, he shall take into account any representations made and evidence produced in the course of the appeal and give to the Secretary of State a reasoned report in writing thereon.

(2) Where the appointed person has proceeded under Regulation 15(b) above he shall expressly state that he has done so in his report.

Dismissal of appeal after appellant's failure to appear

17. – (1) Where it appears from the report of the appointed person that he has proceeded under Regulation 15(b) above the Secretary of State may (subject to paragraphs (2) and (3) below) give directions dismissing the appeal.

(2) Where it so appears from that report and the Secretary of State is minded to give directions dismissing the appeal (whether or not by virtue of paragraph (1) above) the Secretary of State shall (unless it appears that an appointed person has proceeded under Regulation 15(b) above on more than one occasion), not less than 7 days before he gives such directions, give notice to the appellant of the fact that he is so minded.

(3) In a notice given under paragraph (2) above the Secretary of State shall inform the appellant that he will give directions dismissing the appeal unless the appellant satisfies him within a period of 7 days beginning with the date on which the notice is given that there was sufficient reason for the failure to appear; but where the appellant so satisfies the Secretary of State, the Secretary of State shall give such directions as appear to him to be appropriate for a further hearing of oral representations and these Regulations shall apply accordingly.

GENERAL PROVISIONS

Notice of directions disposing of appeal

18. – (1) The Secretary of State shall give notice to the parties of his directions for disposing of the appeal under section 7(2) of the Act and that notice shall in addition contain a statement –

(a) setting out the Secretary of State's reasons for his directions under section 7(2) of the Act;

(b) declaring that if the appellant is dissatisfied in point of law with the decision of the Secretary of State, the appellant may by virtue of section 7 of the Act appeal against that decision to the High Court, the Court of Session or a judge of the High Court in Northern Ireland.

(2) In any case where the directions which the Secretary of State gives under section 7(2) of the Act are not those which the appellant stated that he wished the Secretary of State to give in the notice of grounds, or in that notice as amended under Regulations 6 and 11 above as the case may be, the Secretary of State shall give to the appellant a copy of any report relating to the appeal which was given to the Secretary of State under Regulation 16(1) above.

Appointment of appointed person

19. – (1) The Secretary of State may appoint to hear an appeal on his behalf any person excluding a person who is in the civil employment of Her Majesty ("appointed person") who appears to him by reason of his knowledge or experience to be qualified to do so; and except where he appoints only one such person in relation to an appeal he may determine which of them is to preside.

(2) The Secretary of State may appoint any person to give the appointed person advice on matters of law or on any other matter relating to the appeal.

Evidence
20.   For the avoidance of doubt it is hereby declared that evidence may be admitted in an appeal whether or not it would be admissible in a court of law.

Disclosure of documents
21. – (1) The Secretary of State at any time, or the appointed person during the hearing of oral representations by him, may invite any party to supply to him any document or copy thereof which appears to him to be material to the appeal.

(2) Where any document is supplied by a party under paragraph (1) above –

   (a) to the Secretary of State, he shall send a copy thereof to any other party; or

   (b) to the appointed person, he shall afford to any other party an opportunity to examine it or shall otherwise make known its contents to that party.

Protection of confidentiality, etc. of documents
22.   In any case where under these Regulations he is required to make known in any way the contents of any document to any party, the Secretary of State or the appointed person, as the case may be, may, so far as that is practicable, exclude from any copy of any document or from information about its contents any matter which relates to the private affairs of a person who is not a party and the publication of which would or might in the opinion of the Secretary of State or of the appointed person prejudicially affect the interests of that person.

Abandonment of appeal
23. – (1) The appellant may at any time by notice to the Secretary of State abandon the appeal.

(2) The Secretary of State shall send a copy of any notice given under paragraph (1) to the Director.

Effect of non-compliance with these Regulations

24.   Where, by reason of anything done or left undone, there has been a failure in any respect to comply with the requirements of these Regulations, other than those of Regulation 2(1) above, the failure shall not terminate the appeal unless the Secretary of State so directs; but where there has been such a failure he may give such directions dealing with the proceedings generally as he thinks fit.

Costs of appeals

25. – (1) Any costs directed to be paid under section 7(2) of the Act and required to be taxed shall be taxed by a Master of the Supreme Court Taxing Office.

(2) Any sum payable in respect of any costs directed to be paid under section 7(2) of the Act shall, on application being made to the High Court by the party to whom costs have been directed to be paid, be enforceable as if he had obtained a judgement of that Court in his favour.

(3) In Scotland any expenses directed to be paid under section 7(2) of the Act and required to be taxed shall be taxed by the Auditor of the Court of Session.

(4) The certificate of taxation of such expenses taxed in accordance with paragraph (3) above may be enforced in like manner as an extract registered decree arbitral bearing a warrant for execution issued from the Books of Council and Session.

Extensions of time

26.   At any time the Secretary of State may extend the period, other than the period for giving notice of appeal under Regulation 2(1) above, within which a person is required or authorised by these Regulations to do anything and these Regulations shall have effect accordingly.

Power of Secretary of State to give procedural directions

27.   Subject to the provisions of the Act and of these Regulations, the procedure to be followed in the course of an appeal except in the course of the hearing of oral representations shall be such as the Secretary of State directs.

SCHEDULE 1

NOTICE OF APPEAL

Every notice of appeal shall –

(1) identify the appellant and give his business address and his address for service of documents (if different);

(2) identify the decision against which the appellant is appealing; and

(3) be signed by or on behalf of the appellant.

SCHEDULE 2

(Regulation 3)

NOTICE OF GROUNDS OF APPEAL

Every notice of grounds of appeal shall –

(1) if it is not given to the Secretary of State together with the notice of appeal to which it relates, identify that notice;

(2) contain a concise statement of the grounds of appeal –

(a) indicating –

  (i)   any reason; and

  (ii) any finding of fact

  relied on by the Director for his decision which the appellant disputes;

(b) giving particulars of any reason or fact upon which the appellant relies in relation to the matters disputed under sub-paragraph (a) above;

(c) giving particulars of any other reason or fact upon which the appellant relies; and

(d) indicating any point on which he relies under sub-paragraphs (b) and (c) above which appears to him to be a point of law;

(3) state the nature of the directions which the appellant wishes the Secretary of State to give under section 7(2) of the Act; and

(4) be signed by or on behalf of the appellant.

Department of Trade

26th October 1981.

NOTES

See pp 84–86 and notes to s 7.

STATUTORY INSTRUMENTS

1981 No. 1519

ESTATE AGENTS

The Estate Agents (Entry and Inspection) Regulations 1981

Made	*26th October 1981*
Laid before Parliament	*2nd November 1981*
Coming into Operation	*3rd May 1982*

The Secretary of State, in exercise of the powers conferred on him by section 11(6) of the Estate Agents Act 1979[a] and of all other powers enabling him in that behalf, hereby makes the following Regulations:–

1. These Regulations may be cited as the Estate Agents (Entry and Inspection) Regulations 1981 and shall come into operation on 3rd May 1982.

2. Unless he is authorised by the Director, an officer of a local weights and measures authority is not to be taken to be duly authorised for the purposes of section 11 of the Estate Agents Act 1979 (which confers powers of entry and inspection in connection with the enforcement of that Act on duly authorised officers of enforcement authorities) so far as concerns the exercise of any power under paragraphs (b), (c) and (d) of sub-section (1) of that section in relation to any book or document relating to the business carried on by the Bank of England or a bank which is a bank within the meaning of section 9 of the Bankers' Books Evidence Act 1879[b]: Provided that where a customer on whose behalf a bank maintains an account has consented in writing to the exercise of any power under paragraph (b) of the said sub-section (1) with respect to any such book or document as aforesaid in so far as it

---

a 1979 c.38.
b 1879 c.11.

contains information about the affairs of that customer then, in relation to any suspected offence to which the said paragraph (b) applied before that consent was given, this Regulation shall not apply to the exercise of that power by any such officer as aforesaid with respect to that book or document so far as concerns that information.

Department of Trade

26th October 1981.

Notes

See notes to s 11.

STATUTORY INSTRUMENTS

1981 No. 1520

ESTATE AGENTS

The Estate Agents (Accounts) Regulations 1981

Made	*26th October 1981*
Laid before Parliament	*2nd November 1981*
Coming into Operation	*3rd May 1982*

The Secretary of State, after consulting in accordance with section 30(1) of the Estate Agents Act 1979[a] the persons therein referred to, in exercise of the powers conferred on him by sections 14, 15 and 30(3) of that Act and of all other powers enabling him in that behalf, hereby makes the following Regulations:–

Citation, commencement and interpretation

1. – (1) These Regulations may be cited as the Estate Agents (Accounts) Regulations 1981 and shall come into operation on 3rd May 1982.

(2) In these Regulations –

"accounting period" means a period of not more than 12 months in respect of which accounts required to be kept under Regulation 6 below are drawn up: Provided that an accounting period may end on a date not more than seven days after the end of a period of twelve months;

"the Act" means the Estate Agents Act 1979;

"deposit account" at a building society means an account in which deposits are received in accordance with the rules of the society and the provisions of Part III of the Building Societies Act 1962[b] or the Building Societies Act (Northern Ireland) 1967[c];

---

a 1979 c.38.
b 1962 c.37.
c 1967 c.31 (N.I.).

"employee" means a person engaged in estate agency work under a contract of employment, and "employer" means his employer under that contract.

Authorised Institutions

2. The institutions authorised for the purposes of section 14 of the Act for the keeping of client accounts shall be those listed in the Schedule to these Regulations.

Exempt Persons

3. The obligation imposed by section 14(1) of the Act shall not apply to the persons listed in the Schedule to these Regulations or to an employee of any such person.

Client Accounts

4. – (1) Money other than clients' money may be paid into a client account –

  (a) if it is the minimum required for the purpose of opening or maintaining the account;

  (b) to restore in whole or part any money paid out of the account in contravention of these Regulations,

and in no other circumstances.

  (2) Where –

  (a) part of a contract deposit paid by a purchaser is not, or is not intended to form part of, the consideration for acquiring an interest in land in the United Kingdom or for a connected contract, or

  (b) part of a pre-contract deposit –

    (i) is not paid as an earnest of the payer's intention to acquire an interest in land in the United Kingdom, or

    (ii) is not paid towards meeting any liability of the payer in respect of the consideration for the acquisition of such an interest which will arise if he acquires or enters into an enforceable contract to acquire the interest,

and the money is received in cash or in any other form which it is practicable and lawful to split, then the part of the contract deposit referred to in subparagraph (a) or any of the part of the pre-contract deposit referred to in subparagraph (b) not paid in respect of a connected contract shall not be paid into a client account.

5. The occasions on which, and the persons to whom, money held in a client account may be paid out are as follows –

(a) in the case of money paid into the account by virtue of subparagraph (a) of Regulation 4(1) above, where it is no longer required for the purpose referred to in that subparagraph and is paid to the person entitled to it;

(b) in the case of money paid into the account in contravention of Regulation 4 above, where it is paid to the person entitled to it;

(c) in the case of clients' money –

   (i) where it is paid to the person who is entitled to call for it to be paid over to him or to be paid on his direction or to have it otherwise credited to him;

   (ii) in payment of any remuneration for, or in reimbursement of money expended in, carrying out estate agency work to which the person in question is entitled, with the agreement of the person for whom the money is held;

   (iii) in the exercise of any lien on the money, which is entitled to be exercised;

   (iv) where it is transferred to another client account maintained by the person who received the money or by his employer.

Accounts and Records Relating to Clients' Money

6. – (1) Subject to paragraphs (2) and (6) below, it shall be the duty of any person who receives clients' money in the course of estate agency work and of the employer in the case of money received by his employee to keep such accounts and records relating to clients' money received, held or paid out as are sufficient to show that he has discharged the duty imposed on him by section 14(1) of the Act, and to show and explain readily at any time all dealings with that money, including the title of the client account into which it is paid, the date of such payment and the identity of the institution with which that account is held, any payments out (other than those mentioned in the exception to paragraph (3)(e) below) and all dealings with any other money which may have been dealt with through that account.

(2) The obligations imposed by paragraph (1) above shall not apply –

   (a) to the persons listed in the Schedule to these Regulations or to an employee of any such person;

   (b) to an employee who pays clients' money received by him without delay into a client account maintained by his employer.

(3) Without prejudice to the generality of paragraph (1) above, the accounts and records referred to therein shall –

(*a*) in the case of clients' money received, be such as to show
(i)   the amount;
(ii)   the name and address of the payer;
(iii) whether the sum paid is a contract or a pre-contract deposit and, in either case, whether it is or includes any sum in respect of a connected contract;
(iv)   if the sum paid includes any such money as is referred to in Regulation 4(2) above, for what purpose and in what form it is received;
(v)   the interest in land to which the money relates;
(vi)   the person wishing to dispose of such an interest;
(vii) the capacity in which the money is received and (where known by the person upon whom the duty is imposed by paragraph (1) above) is from time to time held (whether as agent, bailee, stakeholder or in any other capacity);
(viii) the identity of the person for whom the money has been received and (where known) is from time to time held; and
(ix)   the date of its receipt;
(*b*) be kept in such manner as to show separately all clients' money held by reference to the interest in land to which it relates;
(*c*) in the case of any payment out of a client account, be such as to show the amount, the identity of the payee, the date of the payment, any interest in land to which the money relates and such other information as may be necessary to show the corresponding payment into the account, the occasion on which the payment is made and, where the payment is made in accordance with Regulation 5(*c*)(ii) or (iii) above, such particulars as may be necessary to enable any information (and changes therein) required to be given to clients under section 18 of the Act and any Regulations made thereunder to be identified;
(*d*) include counterfoils kept or duplicate copies of all receipts issued in respect of clients' money received which shall contain the particulars required to be shown in the accounts and records under subparagraph (*a*)(i) to (v) and (ix) above;
(*e*) in the case of any sum transferred from one client account to another, be such as to show the occasion for the transfer

and to enable the corresponding payment into the account from which the transfer is made to be identified, except sums transferred between a specified client current account and a specified client deposit account in both of which clients' money is kept generally.

(4) The accounts and records kept under paragraph (1) above shall be retained for six years after the end of the accounting period to which they relate.

(5) Where, under this Regulation, accounts and records are required to be kept so as to show the interest in land to which any clients' money relates, or by reference to such an interest, the requirement shall be taken to be complied with only if the land as well as the nature of the interest therein are identified.

(6) Where a person ceases to be engaged in the estate agency work in which he has been engaged and the accounts and records relating to clients' money received by him are handed over to another person, the latter shall be required to keep the accounts and records required to be kept under paragraph (1) above in place of the former.

Interest on Clients' Money

7. – (1) A person engaged in estate agency work who has received after the date of coming into operation of these Regulations any clients' money and does not hold it as stakeholder on trust for the person who may become entitled to it on the occurrence of the event against which it is held shall account, in the cases prescribed by this Regulation, to any other person who is for the time being entitled to the money –

(a) where the money is or has been held for him in a client account which is a separate deposit account, for the interest earned on it;

(b) where the money is or has been held for him in a client account which is not a separate deposit account, for the interest which could have been earned on it for him if it had been kept in a separate deposit account at the institution concerned;

(c) where, under the Act and these Regulations, the money is required to be held in a client account but is not so held, for the interest which could have been earned on it for him if it had been kept in a separate deposit account at whichever of the institutions listed in the Schedule to these Regulations in which a current or deposit account is held by the person on whom the duty under this paragraph is imposed was, on the day when it could first have been put in such an account, offering the highest rate of interest offered by any of those institutions on money kept in such an account, or if no such account is so held, at whichever of the said institutions was on the day in question offering the highest rate of interest offered by any of those institutions on money kept in such an account;

(*d*) where the person who has received any clients' money is an institution listed in the Schedule to these Regulations or an employee of such an institution, and accordingly under Regulation 3 above that person does not pay it into a client account, for the interest which could have been earned on it for him if it had been kept in a separate deposit account at that institution.

(2) The obligation imposed by subparagraphs (*a*) to (*c*) of paragraph (1) above shall arise in any case where the amount of the sum held exceeds £500 and the interest which is, or, as the case may be, could have been, earned on the money for the person in question during the period for which it is held for him by keeping it in a separate deposit account at the institution concerned is at least £10.

(3) The obligation imposed by subparagraph (*d*) of paragraph (1) above shall arise in any case in which interest is not credited to the person for the time being entitled to the money in the normal course of business and the amount of the sum held exceeds £500 and the interest which could have been earned on the money during the period for which it is held for him if it had been kept in a separate deposit account at the institution is at least £10.

Audit

8. – (1) Any person who is required to keep accounts under Regulation 6 above shall draw them up in respect of consecutive accounting periods and have them audited by a qualified auditor within six months after the end of each accounting period.

(2) Where an employee is required to keep accounts under Regulation 6 above, he shall adopt the same accounting period in respect of those accounts as his employer.

(3) The auditor shall report to the persons who are required to keep accounts under Regulation 6 above whether in his opinion the

requirements of the Act as to the manner in which clients' money is to be dealt with and of these Regulations have been complied with or have been substantially complied with.

(4) The auditor may report that the said requirements have been substantially complied with if in his opinion they have been complied with except so far as concerns certain trivial breaches due to clerical errors or mistakes in book-keeping, all of which were rectified on discovery, and none of which in his opinion resulted in any loss to any person entitled to the clients' money.

(5) If the auditor reports that in his opinion the said requirements have not been complied with or substantially complied with, he shall specify in his report the matters in respect of which it appears to him that the said requirements have not been complied with or substantially complied with.

(6) If the auditor is unable to form an opinion as to whether or not the said requirements have been complied with or substantially complied with, he shall specify in his report the matters in respect of which he has been unable to satisfy himself and the reasons therefor.

(7) For the purpose of making his report under paragraph (3) above, the auditor shall –

(a) ascertain from the person to whom he is reporting under that paragraph particulars of all bank accounts kept, maintained or operated by him or his employee in the course of estate agency work at any time during the accounting period to which the report relates, and

(b) subject to paragraph (8) below, so examine the accounts and records of that person as to enable him to verify whether they comply with the requirements of Regulation 6 above, for which purpose he may ask for such further information and explanations as he may consider necessary.

(8) Nothing in paragraph (7) above shall require the auditor –

(a) to extend his enquiries beyond the information contained in the relevant documents produced to him, supplemented by such information and explanations as he may obtain from the person to whom he is making his report; or

(b) to consider whether the accounts and records have been properly kept in accordance with Regulation 6 above at any time other than the time at which his examination of those accounts and records takes place.

(9) A person who maintains a client account shall produce on demand to a duly authorised officer of an enforcement authority the latest auditor's report relating to the account.

(Regulations 2, 3, 6 and 7)

SCHEDULE

INSTITUTIONS AUTHORISED FOR THE PURPOSE OF SECTION 14 OF THE ACT FOR KEEPING OF CLIENT ACCOUNTS AND TO WHICH THE OBLIGATION IMPOSED BY SECTION 14(1) DOES NOT APPLY.

1. The Bank of England.
2. A recognised bank or a licensed institution within the meaning of the Banking Act 1979[a].
3. The Post Office, in the exercise of its powers to provide banking services.
4. A trustee savings bank within the meaning of section 3 of the Trustee Savings Bank Act 1969[b].
5. A building society which has been designated for the purpose of section 1 of the House Purchase and Housing Act 1959[c].

Department of Trade

26th October 1981.

Notes

See pp 64–70 and notes to ss 14 and 15.

---

a 1979 c.37. This presumably now refers to an "authorised institution" within the meaning of the Banking Act 1987.
b 1969 c.50. Repealed and consolidated by the Trustee Savings Bank Act 1981.
c 1959 c.33.

STATUTORY INSTRUMENTS

1991 No. 859

ESTATE AGENTS

The Estate Agents (Provision of Information) Regulations 1991

Made	*28th March 1991*
Laid before Parliament	*28th March 1991*
Coming into force	*29th July 1991*

The Secretary of State, after consulting in accordance with section 30(1) of the Estate Agents Act 1979[a] the persons therein referred to, in exercise of the powers conferred on him by section 18(4) of that Act and of all other powers enabling him in that behalf, hereby makes the following Regulations:

Citation, commencement and interpretation

1. – (1) These Regulations may be cited as the Estate Agents (Provision of Information) Regulations 1991 and shall come into force on 29th July 1991.

(2) In these regulations –

"the Act" means the Estate Agents Act 1979;

"associate" has the meaning given to it in section 32(1) of the Act;

"client" means a person on whose behalf an estate agent acts;

"connected person" in relation to an estate agent means any of the following–

    (a) his employer or principal, or

    (b) any employee or agent of his, or

    (c) any associate of his or of any person mentioned in (a) and (b) above;

---

a 1979 c. 38.

"estate agent" means any person who in the course of a business (including one which he is employed) engages in estate agency work and includes cases where he is negotiating on his own behalf;

"estate agency work" has the meaning given in section 1(1) of the Act;

"financial benefit" includes commission and any performance related benefit;

"interest in land" means any of the interests referred to in section 2 of the Act and references herein to an "interest in the land" are references to the particular interest in land of which the estate agent is engaged to secure the disposal or acquisition;

"purchaser" means a person to whom an interest in land is transferred or in whose favour it is created;

"services" means any services to a prospective purchaser for consideration, being services which are such as would ordinarily be made available to a prospective purchaser in connection with his acquisition of an interest in land or his use or enjoyment of it (including the provision to that purchaser of banking and insurance services and financial assistance and securing the disposal for that purchaser of an interest in land if that disposal is one which has to be made in order for him to be able to make the acquisition he is proposing or is one which is a result of that acquisition).

Additional information as to services

2.– (1) The following additional information is hereby prescribed and shall be given by an estate agent to his client, that is to say as to the services–

(a) which the estate agent is himself offering, or intends to offer, to any prospective purchaser of an interest in the land; or

(b) which he knows a connected person or (in a case where he or a connected person would derive a financial benefit from the provision of the service) another person is offering, or intends to offer, to any prospective purchaser of an interest in the land.

(2) The additional information referred to in paragraph (1) above shall be given at the time and in the manner specified in Regulations 3 and 4 below.

Time of giving information

3.– (1) The time when an estate agent shall give the information specified in section 18(2) of the Act, as well as the additional information prescribed in Regulation 2 above, is the time when communication commences between the estate agent and the client or as soon as is reasonably practicable thereafter provided it is a time before the client is committed to any liability towards the estate agent.

(2) The time when an estate agent shall give the details of any changes to the terms of the contract between himself and his client are as mentioned in section 18(3) of the Act, is the time when, or as soon as is reasonably practicable after, those changes are agreed.

Manner of giving information

4. The additional information prescribed in Regulation 2 above and the information required to be given under section 18(2) and (3) of the Act shall be given by the estate agent in writing.

Explanation of terms concerning client's liability to pay remuneration to an estate agent.

5.– (1) If any of the terms "sole selling rights", "sole agency" and "ready, willing and able purchaser" are used by an estate agent in the course of carrying out estate agency work, he shall explain the intention and effect of those terms to his client in the manner described respectively below, that is to say–

(a) "sole selling rights", by means of a written explanation having the form and content of the statement set out in paragraph (a) of the Schedule to these Regulations;

(b) "sole agency", by means of a written explanation having the form and content of the statement set out in paragraph (b) of the Schedule to these Regulations; and

(c) "ready, willing and able purchaser", by means of a written explanation having the form and content of the statement set out in paragraph (c) of the Schedule to these Regulations:

Provided that if, by reason of the provisions of the contract in which those terms appear, the respective explanations are in any way misleading, the content of the explanation shall be altered so as accurately to describe the liability of the client to pay remuneration in accordance with those provisions.

(2) Any other terms which, though differing from those referred to in paragraph (1) above, have a similar purport or effect shall be

explained by the estate agent to his client by reference to whichever of paragraphs (a), (b) or (c) of the Schedule to these Regulations is appropriate, subject also to the proviso to paragraph (1) above.

(3) The explanation of the terms mentioned in paragraphs (1) and (2) above shall be given by the estate agent to his client in a document setting out the terms of the contract between them (whether that document be a written or printed agreement, a letter, terms of engagement or a form, and whether or not such document is signed by any of the parties), and shall be given at the time specified in Regulation 3(1) and (2) above.

Prominence etc. of explanation

6.– (1) Subject to the proviso to Regulation 5(1) and (2) above, the explanations set out in the Schedule to these Regulations shall be reproduced in the documents embodying them in the same form as they appear in that Schedule and without any material alterations or additions to the text, and shall be shown prominently, clearly and legibly.

(2) The wording of such explanations shall be given no less prominence than that given to any other information in the document setting out the terms of the contract (as more particularly described in Regulation 5(3) above) between the estate agent and his client apart from the heading thereto, trade names, names of the parties and numbers or lettering subsequently inserted therein in handwriting or in type.

Department of Trade and Industry

28 March 1991

THE SCHEDULE
Regulations 5 and 6

EXPLANATION OF CERTAIN TERMS[a]

(a) *Sole selling rights*

"SOLE SELLING RIGHTS
You will be liable to pay remuneration to us, in addition to any other costs or charges agreed, in each of the following circumstances–

if [unconditional contracts for the sale of the property are exchanged][b] in the period during which we have sole selling rights, even if the purchaser was not found by us but by another agent or by any other person, including yourself;

if [unconditional contracts for the sale of the property are exchanged][b] after the expiry of the period during which we have sole selling rights but to a purchaser who was introduced to you during that period or with whom we had negotiations about the property during that period."

(b) *Sole agency*

"SOLE AGENCY
You will be liable to pay remuneration to us, in addition to any other costs or charges agreed, if at any time [unconditional contracts for the sale of the property are exchanged][b] –

with a purchaser introduced by us during the period of our sole agency or with whom we had negotiations about the property during that period; or

---

a In lieu of the words "us", "we", "our", "you" or "your" may be inserted or printed the name of the agent, the agency or the client, as appropriate, and for "the property" may be inserted the address thereof.
b In Scotland for the words in square brackets there shall be substituted "unconditional missives for the sale of the property are concluded".

with a purchaser introduced by another agent during that period."

(c) *Ready, willing and able purchaser*

"READY, WILLING AND ABLE PURCHASER
A purchaser is a "ready, willing and able" purchaser if he is prepared and is able to [exchange unconditional contracts for the purchase of your property][a].

You will be liable to pay remuneration to us, in addition to any other costs or charges agreed, if such a purchaser is introduced by us in accordance with your instructions and this must be paid even if you subsequently withdraw and [unconditional contracts for sale are not exchanged][b], irrespective of your reasons."

Order made by the Secretary of State, laid before Parliament under section 3(6) of the Estate Agents Act 1979, for approval by resolution of each House of Parliament within 28 days beginning with the day on which it was made, subject to extension for periods of dissolution, prorogation or adjournment for more than 4 days.

Notes

See pp 34–44.

---

a In Scotland for the words in square brackets there shall be substituted "conclude unconditional missives for the purchase of your property".
b In Scotland for the words in square brackets there shall be substituted "unconditional missives for sale are not concluded".

STATUTORY INSTRUMENTS

1991 No. 1032

ESTATE AGENTS

The Estate Agents (Undesirable Practices) (No. 2)
Order 1991

Made	*19th April 1991*
Laid before Parliament	*19th April 1991*
Coming into force	*29th July 1991*

The Secretary of State, after consulting in accordance with section 30(1) of the Estate Agents Act 1979ᵃ the persons therein referred to, in exercise of the powers conferred on him by section 3(1)(d) of that Act and of all other powers enabling him in that behalf, hereby makes the following Order:–

Citation, commencement, interpretation and revocation

1. – (1) This Order may be cited as the Estate Agents (Undesirable Practices) (No. 2) Order 1991 and shall come into force on 29th July 1991.

(2) In this Order –

"the Act" means the Estate Agents Act 1979;

"associate" has the meaning given to it in section 32(1) of the Act;

"client" means a person on whose behalf an estate agent acts;

"connected person" in relation to an estate agent means any of the following–

(a)   his employer or principal, or

(b)   any employee of agent of his, or

---

a 1979 c. 38

(c) any associate of his or of any person mentioned in (a) and (b) above;

"estate agent" means any person who in the course of a business (including one in which he is employed) engages in estate agency work and includes cases where he is negotiating on his own behalf;

"estate agency work" has the meaning given in section 1(1) of the Act;

"financial benefit" includes commission and any performance related bonus;

"interest in land" means any of the interests referred to in section 2 of the Act and references to an "interest in the land" are references to the particular interest in land of which the estate agent is engaged to secure the disposal or acquisition;

"promptly" means within as short a period as is reasonably practicable in the circumstances, from the moment when what is to be done can reasonably be done:

"purchaser" means a person to whom an interest in land is transferred or in whose favour it is created;

"services" means any service for consideration provided, or to be provided, to a prospective purchaser–

(a) by an estate agent or a connected person, or (in a case where the estate agent or connected person would derive a financial benefit from the provision of the service) by another person, and which

(b) is such as would ordinarily be made available to a prospective purchaser in connection with his acquisition of an interest in land or his use or enjoyment of it (including the provision to that purchaser of banking and insurance services and financial assistance and securing the disposal for that purchaser of an interest in land if that disposal is one which has to be made in order for him to be able to make the acquisition he is proposing or is one which is a result of that acquisition).

(3) The Estate Agents (Undesirable Practices) Order 1991[a] is hereby revoked.

---

a S.I. 1991 861.

Undesirable Practices

2. For the purposes of section 3(1)(d) of the Act the following practices in relation to estate agency work are hereby declared undesirable, that is to say as regards–

(a) the disclosure of a personal interest, any failure to disclose that interest as described in Schedule 1 to this Order;

(b) the arrangement and performance of services, any act or omission as described in Schedule 2 to this Order;

(c) other matters in the course of that work, any misdescription or omission of the kind described in Schedule 3 to this Order;

and the provisions of such Schedules shall have effect for supplementing the above paragraphs.

Department of Trade and Industry

19th April 1991

SCHEDULE I   Article 2(a)

Disclosure of Personal Interest

Failure by an estate agent:

1. To make disclosure of his personal interest as required in section 21(1) of the Act promptly and in writing.

2. To disclose to his client promptly and in writing that–

   (a) he himself has, or is seeking to acquire, a beneficial interest in the land or in the proceeds of sale of any interest in the land: or

   (b) he knows that any connected person has, or is seeking to acquire, a beneficial interest in the land or in the proceeds of sale of any interest in the land.

SCHEDULE 2   Article 2(b)

Arrangement and performance of services

1. Discrimination against a prospective purchaser by an estate agent on the grounds that that purchaser will not be, or is unlikely to be, accepting services.

2. In cases where an estate agent has introduced a prospective purchaser to his client and that purchaser had made an offer, failure by the estate agent to forward to his client promptly and in writing at all stages before contracts for the disposal of the interest in the land have been exchanged or in Scotland before a contract for the disposal of the interest in the land has been concluded, an accurate list of services, provided that–

   (a) an application from the prospective purchaser for services has been received by the estate agent or a connected person or (in a case where the estate agent or a connected person would derive a financial benefit from the provision of the service) by another person; and

   (b) the estate agent knows that such application has been received and that it is an application for services, being services in connection with the prospective purchaser's acquisition of the interest in the land or his use or enjoyment of it, or with his disposal of an interest in land which he has to make in order to make that acquisition or which is the result of that acquisition; and

(c) that application has not been refused.

In this paragraph "offer" includes a conditional offer and "forward" means despatch to the client by hand, post or fax at the address or to the number given by the client to the estate agent, which despatch may be made by the person by whom or which the service is being, or is to be, provided.

SCHEDULE 3 Article 2(c)

Other Matters

1. The making by an estate agent, knowingly or recklessly and orally or in writing, of any misrepresentation-
   (a) as to the existence of, or details relating to, any offer for the interest in the land; or
   (b) as to the existence or status of any prospective purchaser of an interest in the land.

2. The failure by an estate agent to forward to his client promptly and in writing accurate details (other than those of a description which the client has indicated in writing he does not wish to receive) of any offer the estate agent has received from a prospective purchaser in respect of an interest in the land.

3. In this Schedule–
   (a) in paragraph 1 a misrepresentation is "recklessly" made if it is made regardless of whether it is true or false, whether or not the estate agent had reasons for believing that it might be false;
   (b) "offer" in paragraphs 1 and 2 includes any conditional offer, but does not include offers of a description which the client has indicated in writing to the estate agent need not be forwarded to him;
   (c) paragraph 1(a) does not affect the right of an auctioneer to bid at an auction in accordance with section 6 of the Sale of Land by Auction Act 1867[a] or in Scotland any rule of law of like effect;

---

a 30 & 31 Vict.c.48.

(d) the "status of any prospective purchaser" in paragraph 1(b) includes the financial standing of that purchaser and his ability to exchange contracts expeditiously or in Scotland conclude a contract expeditiously;

(e) "forward" in paragraph 2 means despatch to the client by hand, post or fax at the address or to the number given by the client to the estate agent.

Order made by the Secretary of State, laid before Parliament under section 3(6) of the Estate Agents Act 1979, for approval by resolution of each House of Parliament within twenty-eight days beginning with the day on which the Order was made, subject to extension for periods of dissolution, prorogation or adjournment for more than four days.

Notes

See pp 45–56.

STATUTORY INSTRUMENTS

1991 No. 1091

ESTATE AGENTS

The Estate Agents (Specified Offences) (No. 2) Order 1991

Made	*29th April 1991*
Laid before Parliament	*29th April 1991*
Coming into force	*1st June 1991*

The Secretary of State, after consulting in accordance with section 30(1) of the Estate Agents Act 1979[a] the persons therein referred to, in exercise of the powers conferred on him by section 3(1)(a)(iii) of that Act and of all other powers enabling him in that behalf, hereby makes the following Order:–

1. This Order may be cited as the Estate Agents (Specified Offences) (No. 2) Order 1991 and shall come into force on 1st June 1991.

2. Offences committed under the provisions of the Acts and Orders listed in the Schedule to this Order are hereby specified for the purposes of section 3 of the Estate Agents Act 1979.

3. The Estate Agents (Specified Offences) Order 1991[b] is hereby revoked.

Department of Trade and Industry

29th April 1991

---

a 1979 c.38.
b S.I. 1991/860.

SCHEDULE
SPECIFIED OFFENCES

Article 2

Act or Order	Provision	Description of Offence
Administration of Justice Act 1970[a]	Section 40(1)(a)	Unlawful harassment of debtors
Administration of Justice Act 1985[b]	Section 35	Pretence of being a licensed conveyancer or recognised body
Building Societies Act 1986[c]	Paragraph 5 of Part III, and paragraph 6 of Part IV, of 8[d]	Performance by building society employee who has certain duties of service for associated body which carries out estate agency work
Company Directors Disqualification Act 1986[e]	Section 11(1)	Undischarged bankrupt acting as company director without leave
	Section 12(2)	Acting as company director without leave where court revokes administration order
	Section 13	Acting as a director in contravention of a disqualification order etc

a 1970 c.31.
b 1985 c.61.
c 1986 c.53.
d Schedule 8 was substituted by the Building Societies (Commercial Assets and Services) Order 1988 S.I. 1988/1141, article 5, Schedule 5.
e 1986 c.46.

Act or Order	Provision	Description of Offence
Companies Northern Ireland) Order 1986[a]	Article 303(7)	Acting in contravention of a disqualification order
	Article 310	Undischarged bankrupt acting as a company director without leave
Consumer Credit Act 1974[b]	Section 7	Provision of false or misleading information to Director General of Fair Trading
	Section 39(1), (2) and (3)	Licensing offences
	Section 46(1)	False or misleading advertisements
	Section 154	Canvassing ancillary credit activities off trade premises
	Section 165(1)	Obstruction of authorised officer
	Section 167(2)	Breach of certain regulations
Consumer Protection Act 1987[c]	Section 20(1) and (2)	Misleading indication of prices of goods, services, etc

a S.I. 1986/1032 (N.I.6).
b 1974 c.39.
c 1987 c.43.

Act or Order	Provision	Description of Offence
	Section 32(1) and (2)(b)	Obstruction of authorised officer
Consumer Protection (Northern Ireland) Order 1987[a]	Article 13 paragraphs (1) and (2)	Misleading indication of prices of goods, services, etc
	Article 24(1) and (2)(b)	Obstruction of authorised officer
Data Protection Act 1984[b]	Section 5	Prohibition of unregistered holding, etc of personal data
	Section 6(6)	Provision of false etc information to Data Protection Registrar
	Section 10(9)	Failure to comply with an enforcement notice
	Section 15	Unauthorised disclosure by computer bureau
Financial Services Act 1986[c]	Section 4	Carrying on investment business without authorisation etc
	Section 57	Issue of investment advertisements not approved by an authorised person

a S.I. 1987/2049 (N.I.20).
b 1984 c.35.
c 1986 c.60.

Act or Order	Provision	Description of Offence
Failure	Section 59(5)	Employment in contravention of disqualification direction
	Section 105(10)[a]	Investigation powers: to comply with a requirement
	Section 111(1)	Furnishing false or misleading information to auditors etc
	Section 130	Restriction on promotion of contracts of insurance
	Section 133(1)(b)	Misleading statements as to insurance
	Section 199(6)[b]	Obstruction of powers of entry
	Section 200(1), (2) and (3)	False or misleading statements, etc
	Schedule 6 paragraph 5(3)	Failure in relation to attendance at, and evidence etc before, Financial Services Tribunal
Malicious Communications Act 1988[c]	Section 1 (1)(a)(i) and (ii)	Sending letters etc with intent to cause distress or anxiety

a Section 105 was amended by section 73 of the Companies Act 1989 (c.40).
b Section 199(6) was amended by section 76 of the Companies Act 1989.
c 1988 c.27.

Act or Order	Provision	Description of Offence
Malicious Communications (Northern Ireland) Order 1988[a]	Article 3 (1)(a) (i) and (ii)	Sending letters etc with intent to cause distress or anxiety
Property Misdescriptions Act 1991[b]	Section 1(1) and (2)	Offence of property misdecription
Trade Descriptions Act 1968[c]	Section 1(1)	Applying false trade description in relation to goods
	Section 13	False representations as to supply of goods or services
	Section 14(1)(b)	False or misleading statements as to services etc
	Section 29(1)	Obstruction of authorised officers

Notes

See pp 78–79.

The Property Misdescriptions Act 1991 was added to this list by the The Estate Agents (Specified Offences) (No 2) (Amendment) Order 1992 (SI 1992 No 2833).

a S.I. 1988/1849 (N.I.18).
b 1991 c.29.
c 1968 c.29.

PROPERTY MISDESCRIPTIONS ACT 1991
(1991 c.29)

ARRANGEMENT OF SECTIONS

Section

1. Offence of property misdescription.
2. Due diligence defence.
3. Enforcement.
4. Bodies corporate and Scottish partnerships.
5. Prosecution time limit.
6. Financial provision.
7. Short title and extent.

SCHEDULE:

Enforcement.

An Act to prohibit the making of false or misleading statements about property matters in the course of estate agency business and property development business.

[27th June 1991]

General notes

Definitions

"conveyancing services": s 1(5)(g).

"England" means, subject to any alteration of boundaries under Part IV of the Local Government Act 1972, the area consisting of the counties established by s 1 of that Act, Greater London and the Isles of Scilly: Interpretation Act 1978, s 5.

"estate agency business": s 1(5)(e).

"false": s 1(5)(a).

"land" includes buildings and other structures, land covered with water, and any estate, interest, easement, servitude or right in or over land: Interpretation Act 1978, s 5.

ɟ": s 1(5)(b).

cludes a body of persons corporate or unincorporate: Interpretation Act
5.

d matter": s 1(5)d.

"property development business": s 1(5)(f).

"Secretary of State" means one of Her Majesty's Principal Secretaries of State:
Interpretation Act 1978, s 5.

"statement": s 1(5)(c).

"the statutory maximum": Magistrates' Courts Act 1980, s 32

"Wales" means, subject to any alteration of boundaries made under Part IV of the
Local Government Act 1972, the area consisting of the counties established by
s 20 of that Act: Interpretation Act 1978, s 5.

Commencement

The Act received the Royal Assent on June 27 1991 and in theory came into
operation immediately. However, the offence which the Act creates consists of making
certain statements about a "prescribed matter", and so the Act could serve no practical
purpose until such matters were duly prescribed by Statutory Instrument. The Property
Misdescriptions (Specified Matters) Order 1992 (SI 1992 No 2834), which contains a
list of prescribed matters, comes into effect on April 4 1993.

Extent

The Act applies to both Scotland and Northern Ireland, though with some minor
modifications.

Parliamentary debates

HC vol 186, col 1219; Standing Committee B, March 20 1991; HC vol 190, col 534;
HL vol 529, cols 82, 714; vol 530, cols 128, 579.

Offence of property misdescription.

1. – (1) Where a false or misleading statement about a prescribed
matter is made in the course of an estate agency business or a
property development business, otherwise than in providing
conveyancing services, the person by whom the business is carried
on shall be guilty of an offence under this section.

(2) Where the making of the statement is due to the act or default
of an employee the employee shall be guilty of an offence under
this section; and the employee may be proceeded against and
punished whether or not proceedings are also taken against his
employer.

(3) A person guilty of an offence under this section shall be liable–

(a) on summary conviction, to a fine not exceeding the statutory
maximum, and

(b) on conviction on indictment, to a fine.

(4) No contract shall be void or unenforceable, and no right of action in civil proceedings in respect of any loss shall arise, by reason only of the commission of an offence under this section.

(5) For the purposes of this section –

(a) "false" means false to a material degree,

(b) a statement is misleading if (though not false) what a reasonable person may be expected to infer from it, or from any omission from it, is false,

(c) a statement may be made by pictures or any other method of signifying meaning as well as by words and, if made by words, may be made orally or in writing.

(d) a prescribed matter is any matter relating to land which is specified in an order made by the Secretary of State,

(e) a statement is made in the course of an estate agency business if (but only if) the making of the statement is a thing done as mentioned in subsection (1) of section 1 of the Estate Agents Act 1979 and that Act either applies to it or would apply to it but for subsection (2)(a) of that section (exception for things done in course of profession by practising solicitor or employee),

(f) a statement is made in the course of a property development business if (but only if) it is made –

(i) in the course of a business (including a business in which the person making the statement is employed) concerned wholly or substantially with the development of land, and

(ii) for the purpose of, or with a view to, disposing of an interest in land consisting of or including a building, or a part of a building, constructed or renovated in the course of the business, and

(g) "conveyancing services" means the preparation of any transfer, conveyance, writ, contract or other document in connection with the disposal or acquisition of an interest in land, and services ancillary to that, but does not include anything done as mentioned in section 1(1)(a) of the Estate Agents Act 1979.

(6) For the purposes of this section any reference in this section or section 1 of the Estate Agents Act 1979 to disposing of or acquiring an interest in land –

(a) in England and Wales and Northern Ireland shall be construed in accordance with section 2 of that Act, and

(b) in Scotland is a reference to the transfer or creation of an "interest in land" as defined in section 28(1) of the Land Registration (Scotland) Act 1979.

(7) An order under this section may –

(a) make different provision for different cases, and

(b) include such supplemental, consequential and transitional provisions as the Secretary of State considers appropriate;

and the power to make such an order shall be exercisable by statutory instrument which shall be subject to annulment in pursuance of a resolution of either House of Parliament.

Notes

See, in general, Chapter 5. For the scope of the Act, which is determined by the meaning of "estate agency business", "conveyancing services" and "property development business", see pp 30–32.

The definition of "estate agency business" relies for the most part on the definition of "estate agency work" in s 1 of the Estate Agents Act 1979. That in turn relies on the definition of "interests in land" in s 2. However, in relation to Scotland, s 1(6)(b) of the 1991 Act adopts a different definition of "interests in land", namely, that contained in the Land Registration (Scotland) Act 1979, s 28(1). The definition is "any estate, interest, servitude or other heritable right in or over land, including a heritable security but excluding a lease which is not a long lease [ie a probative lease exceeding 20 years]".

The "statutory maximum" (s 1(3)(a)) is the maximum fine which may be imposed where a person is convicted summarily (ie by magistrates) of an offence which is triable either way (ie by magistrates or by a jury in the Crown Court). From October 1 1992 this is £5,000: Criminal Justice Act 1991, s 17 and Criminal Justice Act 1991 (Commencement No 3) Order 1992. These provisions also make £5,000 the "prescribed sum" for Scotland.

As to the list of "prescribed matters" (s 1(5)(d)), see the Property Misdescriptions (Specified Matters) Order 1992 (SI 1992 No 2834), which is reproduced in Appendix D.

Due diligence defence.

2. – (1) In proceedings against a person for an offence under section 1 above it shall be a defence for him to show that he took all reasonable steps and exercised all due diligence to avoid committing the offence.

(2) A person shall not be entitled to rely on the defence provided by subsection (1) above by reason of his reliance on information given by another unless he shows that it was reasonable in all the circumstances for him to have relied on the information, having regard in particular –

   (a) to the steps which he took, and those which might reasonably have been taken, for the purpose of verifying the information, and

   (b) to whether he had any reason to disbelieve the information.

(3) Where in any proceedings against a person for an offence under section 1 above the defence provided by subsection (1) above involves an allegation that the commission of the offence was due –

   (a) to the act or default of another, or

   (b) to reliance on information given by another,

the person shall not, without the leave of the court, be entitled to rely on the defence unless he has served a notice under subsection (4) below on the person bringing the proceedings not less than seven clear days before the hearing of the proceedings or, in Scotland, the diet of trial.

(4) A notice under this subsection shall give such information identifying or assisting in the identification of the person who committed the act or default, or gave the information, as is in the possession of the person serving the notice at the time he serves it.

Notes

See pp 97–99.

Enforcement.
3. The Schedule to this Act (which makes provision about the enforcement of this Act) shall have effect.

Bodies corporate and Scottish partnerships.
4. – (1) Where an offence under this Act committed by a body corporate is proved to have been committed with the consent or connivance of, or to be attributable to neglect on the part of, a director, manager, secretary or other similar officer of the body corporate or a person who was purporting to act in such a capacity, he (as well as the body corporate) is guilty of the offence and liable to be proceeded against and punished accordingly.

(2) Where the affairs of a body corporate are managed by its members, subsection (1) above applies in relation to the acts and defaults of a member in connection with his functions of management as if he were a director of the body corporate.

(3) Where an offence under this Act committed in Scotland by a Scottish partnership is proved to have been committed with the consent or connivance of, or to be attributable to neglect on the part of, a partner, he (as well as the partnership) is guilty of the offence and liable to be proceeded against and punished accordingly.

Notes

S 4 makes provision for the personal liability of the senior officers of a corporate body (normally a company, but in Scotland also a partnership), where the corporate body itself is guilty of an offence. "Consent" and "connivance" might be thought to require actual knowledge, but it seems that suspicion may well be enough: see *Taylor's Central Garages (Exeter) Ltd* v *Roper* (1951) 115 JP 445, 449, 450, *per* Devlin J.

"Neglect", according to Simonds J in *Re Hughes, Rea* v *Black* [1943] Ch 296, 298, "in its legal connotation implies failure to perform a duty of which the person knows or ought to know".

As to who is a "manager" or "officer": see *Registrar of Restrictive Trading Agreements* v *WH Smith & Son Ltd* [1969] 3 All ER 1065; *Tesco Supermarkets Ltd* v *Nattrass* [1972] AC 153.

Prosecution time limit.

5. – (1) No proceedings for an offence under section 1 above or paragraph 5(3), 6 or 7 of the Schedule to this Act shall be commenced after –

(a) the end of the period of three years beginning with the date of the commission of the offence, or

(b) the end of the period of one year beginning with the date of the discovery of the offence by the prosecutor,

whichever is the earlier.

(2) For the purposes of this section a certificate signed by or on behalf of the prosecutor and stating the date on which the offence was discovered by him shall be conclusive evidence of that fact; and a certificate stating that matter and purporting to be so signed shall be treated as so signed unless the contrary is proved.

Financial provision.

6. There shall be paid out of money provided by Parliament any increase attributable to this Act in the sums payable out of such money under any other Act.

Short title and extent.

7. – (1) This Act may be cited as the Property Misdescriptions Act 1991.

(2) This Act extends to Northern Ireland.

SCHEDULE

Section 3

ENFORCEMENT

Enforcement authority

1.– (1) Every local weights and measures authority in Great Britain shall be an enforcement authority for the purposes of this Act, and it shall be the duty of each such authority to enforce the provisions of this Act within their area.

(2) The Department of Economic Development in Northern Ireland shall be an enforcement authority for the purposes of this Act, and it shall be the duty of the Department to enforce the provisions of this Act within Northern Ireland.

Prosecutions

2.– (1) In section 130(1) of the Fair Trading Act 1973 (notice to Director General of Fair Trading of intended prosecution by local weights and measures authority in England and Wales), after the words "the Consumer Protection Act 1987," there shall be inserted the words "or for an offence under section 1 of, or paragraph 6 of the Schedule to, the Property Misdescriptions Act 1991,".

(2) Nothing in paragraph 1 above shall authorise a local weights and measures authority to bring proceedings in Scotland for an offence.

Powers of officers of enforcement authority

3.– (1) If a duly authorised officer of an enforcement authority has reasonable grounds for suspecting that an offence under section 1 of this Act has been committed, he may –

(a) require a person carrying on or employed in a business to produce any book or document relating to the business, and take copies of it or any entry in it, or

(b) require such a person to produce in a visible and legible documentary form any information so relating which is contained in a computer, and take copies of it,

for the purpose of ascertaining whether such an offence has been committed.

(2) Such an officer may inspect any goods for the purpose of ascertaining whether such an offence has been committed.

(3) If such an officer has reasonable grounds for believing that any documents or goods may be required as evidence in proceedings for such an offence, he may seize and detain them.

(4) An officer seizing any documents or goods in the exercise of his power under sub-paragraph (3) above shall inform the person from whom they are seized.

(5) The powers of an officer under this paragraph may be exercised by him only at a reasonable hour and on production (if required) of his credentials.

(6) Nothing in this paragraph –

(a) requires a person to produce a document if he would be entitled to refuse to produce it in proceedings in a court on the ground that it is the subject of legal professional privilege or, in Scotland, that it contains a confidential communication made by or to an advocate or a solicitor in that capacity, or

(b) authorises the taking possession of a document which is in the possession of a person who would be so entitled.

4.– (1) A duly authorised officer of an enforcement authority may, at a reasonable hour and on production (if required) of his credentials, enter any premises for the purpose of ascertaining whether an offence under section 1 of this Act has been committed.

(2) If a justice of the peace, or in Scotland a justice of the peace or a sheriff, is satisfied –

(a) that any relevant books, documents or goods are on, or that any relevant information contained in a computer is available from, any premises, and that production or inspection is likely to disclose the commission of an offence under section 1 of this Act, or

(b) that such an offence has been, is being or is about to be committed on any premises, and that any of the conditions specified in sub-paragraph (3) below is met, he may by warrant under his hand authorise an officer of an enforcement authority to enter the premises, if need be by force.

(3) The conditions referred to in sub-paragraph (2) above are –

(a) that admission to the premises has been or is likely to be refused and that notice of intention to apply for a warrant under that sub-paragraph has been given to the occupier,

(b) that an application for admission, or the giving of such a notice, would defeat the object of the entry,

(c) that the premises are unoccupied, and

(d) that the occupier is temporarily absent and it might defeat the object of the entry to await his return.

(4) In sub-paragraph (2) above "relevant", in relation to books, documents, goods or information, means books, documents, goods or information which, under paragraph 3 above, a duly authorised officer may require to be produced or may inspect.

(5) A warrant under sub-paragraph (2) above may be issued only if –

(a) in England and Wales, the justice of the peace is satisfied as required by that sub-paragraph by written information on oath,

(b) in Scotland, the justice of the peace or sheriff is so satisfied by evidence on oath, or

(c) in Northern Ireland, the justice of the peace is so satisfied by complaint on oath.

(6) A warrant under sub-paragraph (2) above shall continue in force for a period of one month.

(7) An officer entering any premises by virtue of this paragraph may take with him such other persons as may appear to him necessary.

(8) On leaving premises which he has entered by virtue of a warrant under sub-paragraph (2) above, an officer shall, if the premises are unoccupied or the occupier is temporarily absent, leave the premises as effectively secured against trespassers as he found them.

(9) In this paragraph "premises" includes any place (including any vehicle, ship or aircraft) except premises used only as a dwelling.

Obstruction of officers

5.– (1) A person who –

    (a) intentionally obstructs an officer of an enforcement authority acting in pursuance of this Schedule,

    (b) without reasonable excuse fails to comply with a requirement made of him by such an officer under paragraph 3(1) above, or

    (c) without reasonable excuse fails to give an officer of an enforcement authority acting in pursuance of this Schedule any other assistance or information which the officer may reasonably require of him for the purpose of the performance of the officer's functions under this Schedule,

shall be guilty of an offence.

(2) A person guilty of an offence under sub-paragraph (1) above shall be liable on summary conviction to a fine not exceeding level 5 on the standard scale.

(3) If a person, in giving any such information as is mentioned in sub-paragraph (1)(c) above, –

    (a) makes a statement which he knows is false in a material particular, or

    (b) recklessly makes a statement which is false in a material particular,

he shall be guilty of an offence.

(4) A person guilty of an offence under sub-paragraph (3) above shall be liable –

    (a) on summary conviction, to a fine not exceeding the statutory maximum, and

    (b) on conviction on indictment, to a fine.

Impersonation of officers

6.– (1) If a person who is not a duly authorised officer of an enforcement authority purports to act as such under this Schedule he shall be guilty of an offence.

(2) A person guilty of an offence under sub-paragraph (1) above shall be liable –

    (a) on summary conviction, to a fine not exceeding the statutory maximum, and

    (b) on conviction on indictment, to a fine.

Disclosure of information

7.– (1) If a person discloses to another any information obtained by him by virtue of this Schedule he shall be guilty of an offence unless the disclosure was made –
  (a) in or for the purpose of the performance by him or any other person of any function under this Act, or
  (b) for a purpose specified in section 38(2)(a), (b) or (c) of the Consumer Protection Act 1987.

(2) A person guilty of an offence under sub-paragraph (1) above shall be liable –
  (a) on summary conviction, to a fine not exceeding the statutory maximum, and
  (b) on conviction on indictment, to a fine.

Privilege against self-incrimination

8. Nothing in this Schedule requires a person to answer any question or give any information if to do so might incriminate him.

Notes

The enforcement provisions are similar to those found under many consumer protection statutes, including the Estate Agents Act 1979: see pp 87–88.

The reason for the restricted powers of local weights and measures authorities in Scotland (para 2(2)) is that all prosecutions there are initiated by the Procurator Fiscal.

"Obstructs" (para 5(1)) includes, it appears, doing anything which makes it more difficult for the officer to carry out his duty: *Hinchcliffe v Sheldon* [1955] 3 All ER 406. It does, however, require some form of positive conduct; hindrance which is purely passive falls under para (c).

The "statutory maximum" (paras 5(4), (6) and (7)) is the maximum fine which may be imposed where a person is convicted summarily (ie by magistrates) of an offence which is triable either way (ie by magistrates or by a jury in the Crown Court). From October 1 1992 this is £5,000: Criminal Justice Act 1991, s 17 and Criminal Justice Act 1991 (Commencement No 3) Order 1992. These provisions also make £5,000 the "prescribed sum" for Scotland.

"Level 5 on the standard scale" (para 5(2)) is a reference to the standard scale of fines laid down by the Criminal Justice 1982, s 37 (and the Criminal Procedure (Scotland) Act 1975, s 289G. From October 1 1992 the relevant amount is £5,000: Criminal Justice Act 1991, s 17 and Criminal Justice Act 1991 (Commencement No 3) Order 1992.

SECONDARY LEGISLATION UNDER THE 1991 ACT

STATUTORY INSTRUMENTS

1992 No. 2834

CONSUMER PROTECTION

The Property Misdescriptions (Specified Matters) Order 1992

Made	*11th November 1992*
Laid before Parliament	*18th November 1992*
Coming into force	*4th April 1993*

The Secretary of State, in exercise of the powers conferred upon him by section 1 of the Property Misdescriptions Act 1991[a], hereby makes the following Order:

1. This Order may be cited as the Property Misdescriptions (Specified Matters) Order 1992 and shall come into force on 4th April 1993.

2. The matters contained in the Schedule to this Order are hereby specified to the extent described in that Schedule for the purposes of section 1(1) of the Property Misdescriptions Act 1991.

Department of Trade and Industry

11th November 1992

---

a 1991 c.29.

SCHEDULE

SPECIFIED MATTERS

1. Local or address.
2. Aspect, view, outlook or environment.
3. Availability and nature of services, facilities or amenities.
4. Proximity to any services, places, facilities or amenities.
5. Accommodation, measurements or sizes.
6. Fixtures and fittings.
7. Physical or structural characteristics, form of construction or condition.
8. Fitness for any purpose or strength of any buildings or other structures on land or of land itself.
9. Treatments, processes, repairs or improvements or the effects thereof.
10. Conformity or compliance with any scheme, standard, test or regulations or the existence of any guarantee.
11. Survey, inspection, investigation, valuation or appraisal by any person or the results thereof.
12. The grant or giving of any award or prize for design or construction.
13. History, including the age, ownership or use of land or any building or fixture and the date of any alterations thereto.
14. Person by whom any building, (or part of any building), fixture, or component was designed, constructed, built, produced, treated, processed, repaired, reconditioned or tested.
15. The length of time during which land has been available for sale either generally or by or through a particular person.
16. Price (other than the price at which accommodation or facilities are available and are to be provided by means of the creation or disposal of an interest in land in the circumstances specified in section 23(1)(a) and (b) of the Consumer Protection Act 1987[a] or Article 16(1)(a) and (b) of the Consumer Protection (NI) Order 1987[b] (which relate to the creation or disposal of certain interests in new dwellings)) and previous price.

---

a 1987 c.43.
b 1987 No. 2049 (N.I. 20).

. Tenure or estate.

8. Length of any lease or of the unexpired term of any lease and the terms and conditions of a lease (and, in relation to land in Northern Ireland, any fee farm grant creating the relation of landlord and tenant shall be treated as a lease).

19. Amount of any ground-rent, rent or premium and frequency of any review.

20. Amount of any rent-charge.

21. Where all or any part of any land is let to a tenant or is subject to a licence, particulars of the tenancy or licence, including any rent, premium or other payment due and frequency of any review.

22. Amount of any service or maintenance charge or liability for common repairs.

23. Council tax payable in respect of a dwelling within the meaning of section 3, or in Scotland section 72, of the Local Government Finance Act 1992[a] or the basis or any part of the basis on which that tax is calculated.

24. Rates payable in respect of a non-domestic hereditament within the meaning of section 64 of the Local Government Finance Act 1988[b] or, in Scotland, in respect of lands and heritages shown on a valuation roll or the basis or any part of the basis on which those rates are calculated.

25. Rates payable in respect of a hereditament within the meaning of the Rates (Northern Ireland) Order 1977[c] or the basis or any part of the basis on which those rates are calculated.

26. Existence or nature of any planning permission or proposals for development, construction or change of use.

27. In relation to land in England and Wales, the passing or rejection of any plans of proposed building work in accordance with section 16 of the Building Act 1984[d] and the giving of any completion certificate in accordance with regulation 15 of the Building Regulations 1991[e].

---

a 1992 c.14.
b 1988 c.41.
c 1977 No. 2157 (N.I. 28).
d 1984 c.55.
e S.I. 1991/2768.

28. In relation to land in Scotland, the granting of a warrant under section 6 of the Building (Scotland) Act 1959[a] or the granting of a certificate of completion under section 9 of that Act.
29. In relation to land in Northern Ireland, the passing or rejection of any plans of proposed building work in accordance with Article 13 of the Building Regulations (Northern Ireland) Order 1979[b] and the giving of any completion certificate in accordance with building regulations made under that Order.
30. Application of any statutory provision which restricts the use of land or which requires it to be preserved or maintained in a specified manner.
31. Existence or nature of any restrictive covenants, or of any restrictions on resale, restrictions on use, or pre-emption rights and, in relation to land in Scotland, (in addition to the matters mentioned previously in this paragraph) the existence or nature of any reservations or real conditions.
32. Easements, servitudes or wayleaves.
33. Existence and extent of any public or private right of way.

Notes

See pp 94–95.

---

a 1959 c.24.
b 1979 No. 1709 (N.I. 16).

INDEX

A

ACCOUNTANT
estate agency work, whether engaged in 17
qualified auditor, as 67, 124

ACCOUNTS
client (see CLIENT ACCOUNT)
regulations 64–70, 124, 126, 173–180

ADVERTISEMENT
publication of, as estate agency work 22,105
unbonded agent, by 62,127

AGENT
clients' money, holding as 57, 58, 60, 61, 69, 122
estate (see ESTATE AGENT)
liability of principal for acts of 53, 81, 107, 142
personal interest of 49, 134

APPEAL
appeals regulations 85, 113, 144, 157–170
court, to 84, 86, 113
order of Director-General of Fair Trading, against 84–86, 112, 157–170
notice of 85, 159
procedure for 85–86, 164–166

ASSOCIATE
business (see BUSINESS ASSOCIATE)
meaning of 49, 50, 146–148
personal interest of, duty to disclose 49–53, 133–135

AUCTION
deposit paid at 61, 68
estate agency work, whether 26
lien of auctioneer 60
personal interest of auctioneer 48
right of auctioneer to bid at 56, 191

AUDIT
client account, of 67–68, 123–124, 178–180

B

BAILEE
  clients' money, holding as 57, 121

BANK MANAGER
  estate agency work, whether engaged in 17, 18

BANKRUPTCY
  disqualification from practice by 71, 78, 137, 142
  trustee in, sale of land by 17, 22

BUSINESS
  course of, as estate agency work 16, 104
  estate agency, meaning of 31, 201–202
  meaning of 17
  property development 32, 200–202

BUSINESS ASSOCIATE
  liability for acts of 50, 53, 81, 107, 145, 147
  meaning of 50, 145

C

CLIENT
  account (see CLIENT ACCOUNT)
  agent, whether negotiating with 52
  disclosure of personal interest to 47, 48, 190
  information on charges to 34–44, 129–131, 181–186
  instructions from 17, 41–42, 104
  money (see CLIENTS' MONEY)

CLIENT ACCOUNT
  accounts regulations 64–70, 124, 126, 173–180
  auditing of 67–68, 123–124, 178–180
  definition of 64, 123
  payments into and out of 64–65, 174–175
  records of 65–67, 175–177

CLIENTS' MONEY
  client account, in (see CLIENT ACCOUNT)
  connected contract as 57, 121
  contract deposit as 57, 121
  definition of 56–58, 121
  duties in respect of 64–70, 123–126, 173–180
  insurance cover for 61–62, 126–129
  interest on 68–70, 125–126, 177–178
  pre-contract deposit as 57, 121
  tracing of 59

trust, held on 58–61, 122

COMMISSION
   information to client on 34–44, 129–131, 181–186
   irrecoverable without court order, when 42–43, 130–131

COMPANY
   associated companies 50, 134–135, 147
   business associate as 50, 134–135, 146
      personal interest of 50, 134–135, 146
   controller of 145–146, 147
   criminal liability of 97, 141–142, 203–204
      liability of director 97, 141–142, 203–204
   liquidator of, whether engaged in estate agency work 17, 22
   minimum standards of competence 73, 136
   order against 75, 76

CONNECTED PERSON
   meaning of 40, 45, 47, 181, 187

CONSUMER CREDIT
   licensing scheme 5, 20

CONTRACT
   connected 57, 121
   deposit 57, 121
   estate agent and client, between 41–42

CONVEYANCING SERVICES
   estate agency business, excluded from 31, 200–202

COURTS
   appeal to 84, 86, 113
   order of, commission irrecoverable without 42–43, 130–131

CREDIT BROKERAGE
   when excluded from meaning of estate agency work 20, 104

CRIMINAL OFFENCES
   banned agent continuing to practise 78, 84, 108, 142
   bankrupt practising as estate agent 71, 78, 137, 142
   clients' money, relating to 62, 64, 67, 124, 127, 129, 142
   company, by 97, 141–142, 203–204
   convictions
      Director-General of Fair Trading, notice to 79, 82, 115
      spent 77, 84, 87, 110, 150
      triggers, as 71, 77–79, 84, 106
   Estate Agents Act, under
      triggers, as 71, 78–79, 106, 193–198

information, failure to give 82, 88, 115, 140–142, 205–208
minimum standards of competence, practice without 73, 78, 136, 142
obstruction, etc. of authorised officer 88, 100, 140–142, 205–208
prosecution
    defences 97–99, 141–142, 202
    intended, notice to Director-General of Fair Trading 79, 139–140
suspicion of, for power of entry 88, 118–120
vicarious liability for 18, 142

D

DEPARTMENT OF TRADE AND INDUSTRY
    estate agency, 1989 review of 10–11

DEPOSIT
    clients' money, as (see CLIENTS' MONEY)
    contract 57, 121
        person entitled to 60–61, 69
    pre-contract 57, 121
        limit on amount of 63, 131–132
        person entitled to 60–61, 69
    prohibition on taking, where personal interest 63, 133, 135

DIRECTOR-GENERAL OF FAIR TRADING
    applications to 62, 86, 87, 111, 114, 128, 156
    Council on Tribunals, supervision by 83, 111, 112, 129, 138
    duties of 87, 113, 138, 139
    enforcement authority, as 74, 139
    estate agency, 1190 report on 11
    Estate Agents Act, 1988 review of 10
    information for
        commissions, from 80, 115
        courts, from 79, 82, 115
        notices requiring 82, 114
    local weights and measures authority, supervision of 74, 139
    notices by and to 82, 114, 142
    orders issued by
        prohibition orders (see PROHIBITION ORDERS)
        warning orders (see WARNING ORDERS)
    powers of 74–87, 106–112, 114

DISCLAIMER
    misdescription, effect on 91, 95

DISCLOSURE
    personal interest, duty of 23, 47, 48–53, 133–135, 190

DISCRIMINATION
    finding of, when no longer effective 80, 84, 110

information to Director-General of Fair Trading of 80, 115
meaning of 79–80, 150–152
purchaser, against, undesirable practice, as 54–55, 190
trigger, as 79–80, 107
vicarious liability in respect of 18, 81

DUE DILIGENCE
property misdescription, defence to 97–99, 202

E

EMPLOYEE
activities of, as estate agency work 18, 23, 104, 105
bankrupt person as 71, 137
client account, no duty to have 18, 123
liability of employer for 18, 81, 107, 134
personal interest of, duty to disclose 50, 134
property misdescription by 97, 200

EMPLOYER
activities on behalf of employee, as estate agency work 24, 105
liability of, for acts of employee
criminal offences 18, 142
discrimination 18, 81
non-criminal breaches 18–19, 81, 107, 135
property misdescription 97, 200
personal interest of, duty to disclose 23, 50, 134

ENFORCEMENT
trading standards officers, by
Estate Agents Act 87–88, 118–120
Property Misdescriptions Act 100, 205–208

ENTRY
power of 88, 100, 118, 206–207

ESTATE AGENCY BUSINESS
meaning of 31, 200–202

ESTATE AGENCY WORK
accountant, whether engaged in 17
advertisement, whether publication constitutes 22, 105
auction, whether 26
bank manager, whether engaged in 17, 18
business, in course of 16, 104
credit brokerage, excluded from 20, 104–105
employees, things done by 18, 23, 104, 105
employers, things done by 24, 105
instructions, pursuant to 17, 104

insurance brokerage, excluded from 21, 104
introduction, based on 15, 104
meaning of 14–24, 26–27, 28–29, 104–105
negotiation, excluded from 16
planning matters, excluded from 19, 104
solicitor, work of, excluded from 21, 104
surveying, whether 19, 104
valuation, whether 19, 104

ESTATE AGENT
  client, relationship with 41
  clients' money, holding (see CLIENTS' MONEY)
  description as, where no insurance cover for clients' money 62, 127
  information to client on charges
    common law rules 44
    statutory rules 34–44, 181–186
  lien of 43, 60, 65, 122, 131
  minimum standards of competence 71–73, 135–137
  personal interest, duty to disclose
    common law, at 48
    statute, under 47, 48–53, 133–135

ESTATE AGENTS ACT
  aims of 8
  background to 1–9
  commencement 103, 127, 129, 132, 137, 150
  consumer protection measure, as 8
  enforcement of 74, 87, 138, 139
  exclusions from 19–24
  framework of 8–9
  interpretation of 103, 148
  Northern Ireland, application to 103, 150
  regulations made under (see REGULATIONS AND ORDERS)
  scope of 14–30, 104–106
  Scotland, application to 103, 149

F

FAIR TRADING
  Director-General of (see DIRECTOR-GENERAL OF FAIR TRADING)

FEES
  prescribed
    application for revocation/variation of order, on 86
    inspection of register of orders, for 87
  meaning of 148

FORWARD
  meaning of 46, 192

FRAUD
  conviction for, as "trigger" 77, 106

H

HOUSING ASSOCIATION
  Estate Agents Act, subject to 17

HOUSING CORPORATION
  Estate Agents Act, subject to 17

I

INFORMATION
  charges, on, to client 34–44, 129–131, 181–186
  Director-General of Fair Trading, to
    convictions 79, 82, 115
    findings of discrimination 80, 115
    judgments of courts 79, 82, 115
    notice requiring 82, 114
    prohibition against disclosure of 82, 116
  false, criminal offence to give 82, 115, 140–142, 205–208
  insurance arrangements, as to 62, 127
  services, on, to client 38, 45, 182, 190

INSTRUCTIONS
  estate agency work done pursuant to 17, 104
  form of, none prescribed 17
  letter confirming, effect of 41, 44

INSURANCE
  brokerage, when excluded from meaning of estate agency work 21,104
  clients' money, cover for 61–62, 126–129

INTEREST
  clients' money, on 68–70, 125–126, 177–178
  land, in, whether within Estate Agents Act 24–30, 105–106
  personal (see PERSONAL INTEREST)
  purchase, in, duty to disclose 47–48, 190

INTRODUCTION
  estate agency work defined by reference to 15, 104

L

LAND
  interest in, whether within Estate Agents Act 24–30, 105–106
  meaning of 103, 199

LEASE
creation or transfer of, whether within Estate Agents Act   25–26, 29–30, 105–106

LIEN
auctioneer, of 60
estate agent, of 43, 60, 65, 122, 131

LOCAL AUTHORITY
Estate Agents Act, subject to 17

LOCAL WEIGHTS AND MEASURES AUTHORITY
authorised officer of 88, 100, 118–120, 140–141, 142, 171, 205–209
Director-General of Fair Trading, relationship to 74, 79, 139–140
enforcement authority, as 74, 87–88, 100, 139, 205
trading standards officer
    entry, powers of 88, 100, 118–120, 206–207
    information to 88, 100, 140–141, 142, 208
    obstruction of 88, 100, 140–141, 142, 208
    seizure, powers of 88, 100, 118–120, 171, 206

M

MINIMUM STANDARDS OF COMPETENCE
practice without 10–11, 71–73, 135, 142

MISDESCRIPTION OF PROPERTY
civil liability for 91
criminal liability for 90
disclaimer, effect of 95
meaning of 92–95, 200–202
prescribed matter, about 94–95, 210–213
price, as to 95, 211

MISREPRESENTATION
offer, of 55–56, 95, 191

MORTGAGE
brokerage, when excluded from meaning of estate agency work 20, 104
disposal of, not within Estate agents Act 25, 106
receiver of income from, sale by 22, 105

N

NEGOTIATION
whether constitutes estate agency work 16

NORTHERN IRELAND
application of Estate Agents Act to 103, 150

application of Property Misdescriptions Act to 200, 205

NOTICE
appeal, of 85, 159
Director-General of Fair Trading, by or to 82, 114, 142

O

OFFER
duty to inform client of 27, 45–47, 191
meaning of 191
misrepresentation of .... : 55–56, 95, 191

ORDERS
commencement 1, 103, 150
prohibition (see PROHIBITION ORDER)
Secretary of State, by (see REGULATIONS AND ORDERS)
warning (see WARNING ORDER)

OVERSEAS PROPERTY
whether within Estate Agents Act 27–28

P

PARTNERSHIP
associate, as 50, 147–148
business associate, as 50, 134–135, 145–146
disclosure of personal interest by 50, 134–135, 190
minimum standards of competence 73, 136
order against 76, 83, 110, 153

PERSONAL INTEREST
estate agent, of
duty to disclose 23, 47–53, 133–135
prohibition against taking deposit 63, 133, 135

PERSONAL REPRESENTATIVE
sale of land by 17, 22

PHOTOGRAPH
misdescription, as 92–93, 201

PLANNING
applications, etc. outside scope of Estate Agents Act 19, 104

PRESCRIBED MATTER
false or misleading statement about 94–95, 210–213

PROHIBITION ORDER

appeal against 84–86, 112, 157–170
company, against 75, 76
   failure to comply with 78, 84, 104, 142
grounds for
   criminal offences, conviction for 71, 77–79, 84, 106, 193–198
   discrimination, finding of 79–80, 107
   excessive pre-contract deposit, taking 62–63, 80, 107
   information to client, failure to give 42, 80, 107
   interest on clients' money, failure to account for 70, 80, 107
   personal interest, failure to disclose 53, 80, 107
   undesirable practices 81, 107
partnership, against 76, 83, 110, 153
procedure for making 82–84, 152–155
register of (see REGISTER OF ORDERS)
revocation or variation of, application for 86, 111, 156
types of 75–76, 107
unfitness to practice, based on 76, 107, 108
vicarious liability, based on 18, 81, 107
warning order, based on 76, 109

PROMPTLY

interest in purchase, duty to inform client 47, 190
meaning of 46, 188
offer, duty to inform client 46, 191
personal interest duty to disclose 51, 190
services requested by purchaser, duty to inform client 45, 190

PROPERTY DEVELOPMENT BUSINESS

meaning of 32, 200–202

                                    R

READY, WILLING AND ABLE PURCHASER

explanation of, duty to give 38, 183–186

REGISTER OF ORDERS

Director-General of Fair Trading, duty to maintain 87, 113
rectification, application for 87, 114, 156

REGULATIONS AND ORDERS

accounts 64–70, 124, 126, 173–180
appeals 85, 113, 144, 157–170
duty to consult before making 144
entry and inspection 120, 171–172
fees, prescription of 86, 87, 148
information to client, as to 34–42, 131, 181–186
insurance cover for clients' money, as to 62, 126
limits on pre-contract deposits, as to 63, 132

minimum standards of competence, as to 71–73, 135
prescribed matters, as to 94–95, 210–213
procedure for making 144–145
undesirable practises, as to 45–48, 51, 52, 54–56, 108, 187–192

RELATIVE
associate, as 50, 134, 146–147

RENT ACT
lettings outside Estate Agents Act 25–26, 29

S

SCOTLAND
application of Estate Agents Act to 103, 149
application of Property Misdescriptions Act to 200

SEIZURE
power of 88, 100, 118–120, 171, 206

SERVICES
information to client of 38, 45, 182, 190
meaning of 39, 182, 188
requested by purchaser, duty to inform client 45, 190

SOLE AGENCY
explanation of, duty to give 38, 183–185

SOLE SELLING RIGHTS
explanation of, duty to give 38, 183–185

SOLICITOR
deposit money, holding 61, 68
Property Misdescriptions Act, application of 31, 201
things done by, outside Estate Agents Act 21–22, 104

STAKEHOLDER
auctioneer as 58, 61, 68
clients' money, holding as 57, 58, 60, 61, 68, 69
estate agent as 58, 60, 61, 68, 69
pre-contract deposit, of 60, 68

STATEMENT
false or misleading, liability for 89–100, 200–209
meaning of 92–95, 210–213

SUB-AGENT
whether within Estate Agents Act 28–29

SURVEY
 when excluded from meaning of estate agency work 19, 104

T

TRIBUNALS
 appeal to, against order of Director-General of Fair Trading 84–86, 112, 157–170
 Council on, supervision of Director-General of Fair Trading by . . . 83, 111, 112,
                                                                             129, 138
 Director-General of Fair Trading, treated as 138

TRUST
 clients' money held on 58–61, 122
 (see also CLIENTS' MONEY)

TRUSTEE
 clients' money, of, estate agent as 58–61, 122
 new, appointment of 59, 75, 122
 (see also CLIENTS' MONEY)

U

UNDESIRABLE PRACTICES
 discrimination against purchaser 54–55, 190
 interest in purchase, non-disclosure of 47–47, 190
 misrepresentation as to offer 55–56, 95, 191
 offer received, failure to inform client 27, 45–47, 191
 personal interest, non-disclosure of 23, 48–53, 133–135
 services to purchaser, failure to inform client of 38, 45, 182, 190
 trigger, as 81, 107

UNINCORPORATED ASSOCIATION
 associate, as 50, 147
 business associate, as 50, 135, 146
 minimum standards of competence 73, 136

V

VALUATION
 when excluded from meaning of estate agency work 19, 104

VICARIOUS LIABILITY
 breaches of Estate Agents Act, in respect of 18–19, 50, 53, 81, 107,
                                                                             135, 145, 147
 criminal offences, in respect of 18, 142
 discrimination, in respect of 18, 81
 employer, for acts of employee 18, 81, 107, 135, 142
 estate agent, for acts of business associate 50, 53, 81, 107, 145, 147
 principal, for acts of agent 53, 81, 107, 142

undesirable practices, in respect of 81, 107

W

WARNING ORDER
appeal against 84–86, 112, 157–170
failure to comply with 76, 109
grounds for 76, 109
procedure for making 82–84, 152–155
register of (see REGISTER OF ORDERS)
revocation or variation of, application for 86, 111, 156
types of 76, 109
unfitness to practise, based on 76, 109